EARSHOT

Earshot: Perspectives on Sound awakens an understanding of the decisive role that sound has played in history and culture.

Although beginning with reference to antiquity, the primary focus is the changing status of sound and hearing in Western culture over the last six hundred years, covering the transition from the medieval period to the contemporary world. Since mythic times, sound has been an essential element in the formation of belief systems, personal and community identities and the negotiations between them. The varied case studies included in the book cover major reference points in the changing politics of sound, particularly in relation to the status of the other major conduit of social transactions, vision.

Earshot is not a work of cultural theory but is anchored in social practices and material culture and is therefore a valuable resource for conveying sound to both undergraduate students as well as the general reader.

Bruce Johnson was formerly a professor of English, and now holds honorary professorships in a range of disciplines including Music, Cultural History and Communications at Glasgow, Turku and University of Technology Sydney. Co-founder of Finland's International Institute for Popular Culture, his academic publications number several hundred, including over a dozen books, mainly on jazz, sound studies and film music. He has also acted as a government advisor on arts policy and is an active jazz musician.

EARSHOT

Perspectives on Sound

Bruce Johnson

NEW YORK AND LONDON

Designed cover image: ilbusca via Getty Images

First published 2023
by Routledge
605 Third Avenue, New York, NY 10158

and by Routledge
4 Park Square, Milton Park, Abingdon, Oxon, OX14 4RN

Routledge is an imprint of the Taylor & Francis Group, an informa business

© 2023 Taylor & Francis

The right of Bruce Johnson to be identified as author of this work has been asserted in accordance with sections 77 and 78 of the Copyright, Designs and Patents Act 1988.

All rights reserved. No part of this book may be reprinted or reproduced or utilised in any form or by any electronic, mechanical, or other means, now known or hereafter invented, including photocopying and recording, or in any information storage or retrieval system, without permission in writing from the publishers.

Trademark notice: Product or corporate names may be trademarks or registered trademarks, and are used only for identification and explanation without intent to infringe.

Library of Congress Cataloging-in-Publication Data
Names: Johnson, Bruce, 1943- author.
Title: Earshot: perspectives on sound/Bruce Johnson.
Description: New York, NY: Routledge, 2023. | Includes bibliographical references and index.
Identifiers: LCCN 2022051611 (print) | LCCN 2022051612 (ebook) | ISBN 9780367487430 (hardback) | ISBN 9780367487423 (paperback) | ISBN 9781003042662 (ebook)
Subjects: LCSH: Sound–Psychological aspects. | Sound–Social aspects. | Hearing–Psychological aspects. | Hearing–Social aspects.
Classification: LCC BF251.J64 2023 (print) | LCC BF251 (ebook) | DDC 152.1/5–dc23/eng/20221102
LC record available at https://lccn.loc.gov/2022051611
LC ebook record available at https://lccn.loc.gov/2022051612

ISBN: 978-0-367-48743-0 (hbk)
ISBN: 978-0-367-48742-3 (pbk)
ISBN: 978-1-003-04266-2 (ebk)

DOI: 10.4324/9781003042662

Typeset in Bembo
by KnowledgeWorks Global Ltd.

CONTENTS

Acknowledgements vi
Preface vii

Introduction 1

1 Acoustemology: Listening to cultural history 15

2 Sound in cultural history 33

3 From hearing to seeing 50

4 The pulpit and the playhouse 66

5 *Hamlet* - The world is out of joint 80

6 Print triumphant 98

7 The aural renaissance 123

8 The aural renaissance and cultural change 144

9 Sound in the contemporary world 164

10 The modern soundscape, social welfare and policy 178

Index *195*

ACKNOWLEDGEMENTS

I would like to thank Professor Helmi Järviluoma-Mäkelä of the University of Eastern Finland, who, from the early 1990s, did so much to enlarge my understanding and give impetus to my further investigation into the cultural history of sound, and kindly assisted with my enquiries specific to this particular book. Dr Paula Hamilton, Adjunct Professor at the University of Technology Sydney made invaluable suggestions after kindly and carefully reading the early drafts of the first seven chapters. As with so many of my publications, the fair hand of friend and colleague Dr Liz Giuffre lies behind the identification of many of the online source materials and the formatting of the final MS. Constance Ditzel, Senior Editor, Music, at Routledge, has guided me through a growing number of books, and her steady encouragement has been especially valuable to me in this project when my own confidence wavered, as well as her time and patience in providing generous advice, particularly regarding structure, pitch and tenor during this work in progress. I want to record my particular appreciation to these four individuals, without whom I would neither have begun nor completed this book.

More broadly, I want in general to acknowledge the contributors to the ever-expanding body of literature on sound studies. When I began working in this field in the 1980s, it was still possible to read pretty much everything on the topic. Forty years later, and especially in the twenty-first century, that body of work is proliferating so rapidly that it is no longer possible to cover and cite it all in detail. There are many significant studies that I have not had the opportunity to cite explicitly, but which inform my understanding of the cultural history of sound. To single out a few for particular mention would be to demean the totality. My thanks to you all.

PREFACE

For 17,000 years, an astonishing secret lay hidden beneath the village of Montignac in the Dordogne region of southwest France. Then in 1940, when a dog called Robot disappeared through a hole in the ground, its owner, 18-year-old Marcel Ravidat, with three friends, went in search of the pet dog by lowering themselves through what turned out to be a 15-metre deep shaft.

What happened to the poor Robot does not seem to have been recorded. It was overwhelmed by the discovery of an enormous system of caves whose walls were covered with images, particularly of animals, the work of generations, dating from the Upper Palaeolithic period. A subsequent archaeological investigation by experts disclosed about 6,000 images in various chambers, which collectively became known as Lascaux.

What had been a secret now became a series of puzzles, including the questions: what was the function of this vast subterranean 'art gallery'? And why, in the uniformly total darkness of the whole complex did the prehistorical graffitists bring their torches to work in some places rather than in others? Expert visual inspection by art historians and anthropologists yielded a range of hypotheses about the purpose of the works, including that they were representations, 'trophies', of hunting successes, or symbolic representations of myths.

But in the 1980s, the range of speculation based on the visual evidence was significantly narrowed by a historian of singing, Iegor Reznikoff. Instead of just looking at the caves, he listened to them. He hummed and sang in them and discovered a connection between various categories and locations of images and the resonance of different parts of the caves. It seemed that the placement of images and their function were related to the otherworldly properties of resonance, that the functions of the images included the accompaniment to shamanistic singing and ceremonies involving forms of sympathetic magic: in some instances, the resonance simulated the sounds of the animals painted on adjacent walls (for a similar case in Mayan culture, see Blesser and Salter 2007: 59, 86, 88).

In this brief account, I am inevitably simplifying Reznikoff's work (see further Reznikoff 2008). But the basic point provides an entrée to this collection: our understanding of culture and society can be unexpectedly and enormously enlarged by listening as well as looking, by attending to the role of sound in human history.

That is what this book is about.

The centre of historical gravity of this study is narrower than the title might imply. Sound is everywhere; nature is literally vibrant (for an overview of the long history of the sounds of the natural world see David George Haskell's book *Sounds Wild and Broken* (Haskell 2022)). My interest is primarily in anthropogenic sounds, which are sounds generated directly or indirectly by human beings. My primary sphere of enquiry is Western cultural history from the medieval period to the emergence of modernity, and the emphasis will be on English-speaking communities. While there will be forays beyond that span, both historically and linguistically, I shall spend most of my time within the boundaries I have just summarised. This is not because I think they are the only ones that matter, quite the contrary, but simply because personally and as a historian, these are the areas I feel best able to speak of.

The running title of this book *Perspectives on Sound* contains a dissonance, but it is unlikely that readers will have noticed. It is a book mainly about sound, but the title invites us to visualise the subject. It offers 'perspectives' – ways of seeing – on 'sound' – what is heard. There is a tension there, but one that we have internalised so deeply that we no longer hear that it is 'out of tune'. We would certainly notice this if we imagined the reverse, if the title were something like 'Listening to Vision'. So, for example, a title like Jonathan Ree's 1999 *I See a Voice* on the history of deafness and the language of signing, or Richard Leppert's 1995 *The Sight of Sound*, produce a sense of disorientation that the title of this study does not. One of the themes of this book is the question of why we do not notice that tension and to make the reader alert to the historical role played by sound in the formation of culture, society and belief.

Seeing and hearing are the primary ways we publicly engage with the world, and that engagement is fundamentally what this book is about. It is less interested in the ontological question – what *is* 'out there' – than the epistemological question – how do we *know* what is 'out there'? How do we know, understand and relate to the world? What is it that makes us attach particular kinds of meaning to our experience? How do those meanings influence the behaviour of individuals and communities? Why do different societies or communities display different tastes and belief systems that affect their relationship with the world? This book is primarily about how we make our way through the world, and how history unfolds, through the realm of sound.

The themes through which these questions are explored are the subjects of each chapter, as follows, and as set out in more detail in the Introduction:

Chapter 1: Acoustemology: Listening to Cultural History presents observations on sound and hearing, their relationship to external space as well as to human physiology and cognition, why certain sounds produce particular responses.

Chapter 2: Sound in Cultural History provides an introductory survey of the kinds of roles sound has played in history and culture, and in particular the way it has functioned in the formation of social identities, both as forces of solidarity and in episodes of conflict.

Chapter 3: From Hearing to Seeing extends and nuances the patterns that were emerging in Chapter Two, to investigate the radical changes in the relationship between sonic and written information networks over the early modern period, that is from roughly the sixteenth to the early eighteenth centuries.

Chapter 4: The Pulpit and the Playhouse investigates the way this transitional moment from the ear to the eye was acted out in the two main arenas of public discourse over the sixteenth and seventeenth centuries: the church and the theatre.

Chapter 5: *Hamlet* – The World Is Out of Joint gives these arguments substance by taking Shakespeare's *Hamlet* as its case study, exploring in detail the operations of the basic argument which drives this study; that is, that an auditory rather than predominantly visual approach to the past produces a different understanding of cultural history.

Chapter 6: Print Triumphant takes us to the 'triumph of the eye' in the eighteenth century, specifically in the form of the written word as the primary authority as the basis of knowledge and social regulation, and the parallel decline of the authority of oral/aural information and tradition.

Chapter 7: The Aural Renaissance explores technological developments during the nineteenth century, from which emerged a renewed attentiveness to the sonic circulation of information, a new soundscape distinctive to modernity, and new ways of listening.

Chapter 8: The Aural Renaissance and Cultural Change draws out some of the less obvious, but far-reaching, cultural changes relating to the dynamics in such areas as gender, class, and politics, that would not have taken place as they did without the sonic revolutions of the Aural Renaissance.

Chapter 9: Sound in the Contemporary World presents an overview of significant acoustic developments through the twentieth century in both the public sphere and in the everyday conditions of domestic life as both streets and households became sites of a new soundscape.

Chapter 10: The Modern Soundscape, Social Welfare and Policy investigates ways in which the technological developments associated with the Aural Renaissance and their social impact require reassessments of social policies and protocols relating to the deployment of sound.

Together, these chapters chart the changing status of sound and hearing in Western society over the last six hundred or so years. They give strength to the argument that we cannot form an adequate understanding of the modern condition if we do not pay attention to the history of sound.

Bruce Johnson
Leura, New South Wales
June 2022

Reading

Blesser, Barry and Linda-Ruth Salter. 2007. *Spaces Speak, Are You Listening? Experiencing Aural Architecture*. Cambridge, MA and London: MIT Press.

Haskell, David George. 2022. *Sounds Wild and Broken*. London: Black Inc.

Leppert, Richard. 1995. *The Sight of Sound: Music, Representation and the History of the Body*. Berkeley, CA: University of California Press.

Ree, Jonathan. 1999. *I See a Voice: A Philosophical History of Language, Deafness and the Senses*. London: HarperCollins Publishers.

Reznikoff, Iegor. 2008. 'Sound Resonance in Prehistoric Times: A Study of Paleolithic Painted Caves and Rocks'. *The Journal of the Acoustical Society of America*, 123 (5): 4137–4141.

INTRODUCTION

The central figure in 'literary' studies, William Shakespeare, had virtually no interest in producing printed versions of his plays. Their scripts were intended to be heard, not read. But he lived through a period when the balance between the authority of the spoken word and the written text, the ear and the eye, was shifting and ambiguous. The title of this book invokes that relationship, with its reference to both sound and the visual concept of perspective. My main objective in what follows is to disclose a body of research, in ways that make it available to general readers who might be curious to consider the role that sound has played in the shaping of history.

Our study of cultural history is dominated by the visual. We know what the battlefield of Waterloo looked like, through maps, paintings and sketches. But we are much more rarely told what it sounded like, and the role that sounds – such as military bands – might have played in its unfolding. The movie footage we have of the First World War suggests silence, yet as we shall read, this omits what participants often identified as its most horrific aspect. Rowland Feilding, an officer serving with the First Coldstream Guards, wrote of going to see the 'Somme film' shown in a field near the lines. It was

> ... really a wonderful and most realistic production, but must of necessity be wanting in that the battle is fought in silence, and, moreover, that the most unpleasant part – the machine-gun and rifle fire – is entirely eliminated. Of the actual 'frightfulness' of war, all that one sees is the bursting shells; and perhaps it is as well. I have said that the battle is fought in silence; but no, on this occasion the roar of real battle was loudly audible in the distance.
>
> Foley and McCartney 2006: 47

DOI: 10.4324/9781003042662-1

Feilding's recollection reminds us that we navigate our way through the world by attaching meanings to it. In studies of human behaviour and taste, the explanation of how we conceive of our individual and collective identities, of how we relate to the world, is for many to be found in our particular culture, the process by which meanings are attached to the world and agreed upon. Through the late twentieth century, cultural studies became a primary avenue of enquiry into human societies and why they behave as they do. Pioneer British cultural theorist Raymond Williams identified different ways in which the word has been used, from capital 'C' Culture, implying refinement and 'cultivation', to more contemporary anthropological and sociological meanings, in which the idea of 'meaning' is significant (Williams 1976: 80).

I give a very simple illustration. Imagine somewhere in a desert wilderness there is a large, flat-topped rock, a piece of 'nature'. But a desert community begins to use it as an altar, perhaps for animal sacrifice. The rock is physically unchanged, but it has now acquired a meaning that is particular to that community. As such, it has shifted from being something 'natural' to something 'cultural'. A similar distinction can be made provisionally for audition. It is because of our body that we can hear some sounds and not others. It is because of our culture that we choose to listen and attach meanings to some sounds rather than others. This is a helpful place to start, but it is simplistic, and later in this book I shall suggest that, understood from a different perspective, the nature/culture distinction, which is so often taken for granted, is by no means so straightforward.

The point here is that our 'culture' is a filter through which we experience and construct the meanings of the world, like different coloured glasses. A scientifically trained geologist would not understand that rock in the same way as the desert community I have referred to. We come to know and understand the world through the 'mediation' or lens of our culture. A member of Islam, a Hindu and a Christian can look at the same thing but form completely different perceptions of it, as for example different kinds of food and drink, gender relations and physical gestures. The cultural difference does not have to be a matter of religion. It can be socio-economic, racial or even generational – what one generation considers to be a fashionable form of dress and conduct is repugnant or ridiculous to another. It is unlikely that any reader would find these ideas surprising, so I want to move beyond them.

There is something that these cultural explanations leave out in our attempt to understand what shapes our way of knowing and relating to the world. That is, the body and its physical senses, the sensorium. Whatever cultural 'filters' we are deploying, without the sensorium, there can be no engagement of any kind with the world. Yet studies of ways of relating to the world have, until relatively recently, taken the body so much for granted as to have ignored it, remaining locked into approaches that even the study of emotions, so clearly rooted in physical experience, is steered 'away from due consideration of the senses' (Boddice and Smith 2020: 7).

Like culture, the body 'mediates' the world for us. But like culture, the senses also filter information. We human beings cannot see all that there is to be seen, such as the ultraviolet and infrared ranges of the visual spectrum. We cannot hear all the sounds that are there to be heard by, for example dogs (who also detect smells that we cannot), and other living creatures, as recorded in detail in David Haskell's 2022 study of sound and hearing that reaches back to Earth's origins and beyond (Haskell 2022). In 2003, astronomers investigating a black hole discovered sound waves 'fifty-seven octaves below middle C', and at the other extreme, university physicists identified a note 'seventeen octaves higher than the limits of human audibility' (Drobnick 2004: 9). In short, we are very far short of being able to take it for granted that what our senses disclose is a full and accurate account of what is 'out there'.

Let us then consider how we engage sensorially with the world. Conventionally, we think in terms of five senses: vision, hearing, touch, smell and taste. But in actual public social practice our channels of engagement are much more limited. In private and intimate relationships we use all those senses. But in our public and professional lives, most of those sensory channels are taboo, or ineffectual for finely discriminated transactions. It would be regarded as grossly improper to communicate with our work colleagues or even close friends, by tasting them. We might admire someone's perfume or aftershave, but interestingly that is actually a manifestation of a desire not to project your identity publicly by the natural smell of your body. And increasingly, touching someone in a workplace or schoolroom is completely out of order.

In short, our primary public sensory engagements with the world are visual and aural. We display ourselves and look at each other. We make sounds and we listen. I want to begin by comparing these two epistemologies, 'ways of knowing': how hearing differs from knowing through seeing, how sound differs from sight. It is necessary to enter a caveat as a context for the comparison: that is, that the distinctions summarised below are not necessarily absolute. To illustrate, I suggest that seeing is spatial – we scan space to look at something, whether it is a panorama, a face, a painting or the page of a book. Hearing on the other hand is primarily a temporal mode – what we hear unfolds in time, like a song, a conversation or a symphony. Music takes place 'in time', in two senses.

In papers published by Ernst Mach over 1863 to 1872, he 'posited that the ear surpasses the other senses in the ability to determine time intervals correctly' (Erlmann 2010: 277), and in fact as we shall note below, in the discussion of how we localize sound sources, the ears have an astonishing sensitivity to extremely minute intervals of time. Some writers have questioned the temporal/spatial distinction I have just made and similar distinctions (see for example Sterne 2003: 14–16; Erlmann 2010: 23), and of course, it is true that we also use our hearing to explore space, as in tapping on a hogshead or a water tank to determine the level of its contents. Sound thus can communicate a sense of space (see further Blesser and Salter 2007, for example on 'Auditory Spatial Awareness', 11–66).

As the later discussion of reverberation argues, we also use our hearing for echolocation, for clues about the nature of the space we occupy, a skill that is particularly relied upon by marine life, by the blind and indeed by all of us albeit subliminally, as experience in an anechoic chamber, discussed below, demonstrates (Ihde 2007: 59, 67, 70–71; for an extended discussion, 85-102). Smith (1999) and Thompson (2004) are only two representatives of a whole branch of scholarship that explores the relationship between physical space and acoustics and the history of that relationship (for an extended study see Blesser and Salter 2007). The word 'primarily' in 'hearing is a primarily temporal sense, vision is a primarily spatial sense' is important. Although vision (say looking at a view), 'primarily' involves the scanning of space, it also takes time; although listening to a symphony requires time, it also takes place in a space that has a bearing on what is heard. Sterne cautions against 'idealizing' sound, and implying that reliance on one sense causes other to atrophy (Sterne 2003: 15, 16).

There is another matter raised by Sterne which I need to address. He attributes to a category of scholars in the field the assumption that 'face-to-face communication and bodily presence are the yardsticks by which to measure all communicative activity … they assume the primacy of face-to-face interaction' (Sterne 2003: 20). I am not sure what 'primacy' means here, but by any definition that I can reasonably imagine, there are a great many writers who do not assign 'primacy' to face-to-face communication, particularly among historians of, for example, film music, or modern politics and demagoguery (for example Birdsall 2012). I am among them. I don't unconditionally assign primacy in any sense to either 'live' or technologically mediated sound. It all depends on context and objective. At the outset, then, let me make it clear that I am not idealizing hearing over seeing, nor do I wish to imply that the dominance of one sense in any given transaction causes the others to atrophy.[1] I am simply making some descriptive comparisons that are generally accepted in the literature.

I am concerned in this book with how the difference between hearing and seeing actually feels, and what are the cultural and social implications. For example, is what we see a more reliable way of representing the 'real' ('Seeing is believing') than listening ('Don't believe everything you hear')? Perhaps we should be more careful about prioritizing vision as our most reliable access to reality, equating what we see with what is there. When we draw a road stretching out before us, gradually converging to a point, it might be what a road looks like, but it is certainly not what it *is* like, or we should soon reach the end of it as disappears in a point. When we draw a cube as it looks to us, we are deforming it, since, unlike that representation, every angle on a cube is a right angle.

Let us pursue this comparison further. First, sound floods the social space, it envelopes all within it. Among other consequences, it makes hearing closer to a shared experience in a way that looking cannot be. In an auditorium, each individual visual perspective is different, ranging from slight to total. Each sees the person on stage from a slightly different angle, and in addition, only that part of the person facing the assembly. But, allowing for acoustic 'dead spots' and 'sweet spots' (see Blesser and Salter 2007: 186), everyone is immersed in the same flood of sounds within that auditorium. And they hear the 'totality' of the sound a speaker makes, but see only one aspect of them. This applies reflexively also: we cannot see ourselves *in toto*, but we can hear ourselves.

Sound can also instantly modify the nature and the horizon of identity. By raising or lowering my voice or adjusting my tone I can instantaneously transform myself in ways that are much more difficult visually. By lowering the volume of my voice, hearing/sounding can thus be a vehicle of closeness rather than of distance (like all senses except for sight, which is often the vehicle and metaphor of distanced analysis, of 'standing back to get the bigger picture'). Sound is therefore a very powerful tool of social negotiation, and in many ways, our projection of our social being is achieved more fully acoustically than visually. As a form of expression, sound can also achieve a terrifyingly high level of intensity. This is reflected in 'stingers' in movies, sharp sonic punctuations that cue moments of danger. A scream uttered and heard is a far more direct and intense experience than one spoken or written of.

Sound also penetrates the body, even entering our own ears *in utero*; in 1998 it was found by Janet DiPietro at Johns Hopkins University that the foetus begins to respond to sound as early as nine weeks after conception (Schwartz 2011: 177, 755). And our voice emerges from within the body; indeed, what we hear of our own voice is not only perceived through our ears but is conducted through our skeletal system, which is why do not hear ourselves as others hear us (Ihde 2007: 247). Vision on the other hand plays over the surface. The sound of a voice whispering in your ear at, for example a dinner table, is an extremely intimate experience, and sets up a separate acoustic reality. As I shall detail later, sound is also in an important sense physiologically processed very differently as compared with the relationship between the eye and the brain. They are, then, different ways of 'being-in-the-world': 'Listening opens our minds to other ways of being' (Haskell 2022: 18).

Most frequently we are not aware of these distinctive characteristics of sound, because generally there is a harmony between visual and auditory information. But when that is not so, it can be deeply disorienting, even horrifying, as in the disparity between what we see – say a child – and hear – a Satanic voice emerging – as in for example *The Exorcist* (dir. William Friedkin 1973). The point is that a world as seen overlaps with a world as heard, but it is not the same world. It is part of the objective of this book to explore this disparity, by attending to history as a soundscape rather than as a 'landscape', to discover a different world. Sometimes it is language itself which is an impediment to this objective. As Haskell notes, 'We have an impoverished vocabulary for hearing' (Haskell 2022: 18). If we could begin to find a language that is not saturated in visual metaphors, we could construct a different representation of human society and the environment.

The dominance of vision is by no mean universal, and the balance between the role of the senses in navigating life varies from culture to culture. In some Inuit communities, the absence of visual markers in a uniformly snowbound environment requires them to rely on other senses, with sonicity playing a major role; as discussed below, communication with the divine in many cultures including Judaism and Christianity is primarily sonic (Blesser and Salter 2007: 72). This is reflected in many indigenous languages and those closer to their oral roots. The example of Finnish makes for an instructive comparison with English, the language in which I am writing, one of the Indo-European language groups. Along with Estonian and Hungarian, Finnish is one of only three major languages in the Finno-Ugric group. Its oral roots are reflected in the fact that if you can pronounce each letter, you can 'speak' the language; that is, the sound of a group of letters will be the same in whatever word they occur. Compare this with English, as for example the letter group 'ough': through, rough, thorough, dough, thought and bough. That is, there is a much closer relationship between how a word is spelled and how it sounds in Finnish.

Finnish culture and language are more sensitive to sound and silence.[2] A few of many illustrations of its sonocentricity:

The timepiece that we call a 'watch' in English is called 'kello' in Finnish, which also means 'bell'. We linguistically model the measurement of time in visual terms, the Finns in aural terms.

In English we bid someone goodbye with the words 'See you later'. In Finnish you can greet someone with 'Mitä kuluu', literally 'What do you hear?' And in fact the word 'kuluu' also represents the notion of a community – a group that hears the same sounds. All forms of the word 'kuulla' (to hear) are widely used in everyday discussion as forms of 'to know', and while in English we use the words 'Let's see' to foreshadow a possible outcome, especially in the east Finnish dialects the more common expression is 'Kuulostellaan', 'Let's hear'.

As in so many languages, proverbial wisdoms are significant, and in Finnish these are notably sonic in orientation, as in:

Respect the deep voice of experience;

'Sitä kuusta kuuleminen jonka juurella asunto' – meaning that wisdom lies in listening to the roots of the fir tree next to your house.

As illustrated (note the visual orientation of the word) below, English terms relating to wisdom and knowledge are overwhelmingly visual in orientation, and in fact many such visual tropes, such as spectacular, envisage, reveal, survey, insight and visualize have no established aural equivalent.

In the foregoing discussion, I referred in particular to the voice. That is because it is one of the most complex and meaningful of all our sounds. Of all the ways we sustain complex relationships with the world, the voice is the one we use most often, it is the most versatile, the most intense, and can be adjusted instantly. The human voice is embodied communication. It IS the body, the irreducible site of our social being. It is the body projected sonically into the social space, and so intimately revealing that we in the mainstream Western world experience embarrassment at certain ways of projecting it publicly, such as singing or yelling. Russian writer Alexander Solzhenitsyn reported that those abducted in the street by the agents of the Stalinist state could well have saved themselves or at least postponed their arrest by not literally going quietly. He cited the example of a woman who grabbed a streetlamp and screamed, 'refusing to submit'; the agents 'got into their car and fled' (Solzhenitsyn 1974: 16). And we are even more sensitive about public involuntary vocalisation such as sobbing.

The voice is an extraordinary instrument, capable of the most finely discriminated expressive gestures. Of all our organs, the larynx has the highest ratio of nerve to muscle fibre; this thing we take for granted is capable of the most astonishingly complex expressive nuances. They are guarantees of our authentic identity, as voice recognition access systems exploit. For all these reasons, playing around with the voice is deeply disconcerting, as in the case of *The Exorcist* mentioned above, and in the more recent movie *The Others* (dir. Alejandro Amenábar 2001) in which, as with so many other films, suspense is generated by sonic/visual incongruities, as for example a young girl's voice coming from an old woman. Likewise the disembodied voice, as in the case of *The Wizard of Oz* (dir. Victor Fleming et al. 1939), who shifts from disturbing preternatural wizard to banal old man when we see where the sound is coming from.

Our most usual way of projecting ourselves vocally is speech, but I am interested in going beyond *what* people say to a broader understanding of vocalising. To illustrate: later I shall discuss one of Shakespeare's most famous plays, *Hamlet*. I am interested in the way sound functions in the play, and of course I am by no means the first to be so. Apart from the myriad commentaries on what Shakespeare's characters say, there have over the decades been studies that embrace broader aspects of sonicity in his work.[3] A study whose title suggests a convergence with my approach is Kenneth Gross's 2001 publication, *Shakespeare's Noise*. He begins his Introduction: 'This book pursues a vision of the work of words in Shakespeare's plays. I look most closely at violent or disorderly forms of speaking: slander, defamation, insult, vituperation, malediction, and curse. Rumor [sic] and gossip play a part as well' (Gross 2001: 1). He includes a chapter on *Hamlet*, but it is not about 'noise' or even 'sound' in the broadest sense. There are references to these, noting that there is much reference to sounding and hearing, often associated with toxicity, slander, damage and a world out of joint. The play is 'full of sounds, of oddly troubled hearings, overhearings, and mishearings. There are, first-off, the literal or non-verbal, though not inhuman, noises that accompany the action', such as the kettledrums and cannon shots at the beginning and end, various footsteps, the thud of a body behind the arras, colliding swords, the clanking of armour, a cock-crow and that these add to a sense of the 'uncanny' (Gross 2001: 12–13). This, however, is something of an aside to his main argument, which is devoted to an instructive analysis based on the lexical components of dialogue, words as meaning something, studying the motif of rumour and slander.

Throughout this book, including the discussion of Hamlet/*Hamlet*, it is what I have referred to as Gross's 'aside' that is my main point of interest: the soundscape in general, encompassing natural and human sounds including speech. As far as speech is concerned, we can think of two dimensions: the lexical content (what the words mean), and the acoustic content (how they sound). Sometimes these converge, as in onomatopoeia, when a word sounds like what it describes: 'miaow', 'woof' and 'thump'. But more often they do not. The sentence 'It looks like a fine day' bears no resemblance to the 'sound' of looking like a fine day. And in fact, often the sound of a statement can take control of the lexical meaning of the written word. 'The voice ... is more than just a bodily device for making sense, for communicating via language. Inevitably it produces an excess: a surplus of sound over sense, of connotation over designation' (Ballantine 2019: 296).

We can express far more emotional complexity in the same number of words – even in the same words – through voice than we can through print. Standing by themselves, the printed words 'I am going home', have none of their expressive possibilities as spoken words: joy, regret, irony, sadness, revulsion and fear, depending on how they are *sounded*. Indeed, the voice does not need 'words' to express emotional states, as a great deal of popular music makes clear, from jovial scat singers like Louis Armstrong and Ella Fitzgerald to Little Richard's ecstatic 'A-wop-bop-a-loo-mop-a-lop-bam-boom'. In all these, meaningful attributes of wordless vocal sounds include rhythm, repetition/disruption and timbre. These are all communicators of meaning, emotion, power, and they are ones which outflank and circumscribe critical discourses obsessed with reason, logic and denotation. Sound can undermine, contest and overwhelm grammatical sense, as any sleepless parent lulling a child to sleep can testify. It's not the words spoken, but the sounds made. At the extremes of experience, words fail us, but sound does not: the scream, the howl, the sob, are incomparably powerful, while at the same time totally unintelligible, resistant to traditional forms of academic analysis, of 'literary criticism'.

So, even when the whole sensorium is brought to bear on the same environment, each component is relating us to that environment in a different way. What I hear and what I see might be the same, but hearing and seeing them are very different kinds of experience. They are such different ways of knowing that anthropologist Steven Feld has coined the word 'acoustemology' as a distinctive form of 'epistemology', of knowledge gained by hearing (Feld 1996).

I want, therefore, to give the strongest emphasis to one central theme which runs throughout the following discussions of apparently disparate subjects, that links such dissimilar phenomena as the Elizabethan playhouse and jet aircraft, the early modern pulpit and the contemporary boom box. That link is sound. Sound seeps into every area of life. As the citations in the final chapters indicate, much has been written about modern sound, because it is so intrusive, from industrial machinery, through road, sea and air traffic, to amplified neighbourhood noise. These are the more obvious impacts of sound on our lives. One of my main arguments is that sound saturates and influences culture in ways that are often less obvious, but nonetheless decisive. The path to discovering that impact is often less direct than the sound of a passenger jet flying overhead, and there will be times when the reader might wonder where the relevance of a discussion lies. Bear with me. This is an important manifestation of a matter of historiographical method: often the relationship between cause and effect is tangled and elusive. But in the end, it is often more revealing of the complex ramifications of sound and its involvement in relations of power than 'the usual suspects' such as the impact of modern traffic noise or a noisy dance club.

The ideas outlined above will be developed in the course of this book, punctuated with various case studies in the cultural functions of sound. This is not a narrative history of sound. That subject is far beyond the compass of any single volume. My primary focus is English-speaking – anglophone – culture, and although I refer to antiquity, most of my attention will be from what is known as the early modern period to the present.

Chapter One presents observations on sound and hearing, their relationship to external space as well as to human physiology and cognition, why certain sounds produce particular responses. This leads to an overview of the history of the relationship between sound, territory and identity, the effects of a shift from spiritual to modern secular sound design and musicality, and the importance of our sense of control over our sonic environment.

Chapter Two provides an introductory survey of the role of sound in cultural history, and in particular, the way it has functioned in the formation of social identities, both as unifying forces and in episodes of conflict. Among the patterns which this discussion foreshadows are, first, that sound is a highly instructive approach to the study of shifting identity formations, alliances and conflicts, and, second, that there appears to be some kind of connection emerging historically between volubility, noisiness and the politics – the power relations – underpinning class and other social hierarchies. A sonically oriented approach to the study of cultures as we approach the modern era might well disclose the existence of 'bottom-up' orally based histories that provide counter-narratives to the 'official' written stories by those in power. The primary case study here involves the relationship between the Irish and the British, both 'home and away'.

Chapter Three extends and nuances the patterns that were emerging in Chapter Two, to investigate the radical changes in the relationship between sonic and written information networks over the early modern period, which is from roughly the sixteenth to the early eighteenth centuries. These changes were particularly reflected in the progress of the English Reformation and the drift towards a more secular culture. In parallel, there is a shift in the balance of authority between oral and written cultures, between unwritten custom and law. That shift is itself associated with changes in the sonic environment, as exemplified in sixteenth-century urban soundscapes, in which sound, and in particular the sound of the human voice was prominent. During this period, the relationship between the sonic and the visual was much more evenly balanced, but in a state of transition from the former to the latter.

Chapter Four investigates the way this transitional moment from the ear to the eye was acted out in the two main arenas of public discourse over the sixteenth and seventeenth centuries: the church and the playhouse. The pulpit was a site for the promulgation of religious beliefs, but at a time when such beliefs were inextricably linked to politics and broader social issues. And one of the themes through which these were debated was whether the road to truth was through the ear – what was heard – or the eye – what was read. The spread of literacy was thus a crucial force in the transition from oral to textual information, from sound to sight. It is of note that over the same period that the secular playhouse was flourishing with its unforgettably eloquent speeches, the record of religious belief – the sermon – was increasingly turning to printed forms and a tightly disciplined, plain style. The playhouse above all proclaims the difference between a live, aural performance, an active soundscape, and the experience of reading a page of print. The dynamic soundscape of the playhouse, and its acoustic properties as compared with those of ecclesiastical architecture, are decisive in the generation of meaning, and in particular in the way it balances what is heard with what is seen.

In Chapter Five these arguments are given substance by taking Shakespeare's *Hamlet* as its case study, exploring in detail the operations of the basic argument which drives this study; that is, that an auditory rather than predominantly visual approach to the past produces a different understanding of cultural history. Attending to *Hamlet* as an acoustic phenomenon provides answers to questions which a study of the printed text cannot easily resolve. For the Elizabethan audience the question of what we know, and how we know it, was very much in the air. The question is explored in terms of a shifting and unstable relationship between the evidence of the eye and the ear. One way of examining the play, then, is to think of it not only as residing at the interface of sight and sound, as exploiting that relationship in its dramatic effects but also in crucial ways that is its actual subject. Standing at a midpoint of a transition from an aural to a visual epistemology, *Hamlet* provides an instructive study in the role of sound in its often confusing relationship with what is seen, exploiting the ways in which sounds – including singing, dialogue, soliloquy, eavesdropping and of inanimate objects such as ordnance and musical instruments, can generate the impression of being neither fully in one world nor the other, of disorder in both the individual and the state. Hamlet himself is torn by these tensions, haunted by voices from which the only 'rest is silence' – the pun is fully intentional.

Chapter Six takes us to the 'triumph of the eye' in the eighteenth century, specifically in the form of the printed word as the primary authority as the basis of knowledge and social regulation. At the same time there is not just a corresponding decline in the authority of sonic information, but a growing active suspicion of noise as a sign of disorder, subversion of authority and a threat to the status quo. This permeates the whole legal apparatus, in tensions between unwritten custom, and written laws which proliferated in parallel with the fetishization of private as opposed to common property, as well as increasing resistance to the 'tumult' of the underclasses. Noise evokes the idea of revolution and resistance, silence signifies dutiful submission to the state. In places of public assembly devoted to self-improvement and education – church congregations, concert halls, libraries, galleries, schoolrooms – the soundscape becomes tightly regulated, and suspicion attaches to places and events where sonic regulation cannot be enforced. The mob, the urban crowd, the embryonic working class or the proletariat, those who were oppressed under capitalism, are all figured as the rise of noise. The connection between public noise, disorder and vulgarity represents a confrontation between the genteel sensibilities of a growing urban middle class and the culture of an urban proletariat. All the forces of modernity converge in the increasingly severe regulation of public noise.

Chapter Seven introduces us to the most influential developments in the history of sound. If the visually oriented Renaissance initiated a major shift in the power relations between the oral and the written, the mid to late nineteenth century saw a revolution that in many ways reversed that shift in favour of sound. Print had enjoyed the great advantage of enabling the storage, standardisation and global dissemination of information. The coming of sound recording broke that monopoly, and opened the way to what could be called an 'Aural Renaissance'. Sound recording radio, amplification, portability and all the technologies that followed through to the digital age meant that sound could be preserved, stored and reproduced in infinite numbers of copies, and circulated internationally on a mass level. That is, it came to possess all the hitting power of print, but in many ways more so. In due course it could also attain a volume and frequency range beyond the tolerance and capacities of the human ear, and could be carried anywhere and delivered through a range of systems that almost anyone can now afford. It became a 'weapon' that almost anyone could possess. Over roughly the same period the Industrial Revolution introduced hitherto unimaginable technological sonorities. These were both quantitative, in the range of volume, and qualitative, in the production of a new sonic vocabulary in terms of frequency, rhythm and tempo of various forms of industrial machinery. The chapter concludes with a discussion of the contribution of the new 'sonic imaginary' made by a watershed event in the transition to twentieth-century modernity, the First World War.

Chapter Eight draws out some of the less obvious, but far-reaching, cultural changes that would not have taken place as they did without the sonic revolutions of the Aural Renaissance. These were not just an extension of an earlier soundscape, but they transformed the way sound was used, imagined and culturally located. The expansion of the soundscape generated new habits of listening, a new interest in the nature and function of sound. This was evidenced in the emergence not just of a new field of study, otology, but the use of sound as itself a means of study, as in the increasing sophistication of the stethoscope as a diagnostic tool. Similarly, the discipline of anthropology was much extended through the use of field recordings, which also had political implications for the (post)colonialist dynamic. These shifts in power relations were also apparent in much less obvious, but equally transformative ways in, for example, gender politics, as exemplified in such areas as stenography and musical performance.

Chapter Nine surveys the soundscape of modernity, significant acoustic developments through the twentieth century. These are to be heard most clearly in public life, particularly but by no means solely in the industrial, commercial and social spheres. But modernity has also transformed the private soundscape. Even everyday households became the sites of a new sonic order. Apart from noises intruding from outside, the modern residence is drenched in sounds largely created by the domestication of electrical and electronic equipment. Apart from the obvious examples of radio, TV and sound reproduction systems, the modern Western home is filled with appliances which emit more or less continuous sounds, accompanied by the *continuo* of mains hum.

Chapter Ten concludes the study with a review of the impact of the modern soundscape on public welfare, the growth of noise abatement campaigns and government interventions through policies related to noise pollution. These raise problems and tensions involving individual rights regarding the sonic environment in densely populated urban centres, and extending to such urgent environmental issues as climate change and the generation of energy, lifestyles and global inequities.

Notes

1 Though in this connection, it is relevant to recall the words of Helen Keller, deaf and blind from eighteenth months old, when she declared that 'the problems of deafness are deeper and more complex, if not more important, than those of blindness. Deafness is a much worse misfortune, for it means the loss of the most vital stimulus the sound of the voice that brings language, sets thoughts astir, and keeps us in the intellectual company of man' (Ihde 2007: 135).
2 In the following, I want to gratefully acknowledge the input by research students, too numerous to name, from Åbo Akademi, Turku, Finland, who participated in discussions of silence and sound in Finnish language and culture.
3 See for example Mahood 1957; Burckhardt 1968; Weimann 1978; Ferguson 1985.

Reading

Ballantine, Christopher. 2019. 'Opera and the South African Political'. In Mark Grimshaw-Aagaard, Mads Walther-Hansen, Martin Knakkergaard (eds), *The Oxford Handbook of Sound and Imagination*, Vol. 1. Oxford: Oxford University Press: 291–312.
Birdsall, Carolyn. 2012. *Nazi Soundscapes Sound, Technology and Urban Space in Germany, 1933–1945.* Amsterdam: Amsterdam University Press.
Blesser, Barry and Linda-Ruth Salter. 2007. *Spaces Speak, Are You Listening? Experiencing Aural Architecture.* Cambridge, MA and London: MIT Press.
Boddice, Rob and Mark Smith. 2020. *Emotions, Sense, Experience.* Cambridge: Cambridge University Press.
Burckhardt, Sigurd. 1968. *Shakespearean Meanings.* Princeton, NJ: Princeton University Press.
Drobnick, Jim (ed.). 2004. *Aural Cultures.* Toronto: YYZ Books.
Erlmann, Veit. 2010. *Reason and Resonance: A History of Modern Aurality.* New York, NY: Zone Books.
Feld, Steven. 1996. 'Waterfalls of Song: An Acoustemology of Place Resounding in Bossavi, Papua New Guinea'. In S. Feld and K.H. Basso (eds), *Senses of Place.* Santa Fe, NM: School of American Research Press: 91–136.
Ferguson, Margaret. 1985. 'Hamlet: Letters and Spirits'. in Patricia Parker and Geoffrey Hartman (eds), *Shakespeare and the Question of Theory.* New York, NY: Methuen: 292–309.
Foley, Robert T. and Helen McCartney (eds). 2006. *The Somme: An Eyewitness History.* London: The Folio Society.
Gross, Kenneth. 2001. *Shakespeare's Noise.* Chicago, IL and London: University of Chicago Press.
Haskell, David George. 2022. *Sounds Wild and Broken.* Collingwood: Black Inc.
Ihde, Don. 2007. *Listening and Voice: Phenomenologies of Sound.* Albany, NY: State University of New York Press.
Mahood, M.M. 1957. *Shakespeare's Wordplay.* London: Methuen.
Schwartz, Hillel. 2011. *Making Noise: From Babel to the Big Bang & Beyond.* New York, NY: Zone Books.
Smith, Bruce. 1999. *The Acoustic World of Early Modern England.* Chicago, IL and London: University of Chicago Press.

Solzhenitsyn, Alexander. 1974 (first pub 1973). *The Gulag Archipelago 1918–1956* (Trans. Thomas P. Whitney.) Vol. 1 of 3 volumes. Melbourne: Collins Fontana.

Sterne, Jonathan. 2003. *The Audible Past: Cultural Origins of Sound Reproduction*. Durham, NC, London: Duke University Press.

Thompson, Emily. 2004. *The Soundscape of Modernity: Architectural Acoustics and the Culture of Listening in America, 1900–1933*. Cambridge, MA and London: MIT Press.

Weimann, Robert. 1978. *Shakespeare and the Popular Tradition in the Theater: Studies in the Social Dimension of Dramatic Form and Function*. Baltimore, MD: Johns Hopkins University Press.

Williams, Raymond. 1976. *Keywords: A Vocabulary of Culture and Society*. Glasgow: Fontana/Croom Helm.

1
ACOUSTEMOLOGY
Listening to cultural history

The power of sounds which seem to come from nowhere but everywhere has been exploited throughout history to inspire fear and awe, by religious communities, playwrights, sound engineers in movies and in military actions. Towards the end of World War II, in December 1944, in a last-ditch effort to regain the initiative by an advance through the Ardennes that became known as the Battle of the Bulge, the Wermacht used sound to disorient the enemy, aided by modern sound technologies. These measures included disrupting US communications by playing recordings at full volume on the wavelengths used by the Americans. As they began night attacks, they yelled and screamed at the enemy and banged on their equipment (Beevor 2015: 157). In the often foggy darkness of the forest, the Germans played American dance band records through loudspeakers, interspersed with promises of showers, warm beds and hotcakes for breakfast if the Americans surrendered (Beevor 2015: 186). Thousands did, the second-biggest mass surrender of US troops in history. Part of the impact of this sonic assault was generated by the 'ubiquity effect' (see below). In the darkness and fog, the apparently sourceless and incongruous sounds of music and propaganda from loudspeakers rigged high in the forest trees exemplify the capacity of unlocalizable sounds to inspire disorientation, anxiety and fear. As a wounded officer was being driven from the battle lines into Bastogne, he heard engines through the fog, and they realized it was the sound of German tanks. Their fear was increased by the fact they could hear them but not see them. 'All you could do was hear' (Beevor 2015: 197). US Colonel William Manley, in charge of the appropriately named Project Jericho, reported the similar use of sonic weaponry in Vietnam:

DOI: 10.4324/9781003042662-2

there is no sound more powerful than the one that conquers your true heart with deep vibrations ... a weapon that uses harmonic infrasound amplified by the power of Evangelical Christian faith to summon and deploy a voice that sounds like it comes from right inside your head but also sounds like it is coming from everywhere else. A voice that comes from everywhere and no where [sic], from everyone and no-one, and when you hear it, you will obey no matter what it says.

Goodman 2010: 16

This chapter discusses both the phenomenology and the physiology of hearing, that is, the nature of the experience of sound and the physical mechanisms by which it is processed to produce particular responses. The physical space in which sound is generated already begins to determine how it will be interpreted, as for example, in the case of reverberant environments and the way we locate sound sources. The listening space will limit and shape affect – our emotional responses – particularly if it makes source location difficult, producing sounds that seem to come from everywhere. Thus, highly reverberant spaces have, since prehistoric times, been sites of shamanistic activity. In 1983, sound archaeologist Iegor Reznikoff noticed that where walls in France's Paleolithic cave, Le Portel carried painted animals, the resonance was more intense; along with colleague Michel Dauvois, he went on to 'sound check' other cave walls in the Pyrenees and found the same relationship, simply by walking in the darkness and using his voice as the sound source. At points of high resonance, he would 'turn on the light, and invariably find a sign, "even in a place unsuited for painting"'. The resonance was so strong 'that when he himself made sounds in the cave Reznikoff felt his whole body vibrating in tandem with the gallery'. He inferred that the connection helped the shaman to identify with the animals, and indeed by making a sound near them, he could make it seem that it was the animal making the sound (Prochnik 2011: 96). Sonic Archaeologist Steven J. Walker visited over 150 sites of wall-cave paintings and observed the same correlations between sonic profiles and categories of painting (Blesser and Salter 2007: 74–75; see further 73–78, and on ancient performance spaces, see for example 67–126; for similar examples of acoustic archaeology, see https://ambpnetwork.wordpress.com/introductions-to-the-field/archaeological-approaches-to-sound/; on Stonehenge, see for example https://www.openculture.com/2021/06/the-acoustics-of-stonehenge.html?fbclid=IwAR09LKadZLPaTZomtHXuQEw9GorjrQ7vyBS-5IkwSBNSKfluQFc0_lCuuyw).

From ancient cave paintings to the acoustics of a cathedral, resonances have created an appropriate sense of other-worldliness, whatever might be uttered. The ancient Greeks applied great ingenuity to 'sound engineering' in their dramatic presentations, as exemplified in the 15,000-seat theatre at Epidaurus (Prochnik 2011: 177–178). Acoustic reflectors and reverberators (large empty pots) enhanced the sense of a different kind of reality from the everyday, of a kind of 'enchantment'. Then the way in which the body/mind processes those sounds and the paths sound takes from the ear to the centre of interpretation influence affect and even dissolve the mind/body distinction itself. Let us begin by returning to some of the distinctive characteristics of sound, concentrating on four features: ubiquity, localization, frequency or pitch and volume.

Ubiquity

When we enter any particular enclosed space, like a theatre or classroom, the sound within that space is ubiquitous. That is, it is everywhere. It floods the space it enters, and unless we have some noise-cancelling apparatus, it is therefore inescapable. Normally, this presents no problems. It is ordinary – but only as long as we can determine where the sound is coming from. At the onset of a new sound, we search for the source. Let us say we are awakened in the night by an unexpected noise, and we can't identify the source. This produces a feeling of uncertainty that can range from mild anxiety through disempowerment to panic. There is a name for sound whose source is concealed: acousmatic. And there is a name for the anxiety it produces: the ubiquity effect (see further Augoyard and Torgue 2006: 130–134; Chion 1994: 71–73, 129–131). We have all experienced it in some form. Apart from the thump at night, hearing a siren while driving, the sound of an aircraft overhead, and a rustling in the bushes and not being able to locate the source are some examples.

That is, if you can detach the sonic from the visual, producing acousmatic sound, you can increase your power of disorientation over the listener, especially if the noise incorporates infrasound (see further below). The ubiquity effect creates the impression that you are in the presence of a hidden, greater power than yourself. This unequal power relationship produces discomfort, nervousness, rising to panic and the desire for flight. This ubiquity effect is caused by our being unable to localize a sound source, which takes us to the second feature of sound referred to above:

Localization

Because of the ubiquity effect, some sounds are more powerful than others; that is, they are harder to source. So how do we localize a sound source aurally? The body employs several systems of sound localization, two of which are most relevant here. One is called interaural intensity difference, that is, a difference in the intensity of the sound (roughly speaking, the volume), reaching each ear. The ear closer to the sound source will experience the sound at greater intensity and facilitate location of the sound source. This works best, however, when the head itself masks the sound, and for this to happen, the wavelength of the sound must be shorter than the width of the head, which in turn means relatively high-pitched sounds. Similarly in the case of a second sound localization system, interaural temporal difference. This refers to the split-second interval between the sound reaching the ear nearer to the source and the other ear. For obvious reasons, both of these systems operate most effectively when the sound is lateral, coming from the side so that there are in fact 'interaural' disparities.

There are two kinds of circumstances which cause these 'interaural' systems of sound localization to break down. First, if the sound comes from above us, it reaches both ears with the same intensity and at the same time, so there is little or no interaural differentiation, and that increases our sense of disorientation. Sometimes it is only mild, as when we hear an aircraft flying overhead but can't locate it visually. But under other circumstances, this can produce panic. The total bomb load of the German Junkers Ju 87 Stuka dive bomber was 500 kilogrammes, a mere mosquito bite compared to, say, the 10,000 kilogramme Grand Slam bomb carried by British Lancasters. Yet the Stuka was a major factor in demoralizing the Poles during Hitler's blitzkrieg of September 1939. And a significant factor in causing panic was its 'Jericho siren' emanating from directly overhead from the aircraft in a vertical dive, and therefore seeming to be coming from everywhere and nowhere. Journalist John Langdon-Davies wrote of the dangers of the noise of bombing in the war on nerves:

> By perpetual bombing, people can be kept awake, kept worried, kept restless, kept unoccupied … and this is exactly what is wanted. Noise is the way to do it. If there could be such a thing as a silent bomb certain to kill ten times as many people as the ordinary bomb, nobody would ever use it. It is the bark of the bomb that is worse than its bite'.
>
> Mansell 2017a: 172

There is nothing exotic or even exclusively modern in the exploitation of vertical as opposed to lateral sound to induce feelings of awe, or fear, of being in the presence of overwhelming power. Any sound coming from above, such as from an organ loft, an elevated pulpit, a highly elevated pop music stadium stage or an apartment above us, is more likely to produce a sense of unequal power relations than sound coming from the same level, as in an upright piano on the floor of a bar, which projects its sound laterally. Consider the very different power relations between two music performance scenarios: an upright piano playing blues in the corner of a pub and a concert grand, lid up, projecting its music both down from a high stage as well as the sound bouncing down from the acoustically engineered high ceiling. The music in the concert hall carries much greater artistic authority, partly because of the more aesthetically 'elevated' music, but this is enhanced by the physically elevated conditions of its presentation, which draw on the ubiquity effect and its corollaries.

The other condition in which our sound localization system breaks down brings us to our third aspect of sonic experience.

Pitch/Frequency

Frequency refers to the number of sound vibrations occurring per second and is measured in Hertz (Hz). One Hz is one cycle per second. The higher the frequency, the shorter the wavelength of the sounds and the higher the pitch. A few examples of what this means in terms of the experience of hearing will give more meaning to the term. The healthy ear can usually hear sounds ranging from 20 to 20,000 Hz, but as we get older, we lose the ability to hear at the upper end of that range. Sounds below the 20 to 20,000 Hz range are called infrasound, and above that range they are called ultrasound. Sounds up to 100 Hz are usually referred to as Low-Frequency Noise (LFN), and we shall return to this below. The human voice usually falls between 100 and 8,000 Hz. It might help think of low, middle and high-frequency sound with respect to musical notes. The lowest note on a piano has a frequency of just over 27 Hz with a wavelength of nearly 13 metres; the highest has a frequency of just above 4,186 Hz and a wavelength of .081 metres. The usual tuning reference point for orchestras, often printed on sheet music, is the A above middle C, which is 440 Hz.

All of these figures will again make more practical sense if we now consider how they impact our emotional responses to sound. In the case of the human voice, we don't just respond to the lexical content of what is spoken; its meanings and emotional impact will be influenced crucially by sonicity itself. For example, whatever words we might be speaking, yelling is unlikely to be understood as the expression of tenderness. In the journey of sound from the ear to what we think of as the 'brain', affect is pre-determined by physiological processes that are involuntary and almost irrevocable. Pitch is a decisive factor. As exemplified below, film composers have long understood that LFN communicates a sense of power in the source and of anxiety in the listener.

The longer the wavelength of a sound, the lower the register, and the less it is screened by physical objects; that is, why so often all we hear of the music being played in the apartment upstairs or coming from CD player in a passing car is the bass 'doof, doof, doof'. As noted above, if the wavelength of a sound is longer than the diameter of the human head, the head will not block the sound to produce interaural differences, so with its long wavelength, LFN is more difficult to localize than higher-pitched sounds in the range of human hearing and is therefore likely to generate the ubiquity effect. Put more simply: for physiological reasons, the lower the pitch of a sound, the more power it projects and the more potentially disturbing and threatening. Conversely, a scream for help is intended to draw people's attention to its source and is therefore spontaneously in a high register.

Extreme bass registers can cause physical damage. Pneumothorax is a condition believed to be characterized by air entering the space between the lungs and their surrounding membranes. Risk factors include, among other things, smoking and alcohol. Symptoms range from chest pain and breathlessness, to lung collapse and consequent life-threatening deprivation of oxygen to vital organs. The physiology underlying such an attack is believed to be the different responses of the two sets of tissue to sound, and the trigger appears to be the presence of LFN at high volume. In one case of pneumothorax, the source was a 1,000 watt bass-box fitted to the patient's car stereo. In another case, a young man experienced an attack while attending a heavy metal concert. In December 2009, a young student attending his first university party in London found himself crowded against a bass speaker. He said to a friend, 'My heart feels funny. I think the bass is affecting me. Oh God, I feel very weird. My heart is beating so fast'. Minutes later, he collapsed and died. Cause of death was recorded as Sudden Arrhythmic Death Syndrome (SADS). But this is a label rather than an explanation and, according to a medical spokesperson, death was possibly attributable to 'a lot of loud noise' (Johnson 2009: 177–178). This bewildered vagueness reflects just how suddenly a new problem has emerged in the contemporary soundscape. Noise pollution is of increasing international concern, but within that general category, it appears that the increase in LFN is in turn the fastest-growing problem, as suggested by the puzzlement of the representative of the medical profession cited above, who attributed the fatal trauma simply to volume. The clue, however, is the reference to the bass speaker, and sound engineers I spoke to immediately understood what the doctor did not: that the student was probably standing in what is known as a 'bass trap'.

We don't have to suffer from these extreme forms of organic damage to experience some form of disempowerment in the presence of low-register noise. In everyday life, lower register vocalization is associated with the site of power and domination, with authority, menace and threat. There is therefore a connection between power and the gendered voice, low voices being most often associated with masculine power. A recent development in the cosmetic surgery repertoire enables individuals to have a 'squeaky voice' surgically lowered in order to enhance their confidence and power in the workplace. The microphone became a performance accessory for popular music vocalists in the early 1930s, to enable them to compete in volume with the big bands, themselves augmented to fill the increasingly spacious urban dance halls. But this technology had further unforeseen consequences, one of which was to enable men to project with a softer and higher pitched voice (crooning), which attracted the charge of feminization and emasculation. At the same time, women no longer had to rely on a piercing high register to project, and lowered their pitch to something approaching normal conversation. The outcome was a narrowing of the discrepancy between the male and the female singing voice and therefore of the gendered power relations (Johnson 2000: 81–135; see further below)). This in turn helped foster a new form of pop lyric in which women could plausibly express themselves more directly and assertively.

This narrowing of the gendered power imbalance can also be traced to the changing register of women's voices in the era of sound movies. When Lauren Bacall was cast in partnership with Humphrey Bogart for the film *To Have and Have Not*, director Howard Hawks directed that Bacall takes months of vocal training to lower her register so that her assertive sparring with her co-star would be more convincing (Johnson 2008: 49). Similarly, Darth Vader's menace in the *Star Wars* movies is communicated through the deep bass voice of James Earl Jones. The sense of power associated with a low vocal register was recognized by Margaret Thatcher in the male-dominated realm of Westminster when she embarked on a programme to lower the pitch of her voice. In Australia, a national election is imminent as I write. In the Prime Minister Scott Morrison's campaign advertising, it has been noted by academic Chris Wallace, author of *How to Win an Election*, that Morrison's voice has, 'lost the treble and upped the bass. He's trying to win this election on the bloke vote and the crude metric he's trying to project is the deeper your voice, the more blokey you are' (The Guardian online 14 April 2022, at https://www.theguardian.com/australia-news/2022/apr/14/wedding-rings-and-political-excuses-scott-morrisons-first-campaign-ad, accessed 14 April 2022).

Film sound engineers have long understood the connection between LFN and power. LFN and Very Low Frequency (VLF) have been used in film soundtracks to enhance fear and alarm in cinema audiences. Examples include the 'Sensurround' of the film *Earthquake* (1974 dir. Mark Robson), producing frequencies as low as 15 Hz, and Peter Jackson's 2005 *King Kong* (Jasen 2017 (2016): 146, 246). In the opening scenes of the film *Jaws*, we know that the young woman swimming is in grave danger long before she does because of the low register music which only we can hear (such sounds are called extra- or non-diegetic, that is, sounds heard by the audience but not by the characters). In the 2002 French film *The Irreversible*, director Gaspar Noe added infrasound at 27 Hz to the soundtrack, saying 'You can't hear it but it makes you shake. In a good theatre with a subwoofer, you may be more scared by the sound than by what's happening on the screen. A lot of people can take the images, but not the sound. Those reactions are physical' (Goodman 2010: 66). LFN is the fastest-growing component of the contemporary soundscape spectrum, and we shall return to this topic as we consider the modern soundscape below.

Volume

A fourth significant aspect of sound in the way it constructs relations of power and associated trauma is volume. This dimension of sound is so familiar and exploited so regularly in public and private that it needs little comment just here, though we shall refer to it again later. Again, volume operates in both the generation of emotional responses and organically. Adolph Hitler was not physically prepossessing, and his normal speaking voice was mild, as revealed in secret recordings made in his discussions with the Finnish leader Gustaf Mannerheim (online at https://www.youtube.com/watch?v=oET1WaG5sFk accessed 3 August 2021). For purposes of public domination, he well understood the performative power of raising his volume, either through a gradual, hypnotic trajectory in his rally speeches or in the form of raging tantrums before his generals.

Volume is not only psychologically intimidating, however. It produces irreversible organic damage. Prolonged exposure to loud noise causes deafness, and in the modern world, we are more than ever exposed to loud noise, in the form of human generated as opposed to natural sounds like thunder. Our modern world is much louder than the pre-industrial world and dangerously so. The noisy work environments of industrialization produced the first cases of industrial deafness in the form of Boilermaker's Disease, but the more pervasive danger, increasing from the late twentieth century, is actually from voluntary exposure in leisure activity: pop concerts, dances, parties and, most insidious, various forms of personal stereo. These not only produce irreversible deafness but reduce awareness of physical threats ranging from assault to traffic hazards. We shall return to this below.

The neuro-physiology of sound reception and affect

There is one more aspect of sonic physiology that needs to be taken into account. So far, our attention has been primarily directed to the relationship between the ear and various characteristics of sound sources. But there is a further stage in the hearing process and its affect: the journey of the sound from the ear to what I will call the mind. Sound produces emotional responses, but that first emotional response is not 'cognitive', but physiological. It can be referred to as 'pre-noetic', that is, it takes place at a stage prior to the conscious activity of the intellect. As far as the distinction can be made, it is our body rather than our mind that determines our first interpretative response to a sound. And, as in the case of LFN in particular, we have no control over that first response.

This is because of how sound, once it reaches the ear, is then processed and interpreted. By 'interpreted', I mean the way we attach significance to what we hear, what it means for us, and in particular sonic affect – the emotional responses to sound. An important source for the following discussion is R.B. Zajonc 2004; all page references are to this collection. Zajonc argues that our first response to a sound is 'affective' (254), and that initial affective response is involuntary, inescapable and difficult to revoke (257, 258). Emotional reactions are controlled in the limbic system which precedes language, the neo-cortex and our cognitive capacities. This means that the affective system does not process, for example, the lexical elements of a message, the literal 'meanings' of the words, but something more primary. In regard to sonic messages (music, speech), this means that 'musicality' and intonation, rather than verbal content, have priority in the formation of emotional responses, as in the cases mentioned above of lulling a baby or yelling at someone.

Zajonc's suggestions have been experimentally reinforced in the work of Joseph LeDoux, much of which is summarized in his 1998 book *The Emotional Brain*. The seat of our emotions is called the amygdala. The amygdala receives stimuli and generates emotional responses: fear, sadness, anger and so on. In particular, the amygdala controls the release of adrenal steroids, which assists the body in preparing to deal with situations of perceived stress or threat. Sound takes two paths from the ear to the amygdala. Both go through the thalamus, but only one then travels via the auditory cortex, the highest processing level in the brain. The other and shorter route bypasses the auditory cortex and goes straight to the amygdala. This route is called 'quick and dirty': quick, because it takes less time than the route via the auditory cortex, and dirty because it has a lower level of discrimination, and it is this route that produces symptoms of fear. This is a survival mechanism, stimulating fight or flight. In simple terms, the quick and dirty path immediately and involuntarily elicits the symptoms of fear, such as goose pimples, the rising hair on the back of your neck or on your pet, and protective 'freezing'. That is, it instantly says 'Watch out', though it can't explicitly tell us what to watch out for. In the meantime, via the slower pathway, the cortex cognitively processes the signal to prepare for action appropriate to the specific fear stimulus.

For example, a low noise is heard, producing involuntarily the physical symptoms of alarm. A cognitive process involving cultural memory then 'puts a face' to the threat: marauding horsemen, tanks, a flash flood, a bush fire and an approaching mob. The immediate point is that the primary response in interpreting the stimulus is physiological.[1] We are accustomed to a model of the human being in which the body picks up information through the physical senses, and then this is sent to the mind for evaluation and interpretation. In this model, the mind and body are separate entities, with the latter in some way subordinated to and serving the former, which is the site of our true identity. This was memorably expressed by Descartes in the statement 'Cogito, ergo sum': I think therefore I am. It is the activity of our mind that proves we exist, that is, our 'essence'. The body is a mere non-cognizant instrument of our mind. By contrast, the slightly later philosopher Spinoza 'describes the essentially indistinguishable nature of mind and body – a "parallelism"' (Jasen 2017 (2016): 11). Descartes' model became dominant.

This discussion raises a very interesting question: when we first 'interpret' a sound as threatening, when we get goosebumps or our hair stands on end, when we become afraid, is that coming from the body or the mind? Clearly, the interpretation of sounds as alarming is pre-cognitive. My general point here is that, in the processes of hearing, the neat division between body and mind becomes unclear. In sonic experience, where do the physical mediations stop and the interpreting 'Me', the 'cogito' begin? Where does the material become cognitive? Judith Becker has written that the study of 'Music and emotion … dissolves intractable dichotomies concerning nature versus culture, and scientific universalism versus cultural particularism' (Becker 2001: 154). The study of sound destabilizes a whole array of conceptual models that underpin cultural theory in its dominant forms. These models involve binaries like 'subjective/objective', 'self/other', 'culture/nature' and of course 'mind/body'. If these are disturbed, it affects the *structures* of our thinking, which in turn affects what we can think.

If the phenomenon of audition challenges the simplistic distinction between mind and body, and the corresponding distinction between nature and culture, then this raises questions about cognition itself. In the mind/body division, we are accustomed to conceiving cognition as an activity conducted by the mind. But if that division is blurred, as in the process of hearing and interpreting what we hear, then cognition is no longer necessarily confined to the 'mind', but is also conducted by the body itself.

Recognition of this has manifested itself directly and indirectly in a range of emerging fields of study, including extended mind theory (Menary 2010; Clarke 2011), embodied cognition (Chemero 2011), cognitive ecology (Tribble and Keene 2011), as well as in studies of sound (Kahn 2001). What these share is a questioning of the sharp distinctions we make between cognitive activity and physical sensations and action, arguing that cognition is a larger complex feedback ecology involving 'mind', 'body' and their interaction with the external world. 'It is a thesis that takes the bodily manipulation of external vehicles as constitutive of cognitive processes' (Menary 2010: 21). Noise abatement campaigns, discussed further below, drew on ideas of sound-induced nervous disorders that emerged 'at the intersection of medicine, literature, and cultural criticism, an intellectual territory in which scientific and cultural representations of nervous illness, and in turn of noise suffering, cannot easily be disentangled' (Mansell 2017b: 279). In the interwar period, the uncertainty as to whether neurasthenia was a physical or a psychic disorder saw a shift from the former to the latter (Mansell 2017b: 285–286; see further, for example Johnson 2017: 15–33).

What is less speculative is that going back as far as creationist myths, sound has always had the power to awaken territorial anxieties and to inspire a sense of awe, of being in the presence of a great power, whether it is benevolent or threatening. Sound and our sense of personal territory are closely connected. Sound is the oldest and most powerful marker of territory and identity and therefore a very powerful vehicle of territorial definition. The oldest continuous civilization on earth, since their origins at least 60,000 (estimates even rise to 400,000) years ago, the Australian aborigines, believed that the land was 'sung' into existence during the Dreamtime. This inscribed 'songlines' that criss-cross the country, and by singing the land, they assert their relationship with it.[2] From mythic times, we have had territorial contests played out sonically, including the power of the music of Orpheus, and Ulysses and the sirens. The Finnish national epic *The Kalevala* presents a battle in which the hero Väinämöinen sings his adversary Joukahainen into the swamp. In biblical times, trumpets brought down the walls of Jericho (hence the name of the siren attached to the Stuka aircraft).

Territorial identities were defined by the range of church bells, as in the case of the cockney defined by living within the sound of the Bow bells. There were bitter feuds in nineteenth-century France between villages in which the sound of their church bells overlapped and disputes as to whether the religious or secular authorities could impose their own temporal order by determining when they were rung (Corbin 1998). Similar disputes arose in England during World War II, though the terms differed. In spite of a shift to the visual measurement of time (watches, clocks in civic clock towers), the sound of village church bells 'remained an important reference point … for the spatialization of identity. In wartime Britain, the sound of church bells, and especially rural church bells, was evoked as an auditory metaphor of the nation' (Mansell 2017a: 154). There was thus widespread opposition both to the banning of church bells under the Control of Noise Order and then to the decision to use church bells as an invasion warning; it was felt that this was silencing, then misappropriating the audible representation of Britain's unity in both a spatial and spiritual sense; the official resumption of church bell ringing on 15 November 1942 was greeted with enthusiasm, reported in the *Evening News* as 'the voice of all this pleasant land and of all its age-old story' (Mansell 2017a: 156, 158). Today, car radios, workplace transistors and aggressive neighbours proclaim themselves with loud music.

As in the cases alluded to above, sound is instrumental in inspiring a sense of supernatural power. Sonicity is the most universal facilitator of ritual, and within that category, the most common is bass register (Jasen 2016: 75). Great bells are immensely heavy, up to 665,000 lbs. It is no light task to manufacture, transport and install such instruments, which is testimony to how important they are regarded in projecting a sense of power. Great bells are rich in bass frequencies, the power of which has been discussed above. They exhibit what is called the 'hum tone', the lowest of its harmonics, usually an octave below its nominal pitch – the 102,000 lb Yong Le Bell in Beijing has a hum tone at 22 Hz – and it is the hum tone that lingers after the strike (Jasen 2016: 76).

In *The Bible*, God is most often manifested as a voice, and God's places of worship exploit echo and reverberation to suggest something otherworldly. Indeed, the shift from an era of magic and religious awe to one of modern technologized secularism can be charted through the shortening reverberation times of historically specific architectural forms. Cathedral architecture has a high level of reverberation, from 4 to 10 seconds. Modern halls and concert halls have a reverb time of 1.5 to 2.5 seconds. Secular theatres, dating from the Elizabethan period, have 1 to 1.5 seconds, and modern cinema is less than 1 second. The history of the progressive reduction of reverberation time in the built environments marks the shift away from the sense of otherworldliness to this one.

This shortening of reverberation times as we approach the modern era also tells us a lot about the changing levels and subjects of discourse. The long decay time of cathedrals achieves a sense of divinity in a number of ways. It produces a shared immersive sound that seems to come from everywhere (like an omnipresent God). The sound is also disembodied – that is, it creates the impression that it comes from a spiritual place. The cathedral acoustics also seem to detach the sound from its source, which activates the ubiquity effect. The progressive reduction of reverberation times became more urgent in the context of modern acoustic design and technology. With the advent of recording technologies from the late nineteenth century, discussed below, reverberation came to be regarded as an obstacle to sound fidelity, compromising the accurate reproduction of sounds in the recording studio. It continued to be a problem with the increased use of amplification in performance spaces and with the advent of 'talkies'; 'reverberation came to be considered an impediment, a noise that only interfered with the successful transmission and reception of the desired sound signal' (Thompson 2004: 234). Thus, reverberation and echo on recordings and sound movies were only introduced for special effects, in the words of Peter Doyle, to 'fabricate' space that had disappeared (see Doyle 2005). Emily Thompson fascinatingly traces the history of the attempts by acoustic engineers to deal with reverberation as 'just another form of noise, an unnecessary sound that was inefficient and best eliminated' (Thompson 2004: 171).

One motif in the history of modern sound is thus the progressive shortening of reverberation times, and while the goal of zero was impossible, on film sound stages, it was reduced to below 0.5 of a second (Thompson 2004: 254, 269). One of the leaders in this enterprise was US acoustic engineer Wallace Sabine, whose 'reverberation equation' was applied in the Boston Symphony Hall, which opened on 15 October 1900, marking what Thompson describes as the beginning of modern acoustics, and which culminated with the opening of the Radio City Music Hall as part of the new Rockefeller Center, on 27 December 1932 (Thompson 2004: 315, 229), in which the acoustics were wholly controlled technologically. The near abolition of reverberation in effect destroyed the relationship between sound and space that had existed since antiquity (see further Kern 2003), that is, the way in which reverberation sends aural signals about the nature of the space in which sound is made and heard. 'Clear, direct, and nonreverberant, this modern sound was easy to understand, but it had little to say about the places in which it was produced and consumed' (Thompson 2004: 3).

The effects of this modern interior soundscape and of the dislocation between sound and space, however, were highly ambiguous. On a personal level, we have already referred to the phenomenon of echolocation, of situating ourselves in space by sound. As I and my students discovered during visits to an anechoic chamber at Australian Hearing in Sydney, to be deprived of the resonance that enables echolocation can be deeply disorienting, including such sensations as the uncertainty of balance and a sense of pressure on the ears (see similar accounts of anechoic environments Blesser and Salter 2007; Schwartz 2011: 585, 638, 803). These are cases in which the environment prepared the auditor for something unusual. When no such contextual framing prepares the listener, the experience can be even more unsettling. On Hitler's 56th birthday on Friday, 20 April 1945, his secretary, Christa Schroeder, was in the antechamber to the bunker, originally designed as a transmitting station for radio broadcasts: 'I had always felt very uncomfortable there, as the ceiling and the walls were covered with soundproofing slabs, which swallowed every sound even as one was speaking. A dead room of oppressive silence like the grave' (Kempowski 2014: 92).

The absence of reverberation in the modern constructed soundscape revealed unexpected anomalies, as illustrated in the case of the new St Thomas's Church in New York. The architect, Ralph Adams Cram, wanted a visually Gothic style but with a modern, low reverberation internal acoustic (Thompson 2004: 180). At the same time, he expressed the desire to build a church that would be 'filled with the righteous sense of awe and mystery and devotion' (Thompson 2004: 181). They sought advice from acousticians including Wallace Sabine, who advised the use of a new tile called 'Rumsford'. According to one commentator, visually, the church was 'a fitting expression of that great spiritual impulse that is slowly leavening the lump of our vast material achievement'; another enthused 'The straight, strong ribs rise from the pavement in aspiring lines that lead the soul of the worshipper heaven-ward' (Thompson 2004: 183).

Acoustically, however, the outcome turned out to be less inspiring. The use of the tile produced a reverberation time ranging from 3 seconds at 250 cycles per second (cps), through 2.6 seconds at 500 cps, to 1.1 seconds at 8,000 cps (Thompson 2004: 383 fn. 54). That is, the lowest-pitched sounds had a 3-second reverberation time, the highest pitched only 1.1 seconds, as compared with a stone-lined medieval cathedral of up to 10 seconds. There is an imbalance here between the medieval appearance and the modern sound. While the eye was drawn up to a higher world, the ear was trapped in this one. One of the primary markers of otherworldliness and the presence of God, reverberation, has been all but abolished. The tension between a medieval Gothic and a modern aesthetic emerges in praise of the new church in 1914 by architectural critic Montgomery Schuyler:

> As to the layman, the requirement of the medieval Gothic church, so far from betraying any disposition to "accommodate" him, was that he should be put in his place and made to feel that he was a worm, blessed above

> his deserts in being permitted to gaze from afar, in the dim recesses of the vaulting of the nave or the aisles, upon the celebration of the "mysteries" which was going on in the full light of the choir. Since then the layman has reclaimed his rights and has refused to be relegated to the shadowy background of what is going on. He pays, and he has to be conciliated.
>
> Thompson 2004: 183

Schuyler's description is accurate, but his evaluation is highly problematic, proclaimed in the demeaning term 'worm'. Of course, it was the function of Gothic architecture to make the individual congregant experience a sense of relative insignificance, a small part of a larger community celebrating a mightier power than him or herself. That is the point of collective worship. And this experience was generated visually, as he notes, not only by the eye being drawn 'heavenward' to a vast spaciousness but also by an acoustic field that, with its long reverberation time as well as its source points (elevated pulpit, choir and organ loft), created the impression of an omnipresent power. Schuyler's elevation of the rights 'paid' for by the secular individual in the framework of modern capitalism is a direct inversion of the theology on which a Gothic cathedral is based. In a Gothic cathedral, the reverberation of speech and music is not 'inefficiency', but quite the opposite in relation to its purpose. Famed organist E. Power Biggs declared 'ample reverberation time is part of organ music itself' (Blesser and Salter 2007: 103; their book is a sustained study of the history and cultural role of echo and reverberation, especially in enclosed spaces, since antiquity).

Schuyler displays the influence of the transactional Protestant ethic, which elevates the individual in his relations with God – eliminating clerical mediation – and replaces the resonant celebratory mass with the expository sermon (see further below). Thompson writes, 'the use of the new tile in St Thomas's was a direct result of his [the architect's] desire, not to recreate the Middle Ages, but to draw upon its spirit to meet the spiritual needs of modern times' (Thompson 2004: 186). I am suggesting that, as Schuyler's comments disclose, the reconciliation was impossible. It was Cram's objective to block out the sounds of modernity: 'Within a church, whatever its environment, the motor-bus and the motorcycle, the moving picture and the electric sky-signs, the newspaper and the billboard and the radio cannot come, and here at least you many demand and receive, peace, harmony and beauty' (Thompson 2004: 180). Ironically, in acoustic terms, while attempting to achieve this objective, what he imported into the church was precisely an acoustic profile of modernity.

Interestingly, the acoustic environments created in chapels and churches using all this anti-reverberant engineering ceased to be satisfactory to their congregations, whose desire for reverberation led to redesigning churches to enhance resonance. 'The reverberation time of Duke University Chapel, for example, was increased from 3 seconds at 500 cps to almost 7 seconds'

(Thompson 2004: 421); such measures created the sense of being enveloped by the sounds, rather than outside them (Thompson 2004: 422 fn. 12). Even secular auditoria came under review for their degree of non-reverberation; 'Audio engineers and serious musicians soon abandoned the aberrant idea that dead acoustics were a sign of quality in live and recorded music alike … recognizing the need for ambient acoustics' (Blesser and Salter 2007: 122); this led to an international race to develop 'high-quality emulators of concert hall acoustics' (Blesser and Salter 2007: 123; on concert hall acoustics see especially 133–161). Reverberation time limits were revised for concert halls, with objections that many of them were too dead (Thompson 2004: 227–278, 319).

The evolution of architectural acoustics has more subtle implications. It doesn't just suggest a movement from an atmosphere of spirituality to this material world. It affects what can be said or sung. Such comparative studies as Bassuet's analysis of the acoustic properties of eighteenth-century opera houses illustrate the relationship between the acoustic properties of a performance space and the kinds of music with which they are most compatible (Bassuet 2004). The reverberation in a cathedral slows down spoken and musical discourse. With a reverberation time of 8.5 seconds, Notre Dame in Paris exemplifies the principle that while such spaces are excellent for slow and stately sacred music, certain kinds of speech are problematic (Von Fischer 2012: 67). You can't have a raging argument in a highly reverberant cathedral; you can't play fast modern music like bebop: that is, the acoustics are best adapted to a dignified, slow and stately discourse in which beliefs are confirmed majestically rather than vigorously debated, and later, we shall compare this to the function of the early secular playhouses.

As exemplified by the congregation of St Thomas, the reduction of reverberation was a triumph of acoustic engineering, but in many contexts, it was inappropriate. In the field of 'mood' or 'easy listening' music, recording bandleaders found it advisable to engineer the sound for added reverberation, as in the cases, for example, of Melanchrino, Ray Conniff and Mantovani, often by recording in churches. The origins of this 'retro-sound' were explicitly evoked by Mantovani: 'I wanted an effect of an overlapping of sound, as though we were playing in a cathedral' (Lanza 2007: 81; see similarly 90, 105). US supermarkets and department stores built in the 1950s also produced reverberation 'as intoxicatingly as a medieval church', perfect for the easy listening background music designed to enhance consumerism (Lanza 2007: 103). This trajectory of sonic history provides a neat and instructive parable of the shift in the function of reverberant sound from the medieval to the era of secular modernity, one of a range of ironies and paradoxes to be considered in more detail in later chapters.

These cases exemplify the proposition that the most complex sounds produced by human beings are those which we classify as music. Perhaps, 'musicality' would be a more appropriate word. Unless we speak like the Daleks of

Dr. Who, we regularly deploy musical effects in our speech, such as rhythm, pitch, tempo and volume variation. In some forms of discourse, such as a black Baptist sermon, it is difficult to identify the point at which speech becomes music, that is, at what point the way something is said becomes more important than what is said. It is partly because, of all expressive practices, musicality is the most accessible and common way of expressing identity.

Music is always used partly to tell people who we are. In addition to aesthetic pleasure, we attend particular kinds of concerts as a way of proclaiming and participating in our 'tribe', identified in various ways. In Germany, during the nineteenth century, 'the song movement became an important part of the German national movement' (Morat 2017: 186; see also Ziemer 2017: 21–211). And in many cases, the formation and proclamation of identity are the primary, if not the sole purpose of music. Obvious examples are national anthems, school songs, sports locker room songs, groups based on religion, ethnicity, gender, colour and the chanting of political demonstrators. Often these converge, as in the controversy called *Hymnen-Streit* (conflict over national anthem) in Germany in 2010 over whether or not the country's football players should sing along to the national anthem at matches regardless of national background; seventy per cent of 50,000 surveyed declared that they should do so as a proclamation of their national identity (Feiereisen and Hill 2012: 2). The morale-building power of chanting and cheering sports stadium supporters has been exploited by electronically boosting their volume (Prochnik 2011: 103). Music is also recognized as the most intense and immediate way of shaping desire and motivation, in advertising, supermarkets, restaurants, workplaces and malls.

Music in particular and sound in general are thus immensely powerful expressive gestures. Unlike vision, sound literally envelops and occupies all the space in which it is present. Unlike taste, touch and that which we smell, it can be massively circulated in finely articulated forms, especially in an age of electronic amplification (you can 'project' smell, in the form of gas attacks, but you can't 'amplify' or finely direct it). Hitler and literary critic F.R. Leavis both recognized that the microphone was perhaps the most powerful tool of modern mass culture and mass persuasion, and Goebbels recognized that what the press had been to the nineteenth century, radio was to the demagoguery (and propaganda and misinformation, including by the BBC – see Rankin 2008: 407–445) of the twentieth.

Notes

1 As in so many (all?) studies of affect, the arguments of Zajonc and LeDoux have been questioned. Apart from the work of Lazarus, which is specifically addressed by Zajonc (Zajonc 2004: 285–296), later differences of opinion are exemplified in Sloboda and Juslin in essays by Davies (27, footnote) and Peretz (118). Zajonc's point, however, that definitions of cognition are at issue (Zajonc 2004: 285), and LeDoux's carefully documented experimental investigations are highly persuasive. At the very

least, the proposition that "separation between affect and cognition may well have a psychological and a biological basis" (Zanjonc 2004: 275) is reinforced experimentally, ethnographically and in the symptoms of everyday experience of anxiety.
2 Although combining non-fiction with a form of speculative fiction, the most famous account of this creationist mythology is Bruce Chatwin's 1987 book, *Songlines*, now available in Vintage Classics 1998.

Reading

Augoyard, J-F and H. Torgue (eds), 2006. *Sonic Experience: A Guide to Everyday Sounds*. Trans. Andra McCartney and David Paquette. Montreal: McGill-Queen's University Press. Originally published in French, 1995.

Bassuet, Alban. 2004. 'Acoustics of a Selection of Famous 18th Century Opera Houses: Versailles, Markgräfliches, Drottningholm, Schweitzingen'. *Acoustical Society of America Journal*, 123: 1645–1650. Online at http://webistem.com/acoustics2008/acoustics2008/cd1/data/articles/003503.pdf, accessed 6 September 2021.

Becker, Judith. 2001. 'Anthropological Perspectives on Music and emotion'. In John A. Sloboda and Patrik N. Juslin (eds), *Music and Emotion: Theory and Research*. Oxford: Oxford University Press: 135–169.

Beevor, Anthony. 2015. *Ardennes 1944*. U.K./New York, NY: Penguin/Random House.

Blesser, Barry and Linda-Ruth Salter. 2007. *Spaces Speak, Are You Listening? Experiencing Aural Architecture*. Cambridge, MA and London: MIT Press.

Chatwin, Bruce. 1998. *Songlines*. London: Vintage Classics.

Chemero, Anthony. 2011. *Radical Embodied Cognitive Science*. Cambridge, MA and London: MIT Press.

Chion, Michel. 1994. *Audio-Vision: Sound on Screen*. Trans. Claudia Gorbman. New York, NY: Columbia University Press.

Clarke, Andy. 2011. *Supersizing the Mind: Embodiment, Action, and Cognitive Extension*. Oxford: Oxford University Press.

Corbin, Alain. 1999 (first pub 1998). *Village Bells: Sound and Meaning in the Nineteenth Century French Countryside*. Trans. Martin Thom. London: Macmillan.

Doyle, Peter. 2005. *Echo and Reverb: Fabrication Space in Popular Music Recording 1900–1960*. Middletown, CT: Wesleyan University Press.

Feiereisen, Florence and Akexandra Merley Hill (eds). 2012. 'Introduction'. *Germany in the Loud Twentieth Century: An Introduction*. Oxford: Oxford University Press: 1–16.

Goodman, Steve. 2010. *Sonic Warfare: Sound, Affect, and the Ecology of Fear*. Cambridge, MA and London: The MIT Press.

Jasen, Paul C. 2016. *Low End Theory: Bass, Bodies and the Materiality of Sonic Experience*. New York, NY and London: Bloomsbury.

Johnson, Bruce. 2000. *The Inaudible Music: Jazz, Gender and Australian Modernity*. Sydney: The Currency Press.

Johnson, Bruce. 2008. '"Quick and Dirty": Sonic Mediations and Affect'. In Carolyn Birdsall and Anthony Enns (eds), *Sonic Mediations: Body, Sound, Technology*. Cambridge: Cambridge Scholars Publishing: 43–60.

Johnson, Bruce. 2009. 'Low Frequency Noise and Urban Space'. Special Issue, 'Music, Characterization and Urban space'. *Popular Music History*, 4/2: 177–195.

Johnson, Bruce. 2017. In the Body of the Audience. In J. Tsioulakis and E. Hytönen-Ng (eds), *Musicians and Their Audiences: Performance, Speech and Mediation*. New York, NY and London: Routledge, 15–33.

Kahn, Douglas. 2001. *Noise, Water, Meat: A History of Sound in the Arts*. Cambridge, MA: MIT Press.

Kempowski, Walter. 2014 (UK), 2015 (US) (1st pub. In German 2005). *Swansong 1945: A Collective Diary of the Last Days of the Third Reich*. New York, NY and London: W.W. Norton & Company.

Kern, Stephen. 2003 (first pub 1983). *The Culture of Time and Space 1880–1918*. Cambridge, MA and London: Harvard University Press.

Lanza, Joseph. 2007. *Elevator Music: A Surreal History of Muzak, Easy-Listening, and Other Moodsong*. Revised and Expanded Edition. Ann Arbor, MI: University of Michigan Press.

LeDoux, Joseph. 1998. *The Emotional Brain*. London and New York, NY: Phoenix.

Mansell, James G. 2017a. *The Age of Noise in Britain: Hearing Modernity*. Urbana, Chicago, IL and Springfield: University of Illinois Press.

Mansell, James G. 2017b (first pub 2014). 'Neurasthenia, Civilization, and the Sounds of Modern Life: Narratives of Nervous Illness in the Interwar Campaign against Noise'. In Daniel Morat (ed), *Sounds of Modern History: Auditory Cultures in 19th- and 20th-Century Europe*. New York, NY and Oxford: Berghahn: 278–302

Menary, Richard. (ed), 2010. *The Extended Mind*. Cambridge, MA and London: MIT Press.

Morat, Daniel. 2017 (first pub 2014). 'Cheers, Songs, and Marching Sounds: Acoustic Mobilization and Collective Affects at the Beginning of World War I'. In Daniel Morat (ed), *Sounds of Modern History: Auditory Cultures in 19th- and 20th-Century Europe*. New York, NY and Oxford: Berghahn: 177–200.

Prochnik, George. 2011. *In Pursuit of Silence: Listening for Meaning in a World of Noise*. New York, NY: Anchor Books.

Rankin, Nicholas. 2008. *Churchill's Wizards: The British Genius for Deception 1914–1945*. London: Faber and Faber.

Schwartz, Hillel. 2011. *Making Noise: From Babel to the Big Bang & Beyond*. New York, NY: Zone Books.

Thompson, Emily. 2004. *The Soundscape of Modernity: Architectural Acoustics and the Culture of Listening in America, 1900–1933*. Cambridge, MA and London: MIT Press.

Tribble, Evelyn B. and Nicholas Keene. 2011. *Cognitive Ecologies and the History of Remembering: Religion, Education and Memory in Early Modern England*. Basingstoke: Palgrave Macmillan.

Von Fischer, Sabine. 2012. 'From Seat Cushions to Formulae: Understanding Spatial Acoustics in Physics and Architecture'. In Florence Feiereisen and Akexandra Merley Hill (eds), *Germany in the Loud Twentieth Century: An Introduction*. Oxford and New York, NY: Oxford University Press 63–80.

Zajonc, Robert Bolesław. 2004. *The Selected Works of R.B. Zajonc*. USA: Wiley.

Ziemer, Hansjakob 2017 (first pub. 2014), 'Listening on the Home Front: Music and the Production of Social Meaning in German Concert Halls During World War I'. In Daniel Morat (ed), *Sounds of Modern History: Auditory Cultures in 19th- and 20th-Century Europe*. New York, NY and Oxford: Berghahn: 201–224.

2
SOUND IN CULTURAL HISTORY

The Irish volunteers were one of a number of groups devoted to Irish nationalism in the years leading up to the Easter Rising of 1916. Inaugurated in 1913, their dedication to the cause was intense, meeting at least three times per week for drills and military exercises, and paying for their own ammunition and other equipment (McGarry 2010: 67). Music was central to their morale:

> Volunteers marched in step to such songs as *Ireland Boys Hurrah, God Save Ireland, The Felons of our Land*, and *Wrap the Green Flag*. Implausibly, it was the Protestant choirmaster of St John's Church in Sandymount, Cecil Grange McDowall, who composed the music for many of the most popular propaganda verses (including such topical numbers as *The Rocky Road to Berlin* and *Pop Goes the Peeler*) on the church organ. He was also responsible for the musical arrangement of *The Soldier's Song*, a song which countless Volunteers could remember where they first heard it, and the powerful impact it had: 'in a few days' time', one recalled, 'every Volunteer in Dublin was whistling or singing it'.
>
> McGarry 2010: 71

One who attended a special mass for the Volunteers recounted,

> Suddenly a rich baritone voice burst into the hymn to our Patron Saint *Hail Glorious St Patrick* and it was taken up by the whole congregation in such a fervent manner that a lump rose in my throat and I wanted to burst out crying or to do something to prove that I was worthy of being in their company.
>
> McGarry 2010: 93

DOI: 10.4324/9781003042662-3

These passages introduce a discussion of the ways in which sound has so powerfully generated and projected collective identity throughout history. In this instance, the 'Us' are nationalist Irish volunteers, and 'Them' is the English colonizers. Yet in an example cited below, from the same year, 1916, the 'Us' is a united Ireland in the service of the British, and the 'Them' is the armies of Germany. These exemplify the ironies, complexities and shifting dynamics that can be mapped through sonicity, which can, as argued below, provide an alternative history 'from below', to the official written accounts. Aspects of the argument of this chapter are neatly encapsulated in Christopher Ballantine's discussion of the problems in establishing a musical archive that encompasses oral as well as written materials, with particular reference to South Africa. He notes the way such an archive '"privileges the official narratives of the state over the private stories of individuals," which also implies that it privileges written documents over oral testimony' (Ballantine 2017: 75). The troubled story of an Ireland divided over its relationship with England points towards what will be the main extended case study of this chapter: a sustained illustration of how the sense of community can be translated and rearticulated to adapt itself across space and time through sound in general and music in particular.

So far, we have talked about the distinctive phenomenology of hearing and the particular power of sound in social groups and formations: it can help form and project individual and collective identity and its territorial spaces. As such, sound has been a major force in historical struggles and transitions. Whenever we study the *'longue durée'*, the long historical epochs, we find it useful to identify major turning points in both material and intellectual history. Major material changes include the invention of gunpowder, the compass, the chronometer, the internet, and the onset of plagues and pandemics. In intellectual history, such transitional moments are often referred to as changes in *'mentalités'*, and these are often marked by terms like the Middle Ages, the Renaissance, the Enlightenment and Modernity.

In later chapters, I will give extended attention to two significant moments of transition which I think represent major turning points in sonic history in the West. The earlier of the two is the Renaissance and the rise of print cultures, which evokes a multiple-cause 'feedback loop' rather than a simple-cause/effect model of thinking about history, as in Fox's observation: 'The rise of print was a phenomenon that was both cause and effect of the expansion of education and literacy in early modern England. Both processes were also inseparable from the progress of the English Reformation. A large part of the market for print was for basic devotional and didactic texts' (Fox 2017: 138). The second transitional moment, from the late nineteenth century, is the arrival of modern sound technologies, to which we turn in Chapter Seven. First, I wish to undertake a very broad survey of sound in the history of power relations, not presented as a comprehensive history, but to illustrate the kinds of role it has played.

As we have glimpsed, the connection we have been considering between sound and power extends back to the farthest antiquity. The power of sorcerers, priests and prophets, and proximity to God was often associated with particular acoustic conditions like echo and resonance, and this of course persists in cathedral worship today. As in the case of religious congregations, sports crowds, national anthems and war cries, one of the sonic power outcomes is to generate and proclaim a sense of collective identity, of a community with shared interests, beliefs and sympathies. In the words of Tom Pickard, a thirteen-year-old member of the Choir of Kings College, Cambridge, 'When we're singing, well it feels like one big mind'.[1] Collective music making can provide consolation even in conditions of terminal peril as in the famous example of the sinking of the *Titanic*, when the ship's orchestra played 'Nearer my God to thee'. It provides hope in times of the most extreme suffering and desperation. Martin Cranz, an inmate of a POW camp near Dülmen, was being convoyed away from the advancing Soviet Army on Wednesday 25 April 1945. The trucks stopped, and the prisoners were told to get out into open fields.

> Barbed wire spirals as tall as men met our frightened eyes, we had to force ourselves through a chaotic wire sluice-gate into a field – crushed beneath the feet of tens of thousands, or was it fifteen thousand men who filled this pen, as if for a count of beasts for the slaughter? Night darkened and it rained, hesitantly at first, then emphatically, then remorselessly. In the middle, the prisoners pushed their way together, they stood packed together with me in the centre. More and more were gathering, to keep their bodies dry and warm – then all of them, a hundredfold, a thousandfold: nursery rhymes, folk tunes, *Heimatlieder*, a monumental chorus, moved by painful longing and aching hope.
>
> Kempowski 2014: 139

And at the individual level, the therapeutic power of music that it 'calms the savage breast', is so well established that it is a cliché. These benign effects, at both the collective and individual levels, are most frequently presented as demonstrations of the positive power of sound and music. One of the most dramatic contemporary examples is the impact on underprivileged children in Venezuela of the music education programme known as 'El Sistema', a 'programme of social rescue and deep cultural transformation' (see at https://www.youtube.com/watch?v=rYXK8TZADws accessed 4 January 2021).

Collective identity is constructed in two ways, however. There can be no sense of 'self' without what is 'not-self'. At the most overt level, we declare who 'we' are, the collective self. But in so doing, we also define an 'Other' as a contrasting entity, with varying degrees of assertiveness, rising to aggressiveness, as in, for example, national anthems. The second verse of England's 'God Save the Queen' runs 'O Lord our God arise,//Scatter her enemies//And make them fall.//Confound their politics,//Frustrate their knavish tricks,//On Thee our hopes we fix,//God save us all'. There can be no 'us' without 'them'. 'The Marseillaise' urges French citizens 'to arms …//Let us march, let us march,// May tainted blood water our fields'. The 1944 version of the Soviet anthem took pride in its citizens having 'Fought for the future, destroyed the invaders'. The 'Star Spangled Banner' of the US, 'the land of the free and the home of the brave', is a sustained call to battle against 'the foe's haughty host'. Although not the country's national anthem, the honorary march of the Finnish defence forces since 1918, *Porilaisten marssi*, is usually heard at state occasions or other highly ceremonial events. Its lyrics include 'Sons of a race whose blood was shed,//On Narva's field; on Poland's sand; at Leipzig; Lützen's dark hills under;//Not yet is Finland's manhood dead;//With foemen's blood a field may still be tinted red.// All Rest, all Peace, Away! begone!' (My thanks to Finnish colleague Johannes Juva for this information). Groups who proclaim themselves sonically, from religious denominations to sports fans, engage in a contest with a vilified other, from Satan or a competing religious community, to a rival football team.

From the most distant antiquity, sound has been a primary inspiration in the definition of individual and collective self, and a primary weapon against 'The Other'. One of the most ancient and durable examples is the war song, or the war cry. Greek galley oarsmen around 400 BC had a range of chants, including one for battle (Proctor 1992: 6). Livy recorded that in the triumph of the Roman army over Hannibal's forces at the battle of Zama in 202 BC,

> There were … factors which seem trivial to recall, but proved of great importance at the time of action. The Roman war-cry was louder and more terrifying because it was in unison, whereas the cries from the Carthaginian side were discordant, coming as they did from a mixed assortment of peoples with a variety of mother tongues
>
> Livy 1965: 661–662

During the war between English colonialists and the tribal nation, the Maroons in eighteenth-century Jamaica, the locals deployed the abeng, a cowhorn that had been used to call the slaves to the canefields. Along with drums, the Maroons used the abeng not only to communicate British troop movements but also just to terrify the enemy (Goodman 2010: 65; for similar examples, see Johnson and Cloonan 2008: 30–35). And In spite of changes in the acoustics of modern warfare, considered below, the unmediated massed voice of the enemy was continued to have a powerful effect on morale well into the twentieth century. On the Eastern front during the Second World War, German General von Mellenthin recalled the terrifying effect of a Russian infantry charge, even on a well-armoured German position: 'A Russian infantry attack is an awe-inspiring spectacle; the long grey waves come pounding on, uttering fierce cries and the defending troops require nerves of steel' (Keegan 2004: 288).

The foregoing is simply a random panhistorical overview intended to exemplify the ubiquity of sound as a way of defining community identity and difference, and in relatively simplistic terms. Let us attend in more detail to a case study that illustrates some of the complex political dynamics in sonic transactions, and which foreshadows later arguments regarding the role of class in the cultural history of sound. The example cited earlier of the sonic space created by the Irish volunteers in their opposition to English colonialism forms an instructive contrast to an incident taking place in the same year, 1916. During the assault on Guillemont in September, Irish of both Catholic and Protestant persuasions were united when 'the pipes of the Royal Irish howled out Brian Boru', and when a 'northern-raised battalion of Irish Rifles met a southern battalion on the march with its band playing the old rebel air "She's The Most Distressful Country", there were cheers of approval' (Holmes 2005: 156).

This case, in which two opposed sections of a community – the Irish Protestants and Catholics – are united by music against a common enemy invites a closer study of the complex ways in which sound and music define boundaries of identity. And it prepares us for two arguments about the cultural history of sound. First, again, it shows how sound can define shifting alliances. At the same time, the predominantly Catholic Volunteers are setting themselves against a largely Protestant English authority, and Catholic and Protestant Irish are inspired by music to unite in the service of the colonial power against Germany. Second, however, the Irish/English dynamic will lead us towards the more general insight that, in such conflicts in the modern era, unauthorized sound is likely to be associated with low rather than high culture. This has extremely broad implications, relating to how a study of sound in the formation of identities can alter how we construct national histories, as well as how we understand the global dynamics of music.

I have referred above to the limitations of simple models of cause and effect in attempting to understand the development of social formations and events. Historical linkages have extremely complex, hidden, and far-reaching root systems, and the journey along them to understand the visible outgrowths, the reasons that certain things take place, is much longer and more indirect than 'X caused Y'. To unfold the arguments, I have just briefly summarized, and it is necessary to begin with a few observations regarding the evolution of popular music throughout the twentieth century and how this has affected attitudes to different kinds of sounds.

Globally, popular music from the early twentieth century was generally dominated by the US, from ragtime and jazz, through swing, rock, pop, rap, hip hop and grunge. On the face of it, this is odd, since the US did not invent the various media through which popular culture was internationally circulated. The French were leaders in the development of moving pictures, and the world's first feature-length movie, at over one hour, *The Story of the Kelly*

Gang (1906, dir. Charles Tait), was produced in Australia, where a thriving film industry flourished in the 1920s. Sound recording could be argued to be the invention of the Germans, radio of the Italians and television of the British. Nonetheless, it was the US who gained control of global music technologies: recording, distribution networks and the film industry. That helps us to understand why the US-dominated modern music, but it doesn't explain why it was *popular* music.

To understand this, it is useful to compare the situation in two countries which had much in common, the US and Australia. Both countries became settler frontier societies that displaced indigenous communities, rich in natural resources, founded during the early modern era. But the founding white settlers of the US arrived voluntarily (though often as political/religious refugees), and nominally based on the rights of free expression of ordinary (white) men and women. The rights to freedom of expression for all are written into the country's founding documents. The volubility of the ordinary man was a testament to the principles of democracy. US popular music is unashamedly self-celebratory. For good or ill, it is muscular, colourful and elbows all else aside. It shows no fear of accusations of vulgarity, theatricality and extravagance. These are its validation, not its embarrassment. It makes no attempts to disguise itself, its US accents, its places and spaces, its own ingenuous hopes and ambitions. It sings of itself.

This is compared with the establishment of white settler Australia, where the 'ordinary people' were in fact criminals. The culture of the ordinary people – popular culture – was, therefore, generally regarded as potentially if not actually criminal culture. The sounds of the everyman, including popular music, were, therefore, regarded with suspicion. It was high art music that reminded us of civilization, and in fact as the country began to develop its own substantial respectable middle class from the mid-nineteenth century, one manifestation of the reaction against the stain of the convict past was the highest rate of domestic piano ownership in the world. High culture represented order, regulation, authority, legality and discipline, and, in an untamed environment, a link with a faraway 'mother country'. By contrast, low culture signified disorder, subversiveness and anti-authoritarianism. The distinction was proclaimed sonically.

That stratification was defined from the first day of permanent European settlement. In 1788, the First Fleet brought with it around one thousand souls, a small proportion of whom were political, religious, administrative and military agents of the state. But the vast majority was convicted felons, mostly men. Few of these wanted to be in Australia, in the sense that they had not freely chosen to make the journey to the farthest reaches of the earth, to be incarcerated in a country generally perceived as savage, desolate and inhospitable. The country was a prison, and its inmates were in the first instance its 'ordinary' citizens. The settlement was founded on the principle of the institutionalized antagonisms of a gaol.

And this dynamic was played out sonically, but in ways that, as we shall see, constitute an alternative history to the official written record. Even before their disembarkation, the convicts had devised an 'instrumental' accompaniment to their singing by banging together the signs of their criminality – the iron chains that restrained them. The first onshore musical event is usually dated on 7 February 1788, when the first official ceremony in the new colony took place. But before we got to that, music making of a very different kind featured as a significant social practice in dramatic circumstances on the previous evening. On that day, the disembarkation of the female convicts had been completed by about six pm. Extra rum rations and shore leave were granted to the sailors. A violent storm ensued, and lightning struck the camp killing precious livestock, a background to the developing 'rum party' involving the female convicts and the sailors. It was reported by a 'gentleman' witness:

> It is beyond my abilities to give a just description of the scene of debauchery and riot ... some swearing, others quarrelling, others singing – not in the least regarding the tempest, tho' so violent that the thunder shook the ship exceeding anything I ever before had a conception of.
>
> Hughes 1996: 89

For the authorities in the new settlement, links were immediately established between demotic or popular recreation, criminal and blasphemous immorality, a hedonistic indifference to signs of divine disapproval, and popular music.

Music was heard again on the following day, setting up a counter discourse that defines the *pas de deux* between high and low and establishes a model for the subsequent history of Australian music. The First Fleet brought with it not only civilian instruments (including a piano) but also military musicians, the musical arm of authority. On 7 February 1788, the Royal Marines played drums and fifes for the first official proclamation in Sydney Cove. Far from the disorder of the previous storm-wracked evening, the physical arrangement of the audience for the music reflected the rigid hierarchical structure of the new colony. Organized in a large circle, the outer annulus consisted of the soldiery, standing and bearing-loaded muskets. The next, inner annulus was made up of the convicts, squatting subordinately. And the inner circle consisted of gentlemen and officers (Hughes 1996: 89).

Thus, from the outset, demotic recreations and popular music were deeply encoded as potentially savage, criminal, immoral and in need of the tightest regulation, sonically embodied in the music of the Royal Marines. The conflict between the two was institutionalized and theatricalized at the 'triangle', to which those sentenced to punitive flogging were bound. This was part of the regular calendar and was 'compulsory viewing' for the convicts. Few activities more grotesquely contest the righteous complacency of 'The Enlightenment' than this motif in its penal settlement. Some sense of this macabre brutalizing of low culture by high culture can be gained by the terrible matter of factness of the punishment reports issued from the Sydney Police Bench, as in the following random sample from September 1833 under the name of the Principal Superintendent of Convicts, Ernest Augustus Slade:

> Daniel Alone, ... grossly neglecting his duty, 50 lashes ... The prisoner cried loudly at the 2d, and repeated his cries at every lash; at the 12th lash the blood was flowing largely; the prisoner seemed to suffer intense agony.
>
> James Clayton, ... absent without leave and neglecting his duty, 50 lashes. The skin was lacerated at the 5th lash, and there was a slight effusion of blood; the prisoner subdued his sense of pain by biting his lips. The skin of this man was thick to an uncommon degree; and both his body and mind have been hardened by former punishments; and he is also known to be what is termed "flash," or "game;" nevertheless, I am of opinion, that if all his former (or perhaps only his first) punishments had been as vigorously administered as this last, his indomitable spirit would have been subdued.
>
> Thomas Holdsworth, ... pilfering from his master, 50 lashes. At the first lash the prisoner uttered piercing screams, and continued screaming at each succeeding lash, and appeared to suffer greatly; the 5th lash brought blood, and the flesh was considerably lacerated at the conclusion of the punishment.
>
> Convict Discipline 1977: 54

Each of these received fifty lashes, while twenty lashes could deeply lacerate the flesh. And beyond that, the flogging could become, literally, a flaying, with reports of the flesh so fully torn away that ribs, pulsating lungs and other organs became visible.

This account is not presented out of any sadistic prurience. If flogging could produce vocalizing on the part of the victim, so could vocalizing produce flogging. The infractions and penalties listed above are compared – absent without leave, neglect of duty, theft – with those of William Riley and Michael Burns, for the offense of 'Singing a Song': one hundred lashes each inflicted under the administration of Major Joseph Anderson on Norfolk Island, notorious for the severity of its discipline and giving its name to the penalty suffered by Riley and Burns: the 'Norfolk dumpling' (Hughes 1996: 480). The crime, the penalty and hints in the names Riley and Burns lead us to the question, 'What kinds of songs could have attracted such extreme measures of repression?'

If any contemporary terms could encompass the range of convict songs, they would be 'vernacular' or 'popular'. Under those umbrella terms, we can identify a number of categories from the collection gathered by Hugh Anderson (2000). Some were songs expressing regret or remorse for the crimes that brought them to the colony. It is unlikely that it was such songs that attracted a penalty of one hundred lashes. Some could be described as 'low life' songs, associated with the earliest 'dancing houses' and strengthening the association between popular music, prostitution, drunkenness and depraved leisure. Many were songs of nostalgia for home and loved ones, and given that for a large number of deportees, home was Ireland, the tone of these could become suspect to the authorities. Demotic music making was one of the flash points between the authorities and the convict/citizens of the penal settlements. You can imprison and chain a man, but it is much more difficult to prevent him from producing any sound. As I write, in Myanmar, a military coup has dislodged the democratically elected government. While various officials have been 'detained' by the generals, in the main city, Yangon, residents are conducting acts of civil disobedience, including by banging on pots and pans outside their houses.[2]

The island now called Tasmania, formerly Van Diemen's Land, to the south of mainland Australia, received 53,000 male and 13,000 female convicts between 1818 and 1853, as compared with 67,000 and 13,000 in New South Wales between the First Fleet in 1788 and 1844. It was one of the most oppressive convict settlements, and the authorities waged 'a war on fiddling' as 'part of a widespread attack on convict culture. The licensing act of 1833 made it an offence for publicans to permit former convicts to "play skittles, bowls, ninepins or any game of chance in a public house, or even to remain on the premises while they were being played"'; in the 1840s, they suppressed public dancing houses because of 'the noise and confusion' they produced (Boyce 2008: 219). Notice how the element of class is entering the sonic discourse: the frequenters of public houses do not dance to music, but to noise. Noise is basically sound unwanted by the dominant class, as discussed further below. In the penal colony, the popular song is not the expression of a democratic principle, as in the US, but contamination of 'cultivated' sonic space.

The earliest colonial hotels incorporated entertainment rooms where the public – largely deportees – could sing and dance, but which the authorities sought to stamp out. In 1848, Lieutenant Governor Denison was petitioned by fourteen Hobart musicians who claimed that 'repeated attempts had been made to deprive them of their only means of subsistence by the interference of the police', arguing that the only recreation available to the 'mechanic and labourer' after work is 'the innocent one of music and a dance'. The police magistrate to whom the matter was referred responded:

> I have with much pains and opposition succeeded to putting a stop to fiddling and dancing in public houses, which have been much improved in conduct and character in consequence. The practice of fiddling in public houses was the means of congregating together vicious and dishonest characters of both sexes, and was the source of much evil to the community.
>
> Boyce 2008: 219

The supposed 'vicious' profile attributed to vernacular music would not have been diminished by local convict compositions which proclaimed defiance of punitive measures by the authorities, as in the 'Rum Song', in which the singer gladly accepted all manner of punishments – flogging, chains, even hanging, 'If you'll only give me rum' (Hughes 1996: 292). Songs of defiance could easily shade into songs implicitly or explicitly fomenting sedition and rebellion, such as celebrations of the working class protest (and sometimes insurrectionary) movement known as the Chartists ('The Chartists are Coming', Anderson 2000: 249–250, music 577); a number of leading Chartists were among the deportees to New South Wales and Van Diemen's Land, including the Monmouthshire Chartist John Frost, the subject of many broadsides (Anderson 2000: 233–257). Other political exiles included Tolpuddle Martyrs (Anderson 2000: 258–265) and the Glasgow cotton spinners whose attempts to raise their wages had extended to acts of violence, and produced the song 'The Cotton Spinners' Farewell' (Anderson 2000: 344–347, music 590).

Among those songs that were evocations of the homes from which they had been deported, a large proportion were of Ireland. Some were simply nostalgia for people and places left behind ('Henry Connor', Anderson 2000: 175–176, music 563). The quotations that opened this chapter remind us of the longstanding hostility between Irish nationalists and England. Among Irish deported to Australia by the English legal system, it would be surprising if that hostility was not especially bitter. By 1800, Irish deportees made up more than twenty-five per cent of the population of the penal colony, and of a disposition, described as 'violent Republicans', which was a cause of considerable anxiety (Hughes 1996: 190). What is notable in Anderson's invaluable collection is that, while many ballads refer to straightforward criminality such as theft, the Irish contributions are overwhelmingly driven politically, by various forms of Irish nationalism: 'The most distinctive feature of Irish crime was the number tried for political or social offences' (cited Anderson 2000: xxx). Given that 'social offences' are related to 'land disputes and rural revolt', often accompanied by eviction by absentee landlords and Protestant/Catholic enmity (as in 'The Banished Defender', Anderson 2000: 351–352, music 592), it is arguable that the line between 'political and social offences' can be seen as highly porous, especially given that there were also exiles from the Irish rebellion of 1798.

Thus, among the popular broadside ballads, 'convict' songs, there is a substantial group that, from the perspective of the singers, would be regarded as political songs, hymns to Irish nationalism, as in the numerous songs about John Mitchell, transported for fourteen years, 'that patriotic man//Who spoke so endearingly of the state of old Erin,//For which he's been banish'd from his dear native land//… The rights of his country he boldly advocated//…And because his country's wrongs he so manfully stated//He has been a victim and his sentence is hard'.[3]

And there were songs that celebrated active rebellion against the authorities. In 1828, when the government brig, *Cyprus*, was transferring convicts in Van Diemen's Land from Hobart to a penal station called Macquarie Harbour, the convicts seized control of the ship under the leadership of an ex-sailor William Swallow. The event quickly became the subject of a ballad, in the category of 'treason songs', banned by the authorities (Hughes 1996: 214). A further 'treason song' accompanied an event at a settlement at Castle Hill, twenty-four kilometres as the crow flies north west of Sydney. In 1804, it was the scene of an Irish rebellion, planned to proceed south to recruit Irish prisoners at Parramatta, then march east on Sydney itself. They marched to the song of the Irish rebellion of 1798, 'Croppy Boy', but the uprising was put down by redcoats dispatched from Sydney at a place that became known as Vinegar Hill, after the site of a battle in Wexford in the 1798 rising, itself commemorated in the broadside 'The Maid's Lamentation' (Hughes 1996: 191–192; Anderson 156, music 560).

Such vernacular songs thus exported a tradition of rebellion against a colonizing authority that extended its power from one side of the world to the other, and who lumped its deportees to Australia into the single category 'convicts'. These forms of the popular song are very significant as a form of oral 'counter-history' that ran in parallel to the official written histories, which represented the underclasses as petty criminals who were either beyond salvation, or who through loyalty to the authorities and hard work could redeem themselves as decent and obedient citizens. By this official written account, the 'penal colony' was occupied by criminals. The oral counter-histories recorded in popular ballads disclose the formation of another community; they 'shape readers and auditors into an imagined community' (Shrank 2017: 32), and in this case, they show a different and much more politicized narrative of struggle against oppression, nationalist or even secessionist movements; the rebels at Vinegar Hill were not simply criminals but were mainly Irish carrying the struggle against the English to the new colony, which was in many cases a concentration camp for political prisoners, and their songs were not just about crime, but about politics and class conflict – the real reason they were suppressed. And it is reasonable to assume that the 'songs' for which men like Riley and Burns were so cruelly punished were songs of political protest rather than criminal defiance.

In the penal settlements, there thus developed a high/low culture divide which equated with other binaries. There was authorized 'art music' as against 'popular music'. This in turn was reflected in instrumental distinctions between concert or genteel instruments, especially the piano as the nineteenth century progressed, and demotic or vernacular instruments like mouth organ or accordion. This in turn corresponded to a distinction between permanence (a piano was a 'stationary' instrument requiring the 'fixed address' of the landed bourgeois home), and transience of the landless (instruments which could be carried around – the mouth organ was known as 'a band in a waistcoat pocket').

Permanent also in that the most respectable piano repertoire was embodied in printed sheet music, while the demotic instruments were vehicles of an ever-developing aural/oral musical culture.

The oral and politically oriented counter-history developed its own adaptive forms native to the new environment. One of the most prolific of these was the bushranger song. Bushrangers were the Australian equivalent of highwaymen. Treated straightforwardly by the authorities as thieves and often murderers, they, in fact, occupied a spectrum running from that official characterization as criminals, to politically driven outcasts at the level of oral culture. I conclude this chapter with a vernacular song that exemplifies this model of a counter narrative which discloses the political resonance of 'low' colonial culture, and in particular of the Anglo/Irish imprint.

The particular bushranger song existed in several forms, the prototype of which was the familiar 'The Wild Colonial Boy', in which the protagonist is referred to as Jack Doolan. The name changes from version to version, but in every case, the initials are J.D., and he is of Irish background, by birth or ancestry, he turns to bushranging, often with a Robin Hood steal-from-the-rich-give-to-the-poor profile, and he is finally tracked down by the police and, defiant to the end, is shot dead. One of the most prolific eponyms is identified in the titles 'Jack O'Donohoe', 'Bold Jack O'Donohoe' and 'The Adventures of Jack O'Donohoe'. Being a form of oral and unauthorized culture, many such songs have not survived, but Jack Donohoe was the first of the bushranger songs to leave a written form (Hughes 1996: 237). Donohoe was sentenced to transportation from Dublin and arrived in Australia in 1825. By 1827, he 'took to the highway', in the words of an early version of the ballad (Hughes 1996: 238). He and his two Irish partners in crime were captured and his henchmen executed, but Donohoe escaped and formed a new gang consisting of Irish and English deportees and resumed an impressively active career of highway robbery, achieving a high level of notoriety and attracting a high price on his head of one hundred pounds. Finally cornered by police near Campbelltown, nearly fifty kilometres west of Sydney, he was shot dead.

Donohoe became the subject of two levels of narrative. In the official written record, he was simply a local criminal who terrorized the communities in which he worked, and who finally received his just desserts, and the evidence is that this characterization had considerable justice to it. But Donohoe also attracted popular admiration for openly defying the authorities and making them look ridiculous with his exploits. Although the song has an Irish analogue, the Australian version is about local events and characters, with local references including the native Australian fauna, dingoes and kangaroos. But in this local narrative, the felon also acquired a political complexion that refers back to Ireland. The activities in his native Ireland prior to his transportation (he was evidently born in Tipperary) were conducted on highways where 'tyrants' feared to walk, as in the first two versions cited from Anderson, and in the third version, he is described as a 'bold United boy', a transplanted representative of the continuing struggle between the Irish and the English oppressors. In the version given by Hughes, the struggle between Donohoe and the police was laminated over with these political overtones. Donohoe's last words to the police who called for his surrender were reportedly a string of abusive obscenities. In the ballads, his last stand became a political statement: 'It shall never be said of me that Donohoe the brave//Could surrender to a policeman or become an Englishman's slave' (Hughes 1996: 239).

As foreshadowed above, as a form of low, oral, culture, the ballad exists in many variants, of which Anderson reproduces three. In all of these versions, Donohoe is accorded heroic status, not as a criminal, but as an Irish patriot resisting the British government:

> 'We've got courage stout and bold and Irish blood also//So this day we'll fight for liberty'
> 'Jack O'Donohoe', Anderson 196, music 568; see also 'The Adventures of Jack O'Donohoe', Anderson 197, music 568.
> 'To resign unto you, you cowardly dogs, it's a thing I ne'er will do,
> I'd rather fight with all my might, says famed Jack Donoghue.
> I'd range these woods and valleys like a wolf or kangaroo,
> Before I'd work for government says bold Jack Donoghue
> Anderson, 'Bold Jack O'Donoghue', 200, music 569.

The song published by Hughes is adapted from Irish sources, the lyrics from an Irish ballad called 'The Adventures of Jack O'Donohoe', and the melody is an amalgam of several Irish songs. So we have here a new 'native' Australian genre – the bushranger ballad – but with its lyrics, melody and politics nourished by a long political tradition of Anglo-Irish relations formed on the other side of the world. As such, it exemplifies an unauthorized 'history from below' presenting the identity of an oppressed community, narrated and sustained primarily through sound: that is an oral tradition.

And that political narrative, which counter-history, would continue to sustain and fortify that identity and its framing politics. About half a century later, on 11 November 1880, the most famous of all Australian bushrangers, Ned Kelly was executed. Born in Australia, his father was an Irish convict, and he became the most 'narrated' character in the history of post-colonial Australia. He was the subject of the first feature film, mentioned above. This was followed by Kelly films in 1920, 1923, 1934, 1951, 1960, 1970, 1993 and 2003. He has been the subject of an abundance of biographies, novels and paintings, most notably the internationally acclaimed mythologizing series by Sidney Nolan. And at least a dozen CDs' worth of songs commemorate and are inspired by Ned Kelly, including two albums by one of Australia's leading jazz composers, Dave Dallwitz.

Again, there are two categories of narrative. The first, and the official one, was of a gang of cattle and horse thieves, and cop killers after an unsuccessful attempt to seek and capture the gang ended with a number of police officers being shot and killed. They were cast by the authorities as vicious and cold-blooded murderers, as in the report from *The Northern Miner* newspaper, 4 November 1880, the week before Ned's execution:

> Ned Kelly bushranger and murderer has been sentenced to death. We should never forget the fact that the first settlers in Australia were convicts of the worst class and that their descendants still retain the traditions, feelings and habits of the criminal classes from which they sprung [sic].
>
> Wilson, 2021: 205

This led to a reward of five hundred pounds being placed on Kelly's head (it later rose to a staggering eight thousand for the four man gang). But there has emerged a second narrative 'from below', an unofficial demotic testimony that emerged from what Alex de Waal, writing of the Irish famine of the mid-nineteenth century, described as the convergence of 'several strands of public life … with the slow sedimentation of oral history' (*London Review of Books*, 7 March 2019: 30). This narrative circulated orally among the largely Irish community within which Kelly circulated and by whom he was often sheltered and was given clearer form and more general circulation by the so-called 'Jerilderie letter'. Jerilderie was a rural village bailed up by the Kelly gang in 1879, and from whence the letter of over fifty pages, dictated by Kelly to a literate member of his gang, was intended to be sent to the press. It was the second time Kelly had sought to present his own account of his career to the general public. The first letter had been sent to the MP Donald Cameron in 1878, but only a brief synopsis found its way into public view. The Jerilderie letter fell into similar oblivion, subjected to political suppression with only brief excerpts convenient to the authorities appearing publicly. The original full text of the letter Kelly dictated was only discovered about half a century later (it can be read on the website of the National Museum of Australia).

Its demotic, often stream-of-consciousness and poetic vigour discloses its origins in the spoken word and exploitation of sonic effects such as alliteration and assonance, often like a hell-and-damnation preacher, as in the vituperative gusto in the description of the 'big ugly fat-necked wombat headed big bellied magpie legged narrow hipped splaw-footed sons of Irish bailiffs or English landlords which is better known as Officers of Justice or Victorian Police'. And, as is hinted here, in addition to giving a detailed account of his supposed crimes and how he was provoked into them, the letter is largely a political statement, as is confirmed more explicitly in the following.

Kelly rails against Irishmen who 'deserted the shamrock, the emblem of true wit and beauty to serve under a flag a nation that has destroyed massacred and murdered their forefathers by the greatest of torture'. He speaks of towns in the colony as 'places of tyranny and condemnation many a blooming Irishman rather than subdue to the Saxon yoke were flogged to death and bravely died in servile chains but true to the shamrock and a credit to Paddy's land'. He imagines the Irish in America declaring war on England to 'fight her with their own arms for the sake of the colour they dare not wear for years. And to reinstate it and rise old Erin's isle once more, from the pressure and tyrannism [sic] of the English yoke'. He concludes by outlining a programme to redistribute wealth and rights, to give money to a fund for widows and orphans and, to any who do not agree with his programme, to leave the state of Victoria as soon as they read his proclamation, otherwise 'The consequences ... shall be worse than the rust in the wheat of Victoria ... I do not wish to give the order full force without giving ... warning, but I am a Widow's Son, outlawed and my orders must be obeyed'.

The dictation in such circumstances of such a long declaration fortifies the sense that, rather than being a common criminal, Kelly, his gang and his numerous supporters saw themselves as victims of Anglo-Irish hostility. His deeper ambition was nothing less than to establish something like an independent republic within Australia. Kelly's last stand is reasonably famous even outside Australia. The gang took over a pub in the small rural town of Glenrowan. They removed railway tracks that would bring the police up from Melbourne, and when the train was derailed, they intended to kill the surviving law officers. Rather than attempting to flee, the gang waited for them in the pub throughout a long night. Among the sixty plus 'hostages' (in many cases supporters) in the pub, he was a local school teacher, Curnow, who persuaded Kelly that he was a sympathizer and sought permission to take his wife home. Curnow alerted the approaching train and the police surrounded the pub. The gang released the occupants of the pub, with whom they had been drinking, talking and singing through the night, and proceeded to shoot it out with the police. Kelly himself could have escaped, but, encased in his home made armour, he emerged from the morning fog in the rear of the besieging police, ultimately to be brought down with numerous gunshot wounds inflicted in areas unprotected by the armour.

This is to be emphasized: the gang could have escaped with ease. They sought the confrontation, as an act of political rebellion, a continuation of a conflict that had begun half a world away. That counter narrative was sustained by an oral tradition, the sound of defiant song. And one of the songs the crowd sang in that pub on the last night was a version of 'Bold Jack Donohue'; one of the 'willing hostages' gave her son sixpence to sing 'The Wild Colonial Boy' for the general entertainment.

At the beginning of this chapter, I suggested that the journey to establish historical linkages is often a long and circuitous one. But, as in this case, it can have greater explanatory power than the quick and easy path. What can we conclude here regarding the cultural role of sound? There are some very significant patterns which are emerging in this tale. They involve the relationships between high and popular culture, authorized and suppressed histories, people with fixed property and those whose legal hold on the land is tenuous. But in addition, there are some interesting collateral correspondences, and for present purposes, we see a general tendency for these relationships to parallel the difference between written and oral cultures. The high, the authorized and the propertied appear to be generally aligned with literate culture, the written law. The low, unauthorized and the transient are aligned with oral culture, unwritten custom (this binary is nuanced below). And there is a further pattern emerging: that sound is a major site over which conflict is negotiated. The struggle over who has the right to make public noise is a way of tracing the history of the emerging modern age and defining its often violent tensions. And we shall see why this became so as we proceed.

Notes

1 *Sydney Morning Herald*, 'Spectrum', 19–20 July 2014: 9.
2 See, for example, *Guardian Online*, 3 February 2021, accessed 3 February 2021.
3 'Trial and Sentence of John Mitchell', Anderson 2000: 354, music 593; on Mitchell see also 'John Mitchell's address' 356–357, music 594; 'Mrs Mitchell's Lament for her Husband' 359–363, music 594; 'Granua's Lament for the Loss of her Blackbird Mitchell', 372–373, music 595; 'John Mitchell, Irish Patriot and Exile', 378–379, music 595; 'John Mitchell's Return' 379, music 596.

Reading

Anderson, Hugh. 2000. *Farewell to Judges and Juries: The Broadside Ballad & Convict Transportation to Australia, 1788–1868*. Hotham Hill Victoria: Red Rooster Press.
Ballantine, Christopher. 2017. 'Song, Memory, Power, and the South African Archive'. *The Musical Quarterly*, 99: 60–80.
Boyce, James. 2008. *Van Diemen's Land*. Melbourne: Black Inc.
Convict Discipline: A Facsimile of the rare Colonial Circular No-33-48 and other related Documents (number 251 of 750). Melbourne: Gryphon Press.
Fox, Adam. 2017. 'Words, Words, Words: Education, Literacy and Print'. In Keith Wrightson (ed), *A Social History of England 1500–1750*. Cambridge: Cambridge University Press: 129–151.
Goodman, Steve. 2010. *Sonic Warfare: Sound, Affect, and the Ecology of Fear*. Cambridge, MA and London.
Holmes, Richard. 2005. *Tommy: The British Soldier on the Western Front 1914–1918*. London: Harper Perennial.
Hughes, Robert. 1996 (first pub 1987). *The Fatal Shore: A History of the Transportation of Convicts to Australia, 1987–1868*. London: Harvill Press.
Johnson, Bruce and Cloonan Martin. 2008. *Dark Side of the Tune: Popular Music and Violence*. Aldershot and Burlington, VT: Ashgate.
Keegan, John. 2004 (first pub. 1976). *The Face of Battle: A Study of Agincourt, Waterloo and the Somme*. London: Pimlico.

Kempowski, Walter. 2014 (UK), 2015 (US) (1st pub. In German 2005). *Swansong 1945: A Collective Diary of the Last Days of the Third Reich*. New York, NY, London: W.W. Norton & Company.

Livy. 1965. *The War with Hannibal* (trans. Aubrey de Selincourt). Harmondsworth: Penguin.

McGarry, Fearghal. 2010. *The Rising, Ireland: Easter 1916*. Oxford: Oxford University Press.

Proctor, David. 1992. *Music of the Sea*. London: National Maritime Museum.

Shrank, Cathy. 2017. 'Crafting the Nation'. In Keith Wrightson (ed), *A Social History of England 1500–1750*. Cambridge: Cambridge University Press: 19–38.

Wilson, Rebecca. 2021. *Kate Kelly: The True Story of Ned Kelly's Little Sister*. Sydney: Allen & Unwin.

3
FROM HEARING TO SEEING

Introduction

The previous chapter explored the relationship between sound, identity and territory, a connection that goes back to the earliest of human communities. The examples cited have begun to hint at a shift in the status of aurality, of the audible, as we move into the modern era. That is, that information circulated aurally has come to be regarded as less trustworthy, less reliable: 'Don't believe everything you hear'. The *Oxford English Dictionary* locates the origins of the word 'hearsay' in the sixteenth century but traces over time its changing status to become an information network lacking the authority of the written record. I want to examine the way auditory cultures and information networks have been given or denied power and who has possessed such power.

Much as it is a cliché of historical writing, the term 'Age of Transition' might well have been coined for England in the early modern period. The term 'early modern' is generally taken to refer to the sixteenth, seventeenth and early eighteenth centuries (Withington 2017: 1) during which, in the words of Wrightson, the idea of 'significant transition in the English economy and society' is

> deeply embedded. It originated in the period itself, in the writings of perceptive contemporaries who believed themselves to be living in changing times …It was elaborated in the work of Scottish Enlightenment thinkers … it informed Marxist historical accounts of the development of industrial capitalism in England; and it was central to the writings of the English Historical Economists.
>
> Withington 2017: 4

In his detailed study of Shakespeare's activities throughout the year 1599, James Shapiro situates *Hamlet* at, and reflecting, 'what it means to live in the bewildering space between familiar past and murky future' (Shapiro 2005: 313). Similarly, the play registers that 'the world had changed. Old certainties were gone, even if new ones had not yet taken hold' (Shapiro 2005: 322).

These changes affected every aspect and level of society, producing optimism, hope and alarm, depending on the situation of the individual (see further Withington 2017: 13). Many of these shocks were associated with, and the product of, the religious reformations 'the most significant extrinsic shock experienced by English society between the Black Death and the Civil Wars of the 1640s' (Ryrie 2017: 107). The drama of the late sixteenth to the seventeenth centuries had 'to engage with a host of new problems. These problems ranged from Luther's doubts about the afterlife to Copernicus' questions about the celestial spheres beyond, from Descartes' paranoia about a deceiving spirit to Hobbes' anxieties about deceiving men' (Fletcher 2011: 12). This has been explained as a sensory revolution in public worship, from vision to audition (see for example Smith 1999: 261–269; Richards 2019: 130–181, and Hunt's full length study of 2010). The break with the Roman Catholic church was experienced as both an intellectual and material crisis. In politico-religious terms, the reformation and shifts in dynastic alliances affected what kinds of values might be safely presented in public spaces such as churches and theatres.

This is compatible with growing materialism that places knowledge based on science, reason and the senses, against revelation by faith in 'The Word', modern scientific enquiry into the natural world against the inherited wisdom of antiquity. The private and individualist entrepreneurialism in open markets which gradually displaces 'closed' and rigid agricultural and ecclesiastical communities creates a new order of ambitions and dilemmas. Among the most fundamental of these relates to the relationship between mind and body. It is notable that the word 'anxiety' appears from the early seventeenth century, 'because this is the moment when the need for such a word enters the language – what anxiety names is the very prospect confronting the early moderns that body and mind might be separable aspects of selfhood' (Johnson et al. 2014: 5).

The psychic trauma hardly requires elaboration, but there were also transforming material reverberations at the social, economic and demographic levels. The sense of approaching political crisis was fed by the threat of a Spanish invasion, military disasters in Ireland, the passing away of a generation of stabilizing forces at court, such as the death of Burghley in August 1599, leaving a visibly ageing monarch who left no heir (Shapiro 2005: 50, 51, 59). There was a destabilizing of traditional social hierarchies, with a redefinition of the elite, the increasingly well-defined and powerful 'middling sort', and often devastating consequences for the hapless labouring classes and the poor (Withington 2017: 11). The dissolution of the monasteries led to 'the largest single transfer of landed wealth in English history' (Ryrie 2017: 109), which in turn destroyed a traditional site of social welfare, with consequences ranging from an increase in infant mortality to mass armed risings in the north in 1536 (Ryrie 2017: 110). The Reformation affected the basic rhythms of life as well as the rituals of worship, 'a stripping away of altars, paintings, ceremonies, vestments, sacramental rituals and beloved holidays. ... Traditional seasonal rhythms were disrupted, the long-standing equilibrium between holiday and workday unbalanced' (Shapiro 2005: 170).

The structure of rural society was changed as new landholding patterns developed, including enclosures of hitherto common lands, which not only increased agricultural productivity for land owners but also displaced sections of the rural populace to towns where they would provide a proletarian labour pool for the coming industrial revolution (Whittle, 2017: 156–157). England was thus becoming urbanized, and more rapidly than any other European country. By 1600, London's population was almost 200,000; by the mid-eighteenth century around 750,000 and by 1700, London was already the largest city in Europe (Cockayne 2007: 7; Withington 2017: 175), with all the attendant infrastructural stresses. Reviewing inflation, crippling taxes, catastrophic crop failures, demographic instability (including vagabond discharged naval and military personnel), a disillusioned and increasingly secularized intellectual class, widening social inequality and a destitute proletariat, suspension of common law, Chris Fitter declares that the politics of late sixteenth century England were in fact marked by 'concentrated distress, revolutionary upheaval' (Fitter 2012: 5).

The sense of change thus percolated through all levels of society including the relationship between unwritten custom and written law. The status of orality during the period under discussion was refracted in legal terms through the idea of custom. For the majority, their local rights and the everyday rhythms of life, such as those which defined conditions of tenancy, grazing rights and land use, were enshrined in traditional customs preserved in the collective memory (Fox 2000: 259–261). These customary frameworks came under pressure from the mid-Tudor period for a range of reasons, not least of which could be traced to the massive transfer of land ownership from the monasteries to

> a new breed of landlords who acquired their land not by inheritance but through investment. Such men had little knowledge of local customs, little empathy with the traditional mores of neighbourhoods, and very often saw such things as inimical to their proprietorial freedoms and commercial interests'
>
> Fox 2000: 271

These changes over the sixteenth and seventeenth centuries would generate confrontations between customary rights and a growing body of legislation, largely controlled by and therefore in the interests of the emerging class of capitalist entrepreneurs, a confrontation between oral tradition and laws inscribed in a rapidly growing written canon (Fox 2000: 271, 280–281), with the authority of unwritten customs gradually losing ground against written contracts. There has been a shift in the balance of authority between the spoken and the written word, the heard and the seen, and I am going to explore how this is related to the way we can use sound to trace the shift from the relatively stable social structures in the Middle Ages, based on status or 'station', to the emergence of the more dynamic model based on a class of the late- and post-Renaissance (for a useful and succinct introduction to the distinction between 'status' and 'class', see Day 2001).

Orality and literacy

To lay down the foundations for that discussion, we need to explore the changing balance between orality and literacy. Earlier I talked about the two most important senses in our public conduct: presenting information in visible form – being seen and being heard, and receiving information by looking and listening. This distinction parallels the distinction between reading/writing and hearing/sounding. It has long been argued that 'Western culture had fundamentally shifted at the Renaissance from a primarily auditory perceptual and cognitive mode to a primarily visual one' and that printing was central to that shift (Fox and Woolf 2002: 5). It is very important to emphasize that while we can make this distinction for purposes of discussion, in practical terms, these two ways of negotiating are not mutually exclusive; that would be patently absurd. Just because someone can read and write, doesn't mean they don't talk and listen. Visual and aural cultures are not neat, mutually exclusive opposites.[1]

The extensive compendium of Fox's scholarship, his 2000 monograph *Oral and Literate Culture in England 1500–1700*, argues that the simplistic binary orality/literacy is a false antithesis (see similarly Davies 2010: 320).

The two in fact interpenetrated each other, often to mutual enrichment. Illiteracy did not mean exclusion from the literate culture but often complemented it (see further, for example Lamb 2006: 10). The basic argument towards which I am working is that the differential spread of literacy ultimately politicized sound. Fox's continuing research has led him to revise some figures, such as data on literacy rates, so I have often cited his more recent publications.

The church was one site at which orality and literacy converged, and especially in rural areas, members of the clergy bridged 'the supposed divide between oral and literate as well as between popular and elite cultures' (Davies 2010: 317). As Fox (2000) has abundantly documented, in many ways, orality and literacy have complemented and interacted with each other, as for example in practice by members of congregations of taking written notes on the sermon they were attending, which 'had become commonplace' by the mid-seventeenth century (Hunt 2010: 139). In sixteenth-century England, 'reading was habitually done out loud' (Fox 2000: 36; see similarly 38) and usually to others (see further on this, for example, Richards 2019: 44, 73, 285) and those unable to afford printed sermons could under various circumstances have heard them read aloud, for example, in households and to serving staff (Hunt 2010: 170, 172). In places of learning of the period, the master would read aloud, followed by his oral commentary and questions for discussion. To complicate the matter further, there are also various degrees and ways of understanding literacy. Some school children, especially girls, would leave school with some rudimentary reading skill but unable to write, while others could read only a limited range of typefaces and scripts (Fox 2017: 136]. What must be kept in mind as our discussion proceeds is that the binaries orality/literacy and literacy/illiteracy are not straightforward (See further Fox 2000: 5). There were degrees of literacy, and just because someone was by any definition illiterate, this did not mean that he or she had no access to the written word.

My interest here is in changes in the relative levels of authority of our two primary public 'information circuits' and how they operate. Let us call one of these the 'Oral' circuit and the other the 'Visual' circuit. In broad terms, each of these involves different modes of transmission, reception and storage of information.[2] The oral circuit transmits information through sound, particularly speech that information is received by hearing – the ear – and is stored in the memory. The visual circuit transmits information by writing, which is received by looking – the eye – and is stored primarily in print. As long as we are equipped with the usual sensory faculties, we activate both at different times, often simultaneously, and in varying degrees of balance. If I read aloud from a text that is being followed by my students, then we are activating both oral and print modes. In any literate society, both circuits are open.

During the period under discussion here, however, the relationship between these two 'information circuits' was in extreme flux, and the authority of the oral/aural was much greater than it is for us. In effect, they are not only complementary but also sometimes competing ways of knowing. Orality carried greater authority, and the elements of its 'circuit' were much more sophisticated than is the case today.

The oral circuit

To an extent barely conceivable to us today, the oral transmission of information was a subject of close study as early as the schoolroom. The field of study called Rhetoric, now virtually extinct, was one of the central pillars of the Elizabethan school and university curricula. But the subject underwent significant changes from the sixteenth through to the seventeenth centuries. It is a sign of the ascendancy of print that this ancient branch of study was shedding its oratorical components, that is, its roots in spoken delivery. Classical or Latin rhetoric had been divided into five major divisions:

1. Inventio, which consisted of the exploration of material in order to discover all the arguments for proof or refutation of propositions;
2. Dispositio, concerning the arrangement of the arguments;
3. Elocutio, concerning the style of presentation, the manipulation of figures of thought and language;
4. Memoria, the memorizing of the arguments;
5. Pronuntiatio, or Actio, involving physical presentation such as speech, gesture and posture.

By the late sixteenth century, largely in association with the influence of the French logician and educator Pierre de La Ramée (latinized as Petrus Ramus), these last two elements of the discipline atrophied – that is, the anchoring of Rhetoric as an art of oral as opposed to written delivery. Teachers of classical and Renaissance rhetoric had been wont to quote Demosthenes in discussing what was the chief part of the study of the subject: 'To pronounce well' – that is, oral delivery (Richards 2019: 87). But the net effect of Ramist reforms was to accelerate 'the shift from aurality to literacy in the age of print' (Richards 2019: 86; Richards summarizes the process succinctly, 84–87). The close study of the techniques and protocols of oratory that were so significant in Elizabethan education has now virtually disappeared from contemporary education, surviving if at all in the withered and now barely remembered practice known as 'elocution'.

The reception phase of the oral 'circuit', interpreting speech, was likewise of a more complex order than is now the case. The Elizabethan ear was more finely attuned to the meanings conveyed through vocalization, picking up signals that are not so clearly inscribed in print. An obvious example that is apposite to discussions below is the delight in puns, through which different orders of experience converge sonically. Now regarded as too trivial to carry any significant burden as a bearer of knowledge, in the Elizabethan era, the pun was a sonic exploration of unexpected resemblances between incongruities and as such formed one of the devices underpinning the metaphysical device called the 'conceit'. In a play that is, as I shall argue, so preoccupied with ambiguity, with the disturbance of order, it is not surprising that *Hamlet* is more densely packed with puns than any other of Shakespeare's works (Delabastita 1993: 249). Delabastita identifies 175 instances of utterances in the play which the Elizabethan ear could have heard as puns (Delabastita 1993: 347–492), minor disorientations that reminded aurally attentive audiences that things might not be entirely as straightforward as they seem – that is, that 'there is more than meets the eye'.

Together with such devices as acousmatic sound, the pun represents a form of acoustically based ambiguity, and as such, it forms part of a theatre soundscape in which other sound effects may also be thought of as related devices, such as the use of bells, invoking a range of cultural meanings that would have been familiar to the alert Elizabethan ear (Kinney 2006: 83). Addressed as an acoustic site rather than a text, such effects may be categorized as puns – similar or identical sounds with several possible meanings – and part of the general soundplay that expresses the ambiguities that pervade the play. It is Hamlet himself who most often plays on these ambiguities, specifically the pun, to advertise what I will argue is his uncertain, transitional state.

The decline in the status of the pun is a marker of more profound changes in the function of language that accompanied the scientific revolution. Delabastita refers to 'a shift in the philosophical *communis opinio* on the relationship between language and thought' (Delabastita 1993: 254). At the obvious level, that shift was part of the programme of linguistic renovation that began with Francis Bacon, and was then formally instituted by the Royal Society, designed to turn the English language into a more efficient instrument of scientific enquiry. That project regarded all figurative language, all forms of ambiguity, as distractions from the basic function of presenting a clear window on the world being catalogued as part of the scientific revolution. Language attained its highest authority as an instrument purged of all functions except denotation, which amounts to the strict meaning given in a dictionary. Like the architectural shift from stained to clear glass in churches, or from early illuminated manuscripts to the austere uniformity of print, the function of the prose was to provide a clear, invisible window to the world, not to distractingly ornament and to titillate the ear.

The pun is essentially a sonic phenomenon which violates the stable protocols of a scientific language, which can best be preserved through the fixity of print as opposed to speech which can destabilize meanings through such effects as tone, timbre, pitch, volume and pace. Print can distinguish 'sun' from 'son', or 'a dew' from 'adieu', confirming the stability of the natural world, but which is unbalanced by sonic ambiguity. Respect accorded the pun up to the early seventeenth century reflected the same appeal of unexpected correspondences that sustained the metaphysical poets, and a world view that found insights rather than obfuscations in these sonic convergences, language as a creative force in itself rather than as the disciplined and tightly regulated handmaiden of scientific rationality.

Complementing the stabilization of meaning through the printed word was the formalization of grammar and spelling – as, for example, through dictionaries. This period also marks the growing consolidation of the visual/print over the aural/oral as the authoritative information circuit, the culmination of which has been dated to the mid-eighteenth century, with the ascendancy of the 'generally accepted view that what is printed is true, or at least truer than any other type of record' (Kernan 1989: 49). When Samuel Johnson produced his watershed *Dictionary* of the English Language in 1755, he made a conscious choice to include no word that had not appeared in print (thus, incidentally, further shifting membership of the English language community towards a matter of class). The *Dictionary* established the English language as a printed, rather than an oral medium, and in particular, a printed language that derives its authority from 'literature':

> But the real poetic power of the *Dictionary* is its print-based ability, like literature itself, to order and fix the language, to abstract it from the linguistic flux of Babel and give it boundaries, stability and meaning. And by treating the printed works of certain famous writers as definitive of what language is and means, it … established that the English language belongs to and is shaped by … "Literature" in its broad eighteenth-century sense of all categories of excellent writing, Hooker and Bacon as well as Sidney and Shakespeare.
>
> Kernan 1989: 197–198

It is thus no coincidence that this is also the period in which Shakespeare's works were translated from the world of the stage to the category of literature, and indeed, his status as a 'man of letters' has so engulfed him that, astonishingly, his best worked was deemed ineffective on stage (Hawkes 1986: 59).

The storage system for 'oral circuits' was also more developed than for communities in which print is dominant. That is, the Elizabethan memory of what is heard seems to have been extraordinary by twenty-first-century standards. Hunt has noted that both theatre audiences and church congregations possessed memories that could assimilate long and complex oral messages (Hunt 2010: 1) and cites the example of the minister John Rogers who recalled in his spiritual biography that he trained himself to repeat 'a sermon to himself every night before going to bed. On Sunday and Friday nights, he repeated the sermon he had heard the previous Sunday morning; on Monday and Saturday nights he repeated the sermon he had heard the previous Sunday afternoon' (Hunt 2010: 101). The possession of such memory skills was also less class dependent and not confined to the literate and educated. 'Such memory skills are a well-known feature of oral culture. … John Norden observed in 1610 that "many unlearned men have better and more retentive memories than have some Schollers", because "such as have not use of a pen, must use the memory only"' (Hunt 2010: 103–104).

While not all members of church congregations were likely to have been as committed as John Rogers, there was an official obligation on all school-boys to undertake exercises involving memory that are difficult to imagine being within the capacities of contemporary students. 'The Constitutions and Canons Ecclesiastical' issued by the Church of England through the Bishop of London in 1604 listed 'The Duty of School-Masters', which included that

> as often as any Sermon shall be upon holy and festival Days, within the Parish where they teach, they shall bring their Scholars to the Church

> where such Sermon shall be made, and there see them quietly and soberly behave themselves, and shall examine them at times convenient after their return, what they have borne away of such Sermons.
>
> Online at https://www.anglican.net/doctrines/1604-canon-law/, accessed 11 May 2021

Richards summarizes an example of the full extent of the exercises from a grammar school in Leicester: boys were required to attend church on Sunday mornings and take notes. On Sunday afternoons, the students were required to take extensive commentaries that they would then deliver to their masters on Mondays (Richards 2019: 81). The taking of notes was highly regulated, and while weaker pupils were allowed to refer to their notes during the 'repetition', the 'older pupils were expected to rely wholly on their memory, using the structure of the sermon as an *aide-mémoire*' (Hunt 2010: 98). It was common practice for families and the servants to gather directly after arriving home from church to repeat what they recalled of the sermon and after dinner that night to discuss what they had learned (Hunt 2010: 73–75).

In our era of technologically sophisticated and largely indiscriminate forms of acoustic and visual information storage, we have, in an important sense, forgotten how to remember. A whole set of memorizing strategies, mnemonics and ways of organizing information have fallen into disuse except as novelty stage and parlour tricks, faint residues of the ancient recognition that there is a direct connection between the level of acoustic attentiveness and the power of memory. In *Institutio Oratoria*, Quintilian made the connection explicit: '… the mind should be kept alert by the sound of the voice, so that the memory may derive assistance from the double effect of speaking and listening' (Smith 1999: 110).

The textual circuit

While the various phases – transmission, reception and storage – of the oral circuit were highly developed, for the textual circuits in general, they were in a much more rudimentary state of development than they are today. Regarding the textual transmission and reception phases, there were fewer people with the literacy to read books. We have noted that the concept of literacy is complex and varied. The ability to sign one's name is an inadequate guide (see Fox 2000: 408–409), but it provides a crude indicator of changes in the culture of literacy. Reports based on parish records and marriage registers vary, depending on the sample, but Fox's survey found that

> in 1500, perhaps 10 per cent of adult males but only 1 per cent of adult females could form a signature. On the accession of Elizabeth I in 1558, these figures had risen to 10 per cent of men and 5 per cent of women; at the outbreak of the Civil War in 1642 they stood at 30 per cent and

> 10 per cent, respectively; and by the time George 1 came the throne in 1714, an average of 45 per cent of men and 25 percent of women could sign, or more than one third of the total adult population, ... between 1754 and 1760, fully 64 per cent of men and 39 per cent of women were able to write their names, or just over half of all people.
>
> Fox 2017: 136–137

At the same time, in regard to storage, there were fewer books to read. In 1500, only forty-six were published in England, as compared with 259 titles a century later, rising rapidly to 577 by 1640 (Fox and Woolf 2002: 22). Fox later revised the earlier figure upwards, to fifty-nine and added the figure of 4,198 in 1642 (Fox 2017: 140).

Furthermore, at least in the secular realm, even the storage phase of the 'visual circuit" was also far more rudimentary than what we now take for granted. The English language itself was in a highly fluid state, with 'relatively little unanimity over correctness and propriety in terms of spelling and pronunciation, grammatical rules, and stylistic conventions' (Fox 2000: 100). Shakespeare's own printed texts exemplify the point. It has been argued that he is one among many dramatists of the period whose work retains a strong element of what Ong has called 'physiological' as opposed to 'syntactical' punctuation (Ong 1944), that is, punctuation reflecting the physiology of vocal declamation, such as pausing for breath, as opposed to punctuation based on grammar; the English forms of which were gradually becoming increasingly standardized from the late sixteenth century. Richards cites numerous examples through which we can trace in 'sixteenth century printed books the beginnings of a transition from a system of punctuation that guides breathing to one that clarifies the syntax of a sentence' (Richards 2019: 46, 53–55). She concludes, 'Thus, the printed page ...is full of cues for reading aloud. Punctuation marks, fount, spelling, even pictures are all features of print that can be seen as "vocal" cues. Pupils learning to read were taught not just to sound the letters but also to note marks like the colon to guide their delivery' (Richards 2019: 66).

The foregoing discussion reflects the broad scholarly consensus on a number of issues. One is that for most of the populace during the sixteenth century, speaking/hearing was the primary if not the only channel through which they could circulate information; another is that by the mid-eighteenth century, the ability to read and write was relatively common, no longer the exclusive preserve of professional elites like the clergy. The sixteenth to mid-seventeenth centuries thus saw a major shift in the balance between orality and literacy, between what is heard and what is seen. The coexistence of the two systems is a transitional moment in the movement, in Smith's words, 'to shift the site of speech from the thorax to the brain - and in that shift to insert one further clause in the Cartesian divorce of mind from body' (Smith 1999: 239).

Around 1600, the great age of the regularization and domination of print still lay in the future. The kinds of organization of written information which today we take for granted, and on which we so heavily rely, were only very erratically used in Shakespeare's time. An organizational principle as basic as alphabetical order only became standard practice in the seventeenth century (see further Burke 2000). The foregoing discussion of the two 'information circuits', the oral and the visual, has already begun to disclose one of the major transitional moments in their relationship. The first is the ascendancy of print in England from the sixteenth to the eighteenth centuries. Let us now examine that gradual transition from, so to speak, the ear to the eye. In our modern cultural consciousness, seeing is generally accorded greater authority than hearing. But what if that difference was not so clear? What if we were at a transitional stage in history where we were not so sure what to believe: to put it simply, what our eyes tell us or what our ears tell us? It is hard for us to imagine this because we take for granted the evidence of our eyes. There are material as well as intellectual reasons for our faith in what we see, and some of these are disclosed if we try to imagine the sensory environment of Elizabethan London.

The Elizabethan acoustic world

The foundational study of sound in sixteenth-century England is Bruce R. Smith (1999), which is the platform on which the following survey is built. Except as indicated, I have broadly tried not simply to duplicate his work, but to add to it.

The general balance between sight and sound in the Elizabethan world was in many ways distinct from today's conditions, and for a host of reasons. Some of these are to do with intellectual factors referred to above, but others, however, are related to the material culture of everyday life. Consider for example the place of light and sight in sixteenth-century London. Relative to today, we find an earlier decline in vigour and acuity with the onset of ageing. Sight deteriorated earlier, and optical devices were less effective and beyond the financial means of most of the populace, leaving them more dependent on hearing (Richards 2019: 2).[3] This was apparent in a range of everyday practices. In a latitude that experienced very wide seasonal variations in the amount of (day)light available, without the benefits of modern domestic and public illumination, when the cost of candles of sufficient brightness to read at night was beyond a large proportion of the populace, relative to a modern city, sight played a very different role as a way of negotiating time and space. The way the individual saw her/himself and others was, over a full lifetime, literally less clear. If primitive optical health and technology limited one's view of others, so too did the more rudimentary and expensive technology of the mirror literally obscure the 'view' of the self.[4] Vision did not carry the same reliable authority as it has subsequently come to enjoy: 'Within the pre-Cartesian context ... eyesight had been associated with the same gross defects that corrupted all human faculties' (Fletcher 2011: 80). This reflected 'a long tradition of doubt about the reliability of eyesight, … that the eye was not a trustworthy guide to the external world' (Hunt 2010: 23; on the historical trajectory of visual authority see further, for example Levin 1993). Discussing the unreliability of vision in *The Winter's Tale*, Michael Schoenfeldt argues that 'anxiety about vision must have produced an interesting dynamic on the Renaissance stage, a space and medium premised on the concept of plausible illusion' (Schoenfeldt 2014: 107; see similarly Chalk 2014). In his benchmark study, Smith summarizes 'Listening, as opposed to looking, seems especially apt with respect to early modern England, as a collectivity of cultures that depended so extensively on face-to-face communication' (Smith 1999: 12).

To be able to define the world acoustically was therefore in practical terms a greater necessity than now and in some ways, it was also more possible to do so. As discussed below, one of the ways in which the modern era may be distinguished from the pre-industrial is the rise in the level of 'white noise' that is so pervasive that we are barely aware of it and its components.[5] Apart from making it much more difficult to isolate and identify particular features of such sound (see below), the rise in the volume of urban modernity has also produced a significant general reduction of hearing acuity.

I am proposing therefore that Elizabethan hearing was likely to be in general more alert, acute and discriminating among the physically healthy than is now the case in urban society. In any case, in relation to identity, for example, the sound of the voice seems to have been much more closely attended to in the process of socialization. We have referred to Shakespeare's contemporary, Francis Bacon. While he centralized vision in the pursuit of scientific knowledge, in his essay 'On Negotiating', he placed sound and speech in positions of primacy for social intercourse:

> It is generally better to deal by speech than by letter … Letters are good when a man would draw an answer by letter back again, or when it may serve for a man's justification afterwards to produce his own letter … To deal in person is good.
>
> Bacon 1985: 203

That Bacon should find this subject worthy of an essay is in itself a significant contrast with the twenty-first century; his 'division of responsibility' of the two senses is also an instructive disclosure of the competing claims of two ways of knowing during this period. And in the essay 'On Discourse', by dealing 'by speech', Bacon meant a civilized transaction as sensitively wrought as a courtly dance:

> The honourablest part of talk is to give the occasion, and again to moderate and pass to someone else, for then a man leads the dance. It is good,

in discourse and speech of conversation, to vary and intermingle speech of the present occasion with arguments, tales with reasons, asking of questions with telling of opinions, and jest with earnest.

...

Discretion of speech is more than eloquence, and to speak agreeably to him with whom we deal is more than to speak in good words and good order. A good continued speech, without a good speech of interlocution, shows slowness; and a good reply or second speech, without a good settled speech, showeth shallowness and weakness.

Bacon 1985: 160–161

Protocols for conversation were, thus, considered worthy of extended discussion, as in John Hopkins' end of century publication *Directions for Speech and Style*.

The sound of the human voice was a major element in the soundscape of Elizabethan England, which was acoustically rich in ways that would surprise us.[6] Visitors from both rural areas and from the major European cities, expressed surprise at the level of noise in London which, in more sudden proximity to forested rural landscapes, could be heard before the city even came into view. But as a 'high fidelity' soundscape, its components were more clearly defined than in today's urban soundscape. And one of the components that would surprise the twenty-first-century urban ear would be the number of voices. Among the various vocal sounds in streets of the early modern period, there were ballads and libels, sung in alehouses, taverns and various public places, and the sound of street criers at market crosses (Fox 2000: 321, 349). Fox instances an obscene ditty from the early seventeenth century that came to be a popular song 'sunge by boyes and others as they went upp and down the towne' in Slapton Northamptonshire, and one called 'Bonny Nell' in Nottingham that 'was hammered out in the streets to the rough music of candlestick, tongs, and basins' (Fox 2000: 319). In London, the sound of voices in conversation and exchanging news was such that in some quarters, such as Paul's walk, in was reported that 'The noyse in it is like that of bees, a strange humming or buzze' (Fox 2000: 346). In 1627, John Earle described the sound of the streets as a 'humming or buzze, mixt of walking, tongues and feet'; it was a 'still roar or loud whisper' (Cockayne 2007: 121).

In a less literate society, the level of visual 'signage' was much lower. Signs for various business premises supplemented print with non-verbal images of the goods or services available: three balls for a pawn shop, a picture of a loaf for a baker and a barrel or bush for a tavern. But there were only rudimentary manifestations of the advertising philosophies and technologies underpinning modern consumerism. There were fewer and less arresting signs, no lights, no flashing neon and no massive electrically activated rotating billboards. In unlit streets, communication is more reliant on acoustics, like the night watch, the hue and cry, the alarm and the street pedlars. This last is a further aspect to

Elizabethan urban commerce that shifted the balance of attentiveness towards sound. That is, more business was conducted from itinerant bases rather than permanent premises or 'stations'. This is another reason that detailed permanent signage was impractical. Peripatetic street pedlars, craftsmen and vendors had to call out their trade using street-cries which have now all but vanished.[7] In day-to-day public life, the Elizabethan voice was called upon to execute more extensive and complex tasks than that is the case in contemporary literate society pervaded by electronic information technologies.

In early modern England, there was thus still a strong residual oral culture in conjunction with an emergent culture of print and literacy. I am going now to try to imagine what it was like to be in a state of transition between hearing and seeing as foundations of our belief, but I also want to make the much more general point, that if we pay more attention to acoustic history, that relationship between what we hear and what we see is a key to a much more complex way of understanding cultural history and all its productions, including architecture, painting, politics, music, literature and technology.

Notes

1 The relationship between orality and literacy has been approached in various ways, much of it pioneered in the work of Walter Ong, going back to the 1940s in such studies as Ong 1944; Ong 1958, and cogently summarized in Ong 1982. His work has been finely nuanced by a succession of scholars on the history of orality and the rise of reading. Important studies on the relationship may be found in the work of such historians as Chartier 1994, Petrucci 1979, and more recently Fox and others cited below.
2 I emphasize the phrase 'in broad terms' to acknowledge nuances and counter-arguments; there has been opposition to the notion that writing reduced reliance on memory and served merely to store knowledge (Harris 2001). On the importance of memory to aural cultures, however, see for example Yates 1966; Carruthers, 2008.
3 On problems of eyesight and lighting in the eighteenth century: Williams 2017: 62–69. On the history of spectacles and spectacle makers from the thirteenth century to 1629 (the founding of a spectacle-makers company in England), Petegree, 2010: 107–110; Ilardi, 2007: 153–205.
4 Thanks to colleague Philippa Kelly, who discussed this topic at length with me, and also gave me a copy of her at that time unpublished paper, 'Surpassing Glass: Shakespeare's Mirrors'.
5 The pioneering work in this area is Schafer 1977. For subsequent studies, see for example, Järviluoma 1994; Järviluoma et al. 2009; and the journal *Soundscape: The Journal of Acoustic Ecology*, inaugurated in 2000. Sound studies have burgeoned over recent decades, see for example the recent compendium, Finch and Bijsterveld 2012. See further Johnson 2017.
6 In addition to Smith 1999 and Schafer 1977, on London in particular see for example Ackroyd 2000: 71–95.
7 I heard one in Hoylake on the Wirral, 'across the water' from Liverpool, in February 1992. I followed the sound to a scrap-iron buyer, wrote down the words and the 'music', and talked to him about where his street-cry had come from. What is relevant to the present discussion of the Elizabethan soundscape is that this, itself a 'residual culture', was the only human voice to be heard in the streets.

Reading

Ackroyd, Peter. 2000. *London: The Biography*. London: Chatto and Windus.
Bacon, Francis. 1985. *The Essays*, John Pitcher (ed.). Harmondsworth Middlesex: Penguin Books.
Burke, Peter. 2000. *A Social History of Knowledge*. Cambridge: Polity Press.
Carruthers, Mary. 2008. *The Book of Memory: A Study of Memory in Medieval Culture*. Cambridge: Cambridge University Press.
Chalk, Darryl. 2014. '"Make Me Not Sighted Like the Basilisk": Vision and Contagion in *The Winter's Tale*'. In Laurie Johnson, John Sutton, Evelyn Tribble (eds), *Embodied Cognition and Shakespeare's Theatre*. New York, NY and Abingdon, Oxon: Routledge: 111–132.
Chartier, Roger. 1994. *The Order of Books: Readers, Authors, and Libraries in Europe Between the 14th and 18th Centuries*. Redwood City, CA: Stanford University Press.
Cockayne, Emily. 2007. *Hubbub: Filth, Noise & Stench in England 1600–1770*. New Haven, CT and London: Yale University Press.
Davies, L.I. 2010. 'Orality, Literacy, Popular Culture: An Eighteenth-Century Case Study'. *Oral Tradition*, 25/2: 305–323.
Day, Gary. 2001. *Class*. London: Routledge.
Delabastita, Dirk. 1993. *There's a Double Tongue: An Investigation into the Translation of Shakespeare's Wordplay, with Special Reference to Hamlet*. Amsterdam and Atlanta, GA: Rodopi.
Finch, Trevor and Karen Bijsterveld. 2012. *The Oxford Handbook of Sound Studies*. Oxford and New York, NY: Oxford University Press.
Fitter, Chris. 2012. *Radical Shakespeare: Politics and Stagecraft in the Early Career*. New York, NY and London: Routledge.
Fletcher, Angus. 2011. *Evolving Hamlet: Seventeenth-Century English Tragedy and the Ethics of Natural Selection*. New York, NY: Palgrave Macmillan.
Fox, Adam. 2000. *Oral and Literate Culture in England 1500–1700*. Oxford: Clarendon Press.
Fox, Adam. 2017. 'Words, Words, Words: Education, Literacy and Print'. In Keith Wrightson (ed), *A Social History of England 1500–1750*. Cambridge: Cambridge University Press: 129–151.
Fox, Adam and Daniel Woolf (eds). 2002. *The Spoken Word: Oral Culture in Britain, 1500–1850*. Manchester and New York, NY: Manchester University Press.
Harris, Roy. 2001. *Rethinking Writing*. New York, NY: Continuum.
Hawkes, Terence. 1986. *That Shakespeherian Rag: Essays on a Critical Process*. London and New York, NY: Methuen.
Hunt, Arnold. 2010. *The Art of Hearing: English Preachers and their Audiences, 1590–1640*. Cambridge: Cambridge University Press.
Ilardi, Vincent. 2007. *Renaissance Vision: from Spectacles to Telescopes*. Philadelphia, PA: American Philosophical Society.
Johnson, Bruce. 2017. 'Sound Studies Today: Where are We Going?'. In Joy Damousi and Paula Hamilton (eds), *A Cultural History of Sound, Memory and the Senses*. New York, NY and London: Routledge: 7–22.
Johnson, Laurie, John Sutton and Evelyn Tribble (eds). 2014. 'Introduction'. In *Embodied Cognition and Shakespeare's Theatre*. New York, NY and Abingdon, Oxon: Routledge: 1–11.

Järviluoma, Helmi (ed). 1994. *Soundscapes: Essays on Vroom and Moo*. Finland: Department of Folk Tradition, University of Tampere.
Järviluoma, Helmi, Meri Kyto, Barry Truax, Heikki Uimonen and Noora Vikman (eds). 2009. *Acoustic Environments in Change*. Includes a reprint of R. Murray Schafer's *Five Village Soundscapes*. Tampere: University of Applied Science.
Kernan, Alvin. 1989. *Samuel Johnson and the Impact of Print*. Princeton, NJ: Princeton University Press. Originally published as *Printing Technology, Letters, and Samuel Johnson*, 1987, same publisher.
Kinney, Arthur F. 2006. *Shakespeare and Cognition: Aristotle's Legacy and Shakespearean Drama*. New York, NY and London: Routledge.
Lamb, Mary Ellen. 2006. *The Popular Culture of Shakespeare, Spenser, and Jonson*. London and New York, NY: Routledge.
Levin, David Michael. 1993. *Modernity and the Hegemony of Vision*. Berkeley, Los Angeles, CA and London: University of California Press.
Ong, Walter J. 1944. 'The Historical Backgrounds of Elizabethan and Jacobean Punctuation Theory'. *PMLA*, 59: 349–360.
Ong, Walter J. 1958. *Ramus Method, and the Decay of Dialogue: From the Art of Discourse to the Art of Reason*. Cambridge, MA: Harvard University Press.
Ong, Walter J. 1982. *Orality and Literacy: The Technologizing of the Word*. London and New York, NY: Methuen.
Petegree, Andrew. 2010. *Reformation and the Culture of Persuasion*. Cambridge: Cambridge University Press.
Petrucci, Armando. 1979. *Books, Writing and the Public in the Renaissance*. Rome-Bari: Laterza.
Richards, Jennifer. 2019. *Voices and Books in the English Renaissance*. Oxford: Oxford University Press.
Ryrie, Alec. 2017, 'Reformations'. In Keith Wrightson (ed), *A Social History of England 1500–1750*. Cambridge: Cambridge University Press: 107–128.
Schafer, R. Murray. 1977. *The Tuning of the World*. Toronto: McLellan and Stewart.
Schoenfeldt, Michael. 2014. 'The Unbearable Permeability of Bodies and Minds'. In Laurie Johnson, John Sutton and Evelyn Tribble (eds), *Embodied Cognition and Shakespeare's Theatre*. New York, NY and Abingdon, Oxon: Routledge: 105–109.
Shapiro, James. 2005. *1599: A Year in the Life of William Shakespeare*. London: Faber and Faber.
Smith, Bruce. 1999. *The Acoustic World of Early Modern England*. Chicago, IL and London: University of Chicago Press.
Whittle, Jane. 2017. 'Land and People'. In Keith Wrightson (ed), *A Social History of England 1500–1750*. Cambridge: Cambridge University Press: 152–173.
Williams, Abigail. 2017. *The Social Life of Books: Reading Together in the Eighteenth Century*. New Haven, CT and London: Yale University Press.
Withington, Phil. 2017. 'Urbanisation'. In Keith Wrightson (ed), *A Social History of England 1500–1750*. Cambridge: Cambridge University Press: 174–198.
Wrightson, Keith. 2017. 'Introduction: Framing Early Modern England'. In Keith Wrightson (ed), *A Social History of England 1500–1750*. Cambridge: Cambridge University Press: 1–16.
Yates, Francis. 1966. *The Art of Memory*. London: Routledge and Kegan Paul.

4
THE PULPIT AND THE PLAYHOUSE

The pulpit

The changes discussed in the previous chapter in the *mentalité* and material conditions of the era are profound and pervasive, ranging from cosmology and religion to the material conditions of everyday life. The debates which they generated were frequently underpinned by arguments over which was the path to truth: the ear or the eye? In religious life, the question was explicit in that ubiquitous public forum in the Elizabethan world, the pulpit. From the late sixteenth century, opportunities to attend sermons in early modern London increasingly abounded. By the mid-seventeenth century, one Nehemiah Wallington reported that he had heard nearly thirty sermons in one month, while in the late sixteenth century, his father in the same parish could not even hear one sermon in eight weeks; this gave the public a wider range of choice and enabled the practice of 'sermon-gadding', that is, crossing parish boundaries to listen to other preachers (Hunt 2010: 188–189).

Pulpit oratory was one of the most sensitive seismographs of the cultural tremors of the era. Everyone from monarch to commoner listened to sermons. And the preacher, like the dramatist, understood that he was a barometer of belief. Preaching 'played an important part in the transmission of news and the formation of public opinion in the early modern period' (Hunt 2010: 3), and as such, it was carefully scrutinized by both a general public eager for information, and government agencies concerned to regulate it. The pulpit was literally a sounding board for the dilemmas of the age.

In his extended study of English preaching from 1590 to 1640, Arnold Hunt documents a broad shift from an emphasis on oratory to a rising interest in the printed sermon. Particularly among Protestants, during the earlier period, a sermon in print 'was arguably not a sermon at all, because it lacked the converting power of the spoken voice', and that when sermons began to be published from the 1590s, they were often regarded with suspicion (Hunt 2010: 10, 12, 123). Access to God's truth was gained through hearing; in the words of Bishop Hugh Latimer, 'No believing without hearing, no hearing without preaching' (Hunt 2010: 22). Physician Hezekiah Cooke declared that: 'a living and audible voice doth better instruct than the silent reading of books' (Richards 2019: 68). So important was the orality/aurality of preaching that it was believed by many that the deaf were, for that reason, barred from salvation (Hunt 2010: 24–25). Unsurprisingly, therefore, from the late sixteenth century, advice was circulated on how to listen to sermons, beginning with Henry Smith on 'The art of hearing' published in 1592 (Hunt 2010: 64).

From the beginning of the seventeenth century, however, there was an upsurge of sermons in print and by the 1630s, and the balance of authority between hearing and reading sermons was undergoing a fundamental reappraisal. By the late seventeenth century, this 'led some writers to argue that the English genius for preaching was manifested in the written rather than the spoken word' (Hunt 2010: 394). Preachers generally revised their sermons for print publication, and by the end of the century, published sermons increasingly became the model for oral delivery (Hunt 2010: 12–13, 182). By the mid-seventeenth century, preaching became less extravagantly oratorical, less stylistically ornate, and less centred on sonic fireworks, part of a general shift towards the 'plain style' of English prose as exemplified in the work of preachers and writers like Joseph Hall and Geoffrey Tillotson, which developed in association with the sonically austere rhetorical programme of the Royal Society.

Thus, the debate over reading and preaching was not just a debate about pulpit protocols. It was associated with the scientific revolution, which centralized vision as the pre-eminent organ of science. As noted in Chapter Four, the function of language was not to call attention to itself in elaborate sonorous displays, but to function as a clear window between the eye and the natural world, not to call attention to the medium, but to make the medium in a sense invisible:

> A number of historians have argued that this period marks the crucial shift from an 'age of the ear' to an 'age of the eye', continuing a process that had begun in the medieval period, but that was greatly assisted and accelerated by the invention of printing. If we accept this thesis, then the reading/preaching debate can be seen as a symptom of the decline of oral culture and the rise of literate culture.
>
> Hunt 2010: 56

For Bishop Hugh Latimer, access to God's truth had been via the ear. By the eighteenth century, in the words of Henry Home, Lord Kames, 'writers,

68 The pulpit and the playhouse

sensible that the eye is the best avenue to the heart, represent everything as passing in our sight, and, from readers or hearers, transform us as it were into spectators' (Hunt 2010: 94).

Thus, there was an active and explicit debate going on about preaching and its relationship to reading, between the aural and the visual, the ear and the eye as pathways to truth. During the period of the English Renaissance, the relationship was contested and dynamic, understood in terms of a number of shifts – literary, pedagogical, socio-political and epistemological. In the present context, the argument is that they are markers of a transition in the balance between the heard and the seen, the spoken and the written. The implications of Ramist logic, discussed above, of the institutionalization of the scientific method, of the ascendancy of the plain style in English prose all converge to lower the status and authority of the ear in the circulation of information in society. Bishop of Salisbury Gilbert Burnet, himself a member of the Royal Society, in his *Discourse on the Pastoral Care*, called for a plain pulpit style, and the balance between his imagery of hearing and looking suggests the re-modelling of knowledge from oral to visual modes. He warned against a style which

> … may be pretty, but it only tickles the Imagination, and pleases the Ear; whereas that which goes to the Heart, and wounds it, makes the Hearer rather look down, and turns his Thoughts inward, upon Himself.
>
> Burnet 1713: 200

In Shakespeare's England, the balance between the oral and visual knowledge circuits was thus both less stable and more equal, with the authority of the oral in decline. This transition was largely enabled by the increased availability of printed and cheaper texts and a massive expansion of educational opportunities (Fox 2017: 129). This was seen by conservative forces as part of an alarming shift in the balances of intellectual politics. Thus, Anglican Bishop Montagu, writing on the effects of such reforms in his *Diatribe upon the first part of the late History of Tithes*, complained of

> …plagues of Learning, and learned men. It maketh men idle, and yet opinionative, and well conceited of themselves … In a day he is taught, but to little purpose, as much as others can learne in a whole yeere.
>
> Howell 1956: 201

Montagu's anxiety was associated with the Protestant belief that on the path to truth, mediation by clerical oratory could be bypassed in favour of reading the Word of God for one-self (Fox 2017: 134). Print brought with it a boom in the publication of Reformation texts including sermons, from which Protestantism in particular benefited, and some of these texts, like the Book of

Common Prayer and the metrical psalms became 'foundational' in the imaginations of the English. 'Thanks to print and collective repetition, these works came to provide the foundations of a national culture' (Fox 2017: 139).

This underscores one of the most fundamental tendencies of print: that is, towards forms of national standardization. It meant that 'the letter of the law as well as Latin grammar was identical across the nation' (Shrank 2017: 26). As such, print had consequences that went far beyond the basic issue of literacy, and in unforeseeable ways. These included the development of a shared idea of 'nation' (Shrank 2017: 25–26) and also changed the concept of 'the market', enlarging it from a local 'fixed place of exchange, as it had [been] since early medieval times … [to] … the abstract notion of potential consumers anywhere', through the proliferation of printed advertisements (Green 2017: 248). The printed text also enabled the circulation of scientific developments as for example in the case of the anatomy studies of Andreas Vesalius. From the seventeenth century, rising literacy also contributed to the national 'culture of commemoration' – memorials in churches and churchyards, which carried detailed summaries of the achievements of the commemorated, especially of the 'of the prosperous middling sorts' families (Green 2017: 255).

The reference to social class here points the way forward to one of the central arguments of this book: the resituating of sound in class terms. The main readership of the proliferating published sermons was 'probably drawn from the ranks of the better sort, members of the London mercantile and professional élite' (Hunt 2010: 163–164, see also 167), as well as the 'middling sort', but not among the poor (Hunt 2010: 169). That is, there was a class, as well as a gender, dimension to these changes. While the general level of literacy increased, it did not do so uniformly throughout society but worked downwards in terms of class (see Fox 2000: 18). The emerging mercantile bourgeoisie enjoyed the benefits of literacy, and the printed word became the means by which they exercised power. The lower orders were illiterate and largely confined to an oral/aural information economy, a network sustained by speech and hearing. The advent of print in the West created a new way of demarcating class: those privileged who could read and write, and the lower orders who could not.

As the practice of silent reading and learning became more widespread, so did the idea that the authority of information lay in the fact of its being in written rather than in oral form. In western societies, print carries authority, and orality became (and still remains) associated with unauthorized, unreliable and even subversive sites of knowledge, likely to disturb those who are concerned with the higher powers of the mind. The rise of a textual information economy parallels the ascendancy of the bourgeoisie, and the two found a powerful alliance: print as an instrument of authority for the emerging new classes. So, the difference between a reading culture and an oral culture became a class issue (among many other things), implicated with the importance of fixed property, and the threat of mobility (social as well as physical) among the underclass: migrant labour, the homeless, the displaced, the vagabond and information circuits that do not have written stability; in music, oral forms, not written down, are regarded as inferior and untrustworthy, rooted in the mobility of the body, not preserved in the permanent shrine of written ideas.

Class conflict is typically associated with the power and authority of sound. The complicity of class in the transitions we are tracing is unsurprising; it is easy to forget just how many privileges are required to participate in the print culture of the early modern period. Education still required money, including sufficient affluence to be able to spare a child from commitment to domestic duties. It required leisure, both to learn to read, and then for reading itself; consider the size of those printed books, from Sir Philip Sidney's *Arcadia* in the late sixteenth century (over 800 pages in my Penguin edition), growing to Samuel Richardson's *Clarissa* of the mid-eighteenth century and running to around 2,000 pages in my Everyman edition (Richardson 1967; Sidney, 1977).[1] In the absence of public libraries as we now understand them, it required sufficient means to buy books, the cost of which happened to place them within reach of the emerging middle classes (see Ian Watt's pioneering 1957 study, *The Rise of the Novel*). It required space to store books, and good-quality candles by which to read them. As the level of literacy increased, it became a marker of social distinction between, for example, the 'middling sort' and the labouring classes (Fox 2017: 147; French 2017: 269). Thus, as literacy percolated down through the social scale, it became a new line of social differentiation and began to politicize the relationship between silence and volubility, as will be elaborated further below.

Montagu's lament, cited above, was published in 1621. By 1690, the literacy rate had risen to thirty per cent among males and ten per cent among females, producing increasing alarm among intellectual and political authorities as evidence of the spread of potentially seditious opinion (Wheale 1999: 39, 53). As these comments disclose, the question of who could read and who should not resonated with larger issues that were 'in the air', debated not only in the pulpit but also in universities, literary texts, print media and that other major Elizabethan public forum: the stage.

The playhouse

The transition from the world of church and pulpit to secular stage is at one obvious level a considerable leap. But my primary interest here is in soundscape, and in this respect, there are similarities as well as differences. The differences I shall discuss below, but some account of similarities will make that leap less implausible. Both venues were immensely popular. We have already noted the considerable role sermon attendance played in Elizabethan life. Likewise, the theatre: it has been estimated 'that over a third of London's adult population saw a play every month …the most experienced playgoers in history' (Shapiro 2005: 10). The apparent incongruity between the place of worship and secular playhouse diminishes further in terms of the audience profile and soundscape. Unlike, say, an opera house today, both venues were attended by audiences that were heterogeneous across class lines, from monarch to ordinary folk, and indeed, there was probably a considerable audience overlap between the two public venues (Hunt 2010: 164, 223, 293). The boisterous interactivity between Elizabethan theatre audiences and the stage action is well known, but church congregations were by no means silently passive. In a sermon at Pauls Cross, John Donne noted that when the preacher made a point, the congregation might then conduct a discussion over it that could last for a quarter of an hour (Hunt 2010: 6). In instructions on congregational conduct, it was advised that if attendees felt sleepy, they should stand up, move around and respond vocally to the preacher (Hunt 2010: 67). The more emotionally charged sermons were expected to elicit weeping and exclamations from the listeners (Richards 2019: 91), and the soundscape of an Elizabethan parish church would have included 'feet shuffling, people talking, snoring, walking, pew doors banging and dogs barking' (Richards 2019: 134). Richards cites a case in 1570 of a priest reprimanding a congregant, a blacksmith who was reading a book during the service: not for reading, but for reading too loudly (Richards 2019: 44; see further Brown 2003; Craig 2005). Unlike the reverential silence that we have now come to expect from theatre audiences and church congregations, audience protocols allowed for considerable interplay with the 'performance' in both venues.

The emergence and flourishing of secular theatre in sixteenth-century England are in itself one of the signals of a cultural rupture. Over the last century or so, there can be few anglophones who have not had some exposure to Elizabethan theatre, most frequently through the work of Shakespeare. Some filmed versions of his work have enjoyed mainstream popularity, but the continuing day-to-day site of this contact is the classroom, through printed texts which form part of a curriculum. Thus, the least likely form of initial contact for contemporary students was the primary, and for many the sole, medium for the Elizabethan audience: live theatre.

While what can ironically be called 'lip-service' is paid to this difference, Shakespearean scholarship has increasingly come to recognize the importance of the distinctive embodiedness of Elizabethan theatre as a total sensory experience unfolding 'through action of a stage, not the turning of a page', recognizing 'the impact of auditorium location, music, costuming, blocking … gesture, intonation, and manipulated audience interaction' (Fitter 2012: 34–35). In a theatre, we are in close proximity to hundreds, perhaps thousands, of audience members, whose conduct becomes part of the experience through, for example, applause and other interjections, the obstruction of sightlines, talking or coughing. And in the Elizabethan theatre, these experiences would be more vividly imprinted with a range of other sensations including the heat of others, smells of bodies, timber and lathe, perhaps of fruit, sweetmeats and pomades, the close jostling of bodies. We are experiencing the 'artwork' itself as an embodied activity with actual people moving, speaking and gesturing. 'When we teach or write about Shakespeare's language as silent literature or cultural artefact rather than as latent aural, kinetic experience, … we are looking at less than half the picture' (King 2014: 33).

The distinction between theatre and print is not absolute. The Elizabethans also wrote 'closet dramas', not intended to be performed, but read; and 'salon' readings of prose romances and verse were much more common than has later become the case. The plays by Fulke Greville were examples of such 'closet' dramas. We tend to think of poetry as a literary form, on a printed page, but treatises on poetry placed a great deal more emphasis on what the ear heard than what we are now accustomed to. In *A Discourse of English Poetrie* (1586), William Webbe spoke of poetry in terms of 'sweet measure of sentence and pleasant harmonie' (Smith 1964 vol. 1: 231); for George Puttenham in *Arte of English Poesie* (1589), it was 'a pleasant maner of utterance' in which the poet sought to compose his material 'as may best serve the ear for delight' (Smith 1964 vol. 2: 88). In general, the experience of theatre may be distinguished from these other 'literary' forms by even more intense embodiedness, and by the balance of the senses engaged. These affect the expressive resources available to the playwright in the attempts to 'make meaning'.

There are many channels of communication in the theatre which are closed in the case of a printed text. For example, the actual presence of human beings as both actors and spectacle allows for a much more intricate expressive management of space, on and off stage. Unlike the relatively simple spatial relationship between a reader and a book, the large assembly of people entails certain kinds of spatial arrangements that send messages about power relations not only in the audience but also within the play. Audience members could be differentiated by class according to what seating, if any, they could afford. Elizabeth herself never attended the public theatres, but there was nonetheless a very strict set of protocols as to who could sit where in the performance spaces she did attend, as for example in the great chamber of Whitehall (Shapiro 2005: 16, 36). The Elizabethan public stage itself, its depth, its access points and its sets provided a three-dimensional space within which relationships could be disclosed physically (see for example Tribble 2011: 38–40).

Tribble's point is that the manipulation of space is crucial, and I want to argue that this is true both acoustically as well as visually. Ambiguity is, as I shall argue, absolutely central to *Hamlet*, and space can be 'ambiguated' acoustically much more effectively than visually on that stage. As the conversation between Hamlet and Polonius regarding the shapes of clouds indicates (III. ii lines 367–373),[2] in the pre-modern technology of the Elizabethan theatre, visual ambiguity can most easily, if not only, be represented through speech. But acoustic ambiguity can actually be created. This 'meaning-making' through space and sound applied not only diegetically (the world portrayed on stage), but also the relationship of that world to the audience (the world outside the play), could be adjusted in spatial terms, as for example by an actor moving forward to deliver an aside.

The moving, speaking actor is central to the difference between stage and page. Regarding the first – movement – the surviving texts give little guidance to the importance of the actor's gestures in engaging the audience. Yet for the actors of Shakespeare's time, action was a crucial complement to speech in the manipulation of the audience's responses. Rhetoric framed all forms of public address, from preaching to acting. As we have noted, the formal art of rhetoric was becoming unmoored from its foundations in oratory over the period under discussion. This led to the atrophy of its oratorical disciplines: pronuntiatio and actio, or speech and action, which is one of the reasons they were neglected when Shakespearean studies were absorbed into the category of literature. Shakespeare was moved from the stage to the page, obsessively textualized (Dawson 1995: 33). In their 'Introduction' to the 2016 Arden edition of *Hamlet* used in this study, the editors Thompson and Taylor note that from the time of its composition, the play was progressively altered through successive printings, until by the late seventeenth century, Sir William Davenant's version had about a quarter of the text removed 'on grounds the play was a "literary text", and "too long to be conveniently acted"' (100–101). When Samuel Pepys attended a performance of *Henry the Fourth* in December 1660, he found it disappointing when compared to reading the 'book' which he had recently bought (Pepys 1970: vol 1: 123; see further Murray 2001).

What is disappearing in these developments is of course the dynamic soundscape of live theatrical performance. Let us then consider the conditions in which sound and speech were produced and consumed. Of crucial importance is the fact that, as we have noted, Elizabethan England was moving from being primarily an oral towards a print culture. We can begin to appreciate the character of this liminal stage if we think in terms of the two 'knowledge circuits' discussed above. We must imagine, in Shakespeare's day, a balance between these two circuits as being very different from what we take for granted. We think of the England of Shakespeare, Ben Jonson, John Donne, as a society rich in literary texts. To a very large extent, however, this is in the eye of retrospective beholders, the receivers and conservers of what has become the English literary tradition. But in Shakespeare's day, as we have seen, print culture was directly available to only a small minority of the total population. For nearly everyone, speech rather than writing was the everyday mode of information circulation; for the majority of the population, it was virtually the only one, with, as we have seen, memory playing a crucial role. A study of memory in *Hamlet* – 'Remember me', commands the ghost – would provide another entry into the argument forming here. There are two parts to the argument. Shakespeare is writing for a society in which oral culture was still powerful enough to represent a significant 'way of knowing', an epistemology. Yet at the same time, as we have noted, that culture is under increasing challenge by the growing visual authority of print. At both popular and academic levels, Shakespeare's world was actively preoccupied with a crisis in what constituted the grounds of knowledge and evidence, and this dilemma could be resolved into the competing claims of the visual and the acoustic. This transition from oratory to print, from ear to eye is especially significant if we remind ourselves that the dramatist is constantly balancing what is seen with what is heard:

> The importance of auditory reception and perception in comparison to visual was more significant in Shakespeare's theatre than many modern commentators have allowed. The soundscape of the early modern English theatre in its contemporary acoustical environment is vital to an understanding of the impact and meaning of a play.
>
> Wilson and Calore 2005:155

The shifting and precarious balance between sound and sight affects our 'reading' of *Hamlet* in two ways. Technically, in terms of the resources that Shakespeare draws upon, sound is used in very complex ways to communicate his themes. But this has a thematic resonance also. Shakespeare is writing for a society that is experiencing a transition, and therefore a tension, between two modes of knowing which can be simplistically modelled as the visual and the aural. I will suggest precisely that tension is an important presence in Hamlet as he ponders the dilemmas of his personal, political and cosmological situation. In a society more aware of its orality, in which far more hangs on acoustic articulation, vocalization is the subject of much greater attentiveness. As we have seen, Elizabethans paid great attention to the enhancement of the expressive powers of speech. Apart from the oratorical residue in the study of rhetoric, in everyday life, the manner of person you were and the effectiveness of your social transactions, relied decisively on the cultivation of speech protocols. As Smith documents, conduct books, school curricula, general essays of the kind we might now find in life-style magazines, invariably included guides to effective speech including pace, tone and diction (Smith 1999: 252–261). This was especially pertinent to the Elizabethan stage. The playwright needed to establish character, setting, time of day and trajectories of plot and relationships, in theatres which did not have the elaborate representational technologies of film, TV, or even the modern theatre of *Phantom of the Opera*. There was no instant adjustment of light, with dimmers or spots, no elaborate sets, electrical or electronic stage effects. The unaided voice carried the major expressive burden, as is suggested in the players' scene, in which Hamlet gives instructions to the actors before they perform the play. The burden which falls upon dialogue is reflected in the dearth of stage directions, relative to twentieth-century dramatists like George Bernard Shaw, or to a film script. Elizabethan 'stage directions' were to a much greater extent lodged in the dialogue (see for example Tribble 2011: 62; see further on stage directions during the period Dessen and Thomson 1999). It is the dialogue which largely determines the pace of disclosure: where we are, what time of day, what season, what country. As a theatrical resource, dialogue thus carried a heavy burden in regulating the flow of information to create continuity, suspense, puzzlement and ambiguity.

For this reason, the acoustic properties of the auditorium are also relevant to our understanding of what could be presented. The Elizabethan theatre was very much a sound studio, and the playwright was a sound engineer. Of course, in a pre-microphone era, all public auditoriums were designed with close attention to acoustic properties, as 'sound-spaces'. But attention was also paid to the relationship between the social function of the auditorium and the kinds of sounds to be made in it, and the meanings of those sounds. Two major categories of 'enclosed' spaces built specifically as public auditoriums in Shakespeare's London happen also to represent two ways of understanding experience; they are the two under discussion: church and playhouse.

Not coincidentally, these two sites of contrasting 'cultural authority' (Fitter 2012: 41) exemplify two contrasting ways of processing sound. If we think about the kinds of function they fulfilled and the social structures and beliefs they corresponded to, we will understand that the different acoustic profiles of these two forms of public auditorium were specifically compatible with the kinds of discourses which each hosted. These acoustic qualities were developed through different building materials and interior design. These differences can be most forcefully disclosed if we concentrate our attention on the apex of places of public worship, the cathedral. With its long reverberation time, it narrowed the dynamic range of intelligibility, with a tendency to favour Low-Frequency Noise (LFN), which, being difficult to localize, enhanced the sense of being in the presence of otherworldly power, and has played a significant role globally in religious cultures.

Long-reverberation times favoured speech and music that were slow, majestic, ritualized and largely familiar discourses rooted in agreed certainties, with repetitive slow antiphony (by contrast, the 'dry' acoustics of modern performance spaces would enable the composition of different kinds of music, including 'faster tempi, more delicate transients, stronger rhythms, and discordant harmonies' (Blesser and Salter 2007: 111)). Although often the site of polemic, of politico-religious commentary, cathedral discourse like the mass was conducted within the parameters of highly ritualized and relatively 'closed' belief systems. These focussed ultimately on timeless static, otherworldly states, in which the coherence of a community and its commonality of belief within an all-encompassing divine order were reasserted. The cathedral was a place built to celebrate shared religious traditions. The cathedral favoured the monophonic end of the spectrum of musical complexity and the single voice of the preacher over the hubbub of the crowd. The dialogue from Act 1, scene 5 of *Hamlet*, discussed in the next chapter, could not be made intelligible in the long reverberation times of a medieval-built cathedral.

The acoustic profile of the playhouse was very different (see especially Smith 1999: 206–245; Blesser and Salter 2007: 97–199). While *Hamlet* was first presented at another venue, we can take The Globe as representative of the public playhouse. The building materials were acoustically dead and this non-reverberant character was enhanced by the close-packed human bodies. Despite supposedly being built for 1500 people, apparently up to 2500 were squeezed in.[3] Compared to the otherworldliness of a cathedral mass with its slow reverberant echoes, the playhouse was very this-worldly, with the smell, the heat, the jostling and the boisterous interactivity of the occupants. The absence of reverberation enabled the on-stage speech to be fully intelligible at any pace and register. This secular auditorium could present rapid-fire dialogue, with wide dynamics and cacophonous disruptions, serving as a vehicle for social, psychological and moral conflict, doubt and ambiguity, and complex nuances of individualization. The playhouse was a contemporary site in which belief systems were questioned and tested in relationships charged with tension. These focussed on this secular world, full of heterogeneous individuals whose beliefs and interests were often in deep conflict. The playhouse was a place of vocalized enquiry and sonic conflict.

The difference between the acoustics of the cathedral and the playhouse provides both vehicle and metaphor for the transitional nature of the age. The playhouse can allow the projection of a less constrained range of vocal practices, timbres and volume, from majestic oratory to the disruptive and ironic aside. That is, it can recognize and accommodate the relationship between the private and the public realms. It can allow a faster rate of exchange, so that dramatic tensions can be rapidly built up and released. It can allow for the clear projection of extremely complex and exploratory reflections and debates. In the 'dry' acoustic of the secular playhouse, sounds can be immediately sourced to particular individuals; it could be said elliptically that it is an acoustic that brings the modern individual into existence.

This discussion does not pretend to present new information in all its details. Rather it seeks to assemble what are already established, but generally unrelated data, in order to give a deeper understanding of the acoustic order and its implications for engaging with the culture of the time. I began by pointing out that the normal exposure to drama for the Elizabethan was in the playhouse, as opposed to the printed page which is the most usual form of contact for the modern student. I now repeat this, as its implications are teased out. Shakespeare wrote his plays for sound, not print. The textual inconsistencies and ambiguities that have produced the academic Shakespeare literary industry largely arise from this fact. The assiduousness that Shakespeare brought to overseeing the publication of his poetry is conspicuously absent in his attitude to the printing of his plays (Brooks 2000: 9; Shapiro 2005: 212–213). Debates ranging from the overall question of the authoritative texts to such details as to whether Hamlet regarded his flesh as 'sullied', 'sallied' or 'solid', remind us that Shakespeare was primarily interested in his plays as 'embodied' acoustic and visual stage events, not their printed form. Even controversies over dates and influences can be linked to what appears to be the relative indifference of the era to the 'authentic' printed text authorized by the playwright himself. As live performances, successive presentations of the same play would be 'workshopped' in relation to current events and other contemporary theatrical productions, an organic response to the lived issues of the day.[4]

Textual authenticity, at least in secular artistic works, is a modern fetish. Producing a printed text of an Elizabethan play was in many ways a secondary process, reminding us of the different balances of importance between play as a performance and as a written text. The study of Elizabethan type-setting disclosed casual and pragmatic liberties which have later puzzled readers as to what the great literary genius Shakespeare really meant.[5] Apart from spacing out text to fill unexpected gaps on the page, printers undertook unauthorized editing for various reasons, including simply to reduce what could at that time be regarded as superfluous text so that it would fit on the last page of a gathering of pages. This offhand attitude to the printed text both emphasizes the changes that have since occurred in attitudes to the written record, and will also have echoes in our attempt to engage with the acoustic semiotics of *Hamlet*, to which we now turn.

Notes

1. In the context of the larger arguments relating to social change, literacy, secularization and the emergence of a new and growing middle class, it is significant that this massive epistolary novel (that is, structured as a succession of personal letters) can be seen as a guide to conduct for a young genteel woman of the period.
2. All citations from *Hamlet* are from The Arden Shakespeare, Third Series, ed. Ann Thompson and Neil Taylor, London: Bloomsbury, 2006.
3. Apart from the published literature on the subject, and in particular Smith 1999, I wish to thank my late colleague, Dr Richard Madelaine, for his discussions in this connection. In addition to being a specialist in Elizabethan and Jacobean stage conventions, his opinions are also informed by his attendance at numerous performances in the reconstructed Globe Theatre in London. In his experience, based on having sat in many different sections of the auditorium, the clarity of the dialogue is uniformly excellent.
4. As a succinct and accessible exemplification of these textual problems, see Ann Thompson and Neil Taylor's Introduction to the 2006 Arden edition of *Hamlet*.
5. On type-setting practices and their impact on Shakespeare's texts, see for example the pioneering work of McKerrow 1927.

Reading

Blesser, Barry and Linda-Ruth Salter. 2007. *Spaces Speak, Are You Listening? Experiencing Aural Architecture*. Cambridge, MA and London: MIT Press.

Brooks, Douglas A. 2000. *Drama and Authorship in Early Modern England*. Cambridge: Cambridge University Press.

Brown, Laura Feitzinger 2003. 'Brawling in Church: Noise and the Rhetoric of Lay Behavior in Early Modern England'. *Sixteenth Century Journal*, 34 (4): 955–972.

Burnet, Gilbert. (1713, 3rd edn.). *Discourse on the Pastoral Care*. London, St Paul's Churchyard: D. Midwinter and B. Cowse.

Craig, John. 2005. 'Psalms, Groans, and Dogwhippers: The Soundscape of Worship in the English Parish Church, 1547–1642'. In Will Coster and Andrew Spicer (eds), *Sacred Space in Early Modern Europe*. Cambridge: Cambridge University Press: 104–123.

Dawson, Anthony B. 1995. *Hamlet*. Manchester and New York, NY: Manchester University Press.

Dessen, Alan C. and Leslie Thomson. 1999. *A Directory of Stage Directions in English Drama 1580–1642*. Cambridge: Cambridge University Press.

Fitter, Chris. 2012. *Radical Shakespeare: Politics and Stagecraft in the Early Career*. New York, NY and London: Routledge.

Fox, Adam. 2000. *Oral and Literate Culture in England 1500–1700*. Oxford: Clarendon Press.

Fox, Adam. 2017. 'Words, Words, Words: Education, Literacy and Print'. In Keith Wrightson (ed), *A Social History of England 1500–1750*. Cambridge: Cambridge University Press: 129–151.

French, Henry. 2017. "Gentlemen': Remaking the English Ruling Class'. In Keith Wrightson (ed), *A Social History of England 1500–1750*. Cambridge: Cambridge University Press: 269–289.

Green, Adrian. 2017. 'Consumption and Material Culture'. In Keith Wrightson (ed), *A Social History of England 1500–1750*. Cambridge: Cambridge University Press: 242–266.

Howell, W.S. 1956. *Logic and Rhetoric in England, 1500–1700*. Princeton, NJ: Princeton University Press.

Hunt, Arnold. 2010. *The Art of Hearing: English Preachers and Their Audiences, 1590–1640*. Cambridge: Cambridge University Press.

King, Ros. 2014. 'Plays, Playing and Make-Believe: Thinking and Feeling in Shakespearean Drama'. In Laurie Johnson, John Sutton and Evelyn Tribble (eds), *Embodied Cognition and Shakespeare's Theatre*. New York, NY and Abingdon, Oxon: Routledge: 27–45.

McKerrow, Ronald B. 1927. *An Introduction to Bibliography for Literary Students*. Oxford: Clarendon Press.

Murray, Barbara A. 2001. *Restoration Shakespeare*. Madison, NJ: Fairleigh Dickinson University Press.

Pepys, Samuel. 1970. *The Diary of Samuel Pepys. 3 Volumes*. John Warrington (ed). London: Everyman Dent, vol 1.

Richards, Jennifer. 2019. *Voices and Books in the English Renaissance*. Oxford: Oxford University Press.

Richardson, Samuel. 1967 (first pub 1753–1754). *Clarissa*. John Butt (ed) in 4 volumes. London and New York, NY: Dent, Everyman's Library.

Shakespeare, William. 2006. *Hamlet*. The Arden Shakespeare, Third Series. Ann Thompson and Neil Taylor (eds). London: Bloomsbury.
Shapiro, James. 2005. *1599: A Year in the Life of William Shakespeare*. London: Faber and Faber.
Shrank, Cathy. 2017. 'Crafting the Nation'. In Keith Wrightson (ed), *A Social History of England 1500–1750*. Cambridge: Cambridge University Press: 19–38.
Sidney, Philip. 1977 (first pub 1593). *The Countess of Pembroke's Arcadia*. Maurice Evans (ed). Harmondsworth Middlesex: Penguin.
Smith, Bruce. 1999. *The Acoustic World of Early Modern England*. Chicago, IL and London: University of Chicago Press.
Smith, G. Gregory. 1964 (first pub 1904). *Elizabethan Critical Essays*, 2 Vols. London: Oxford University Press.
Tribble, Evelyn B. 2011. *Cognition in the Globe: Attention and Memory in Shakespeare's Theatre*. New York, NY: Palgrave Macmillan.
Watt, Ian. 1957. *The Rise of the Novel: Studies in Defoe, Richardson and Fielding*. Harmondsworth Middlesex: Penguin.
Wheale, Nigel. 1999. *Writing and Society: Literacy, Print and Politics in Britain 1590–1660*. London and New York, NY: Routledge.
Wilson, Christopher R. and Michela Calore. 2005. *Music in Shakespeare: A Dictionary*. London: Bloomsbury.

5
HAMLET – THE WORLD IS OUT OF JOINT

The basic argument which drives this study is that an auditory rather than predominantly visual approach to the past produces a different understanding of cultural history. In the case of *Hamlet,* I suggest that attending to the play as an acoustic phenomenon might provide answers to questions which a study of the printed text cannot easily resolve.[1] Others have contributed significantly to the play of acoustics in his work and it is appropriate that they be acknowledged. Apart from Smith's work (1999), there have been several book length studies relating to aurality in Shakespearean England (see for example Crockett 1995; Gross 2001; Folkerth 2002). Folkerth specifically focuses on Shakespeare, and makes the case that hearing was not so much a supplementary source of information to vision, but a different and in many ways a superior one. He also presents a fascinating study of the way music is used to signal to a contemporary audience that there is something deeply amiss in the state. While my discussion draws on such work, my emphasis differs in significant ways, particularly its analysis of the role of sound in general in the experience of one play.

Let us now turn to that play, *Hamlet*, framed by its soundscape, keeping in mind the transitions being experienced and debated by Shakespeare's society. For the Elizabethan audience, the question of what we know, and how we know it, was very much in the air. The question is explored in terms of a shifting and unstable relationship between the evidence of the eye and the ear. One way of examining the play, then, is to think of it not only as residing at, but being very much about, the interface of sight and sound. Once this particular key is turned, every scene is amplified by the exploration of the relationship between Hamlet/*Hamlet* and these two regimes of knowledge and understanding. We thus rediscover 'meanings' in actions which, innocuous to today's audiences, would have sent significant signals to Shakespeare's contemporaries. To illustrate, one such example is when Hamlet enters at II.2,165, and the Queen observes that 'the poor wretch comes reading'. Nothing is remarkable here for today's audience. But in Shakespeare's day, reading was most commonly conducted aloud (Fox 2000: 36, 37), to others and therefore from a stationary position. To be walking and reading a book in silence would have been a clear warning of something dissonant.

One source of such dissonance is the use of music, on which Sternfeld remains a major authority, exploring its role in articulating the idea of impropriety which pervades *Hamlet*.[2] Music that is presented with due respect for form and occasion signified civil and political order. As Sternfeld points out, the experience of tuning was different for the Elizabethan, because equal temperament did not come into universal use until the nineteenth century. The Elizabethan ear thus had regular access to a degree of musical consonance, and also of dissonance, greater than the modern ear. Its sense of both was thus more highly developed, and the notion of a whole consort of strings (which are not fixed pitch instruments) was a 'striking restoration of law and order' (Sternfeld 1963: 241). The disorder in Hamlet is also signalled musically, in improper, indecorous interpolations (Sternfeld 1963: 210–212). Ophelia is the most striking 'singer' in the play, and even before she appears as such, Horatio's report of her changed behaviour prepares us for someone who has passed into a disordered, liminal world of 'half sense' (IV.5.7). A moment later she enters, and during the remainder of the scene, her dialogue alternates erratically between speech and fragments of song. Sternfeld has sourced and identified all seven of these songs (on Ophelia's singing, see also for example Trudell 2012). It is significant that all the songs are pre-existing. One of the songs, for example is 'Bonny Sweet Robin', the music for which was also used for other lyrics. The song was even more popular in Shakespeare's day than the now clichéd signal of Merrie England, 'Greensleeves'. In using such a song, Shakespeare was able to evoke shared memories that would proclaim the full extent of Ophelia's derangement. The use of songs already known to his audience, but in sometimes grotesque ways and contexts, give him a shorthand way of telling the audience that all is not well.

Apart from proclaiming a mind unable to maintain a coherent narrative, Ophelia's songs are evidence of a disturbing violation of social protocols. Sternfeld observes that other Elizabethan heroines 'would regard with the utmost disdain such uncontrolled behaviour'. They would not sing but would 'command their servants to do so' (Sternfeld 1963: 64). Ophelia's surrender of all dignity and power is also proclaimed in her reversion 'to the songs a nurse may have taught her; not the aristocratic ayre, but crude songs of the common folk' (Sternfeld 1963: 65). They are also aesthetically disordered, not simply in being fragmented, but in their being a disorderly mix of genres and non-song. Laments are mixed with non-sense lines usually associated with light-hearted

'May-time' popular songs. Finally, they are also morally indecorous, especially in the mouth of a young woman of Ophelia's rank, in that many of them deal with extramarital affairs (Sternfeld 1963: 57–58). Ophelia's disordered and rambling performance of popular song is itself evidence that something is rotten in the body politic. In every way, through her songs, Ophelia stands at the doorway to the parallel disordered universe opened up by Hamlet, somewhere between normal life of the court, and 'that other bourne' – death – which is the subject of her delirium, and its destination. It is the juxtapositioning of the normal with the disordered which is disturbing, because it emphasizes the proximity of the two and therefore the fragility of the former. *Hamlet* is largely about the thinness of the membrane between two orders.

Music functions in a similar way when put into the mouths of the clowns/gravediggers in V.1. This funeral scene is the blacker for the apparent lack of fitness to the usual obsequies. Even Hamlet, himself drifting between perspectives, is offended: 'Has this fellow no feelings of his business, that he sings at grave-making?' (V.1.61–62). Shakespeare's decision to put comic songs at the site of funerary solemnity would in itself have struck the audience as generically unsettling (Sternfeld 1963: 7), rather like the song 'Always look on the bright side of life', in the concluding crucifixion scene of the film *The Life of Brian* (dir. Terry Jones, 1979). Through the persistent violation of the musical conventions of the period, the contemporary audience would understand all the more clearly just how deeply the times were 'out of joint'.

The singing gravediggers remind us that death and the acoustic realm are intimately connected in this play. The one thing that distinguishes the dead is that they cannot 'sound' and cannot be 'sounded': 'The ears are senseless' (V.2.353). Shakespeare is so explicit on this distinction that it is hard to believe it was not part of his conscious motivic scheme. The dead remains accessible through every other physical sense. Obviously, they may be seen; true to the genre of Elizabethan/Jacobean revenge tragedy, the play seems to revel in the spectacle of the dead. They can be touched, as when Hamlet 'lugs the guts' of Polonius' dead body into another room, or when he holds the skull of Yorick. They may be smelled: when the king asks the whereabouts of Polonius, Hamlet replies, '… if indeed you find him not within this month, you shall nose him as you go up the stairs into the lobby' (IV.3.34–36). Contemplating Yorick's skull, he wonders if the great Alexander looked, thus, in death, 'And smelt so? Pah!' (V.1.190). The dead may even be tasted. Polonius is now a meal for a 'convocation of politic worms'; both king and beggar become meat for maggots, and a man may eat the fish caught by the worm that ate the king (IV.3.19–30). But the dead may not be heard. They cannot speak, they cannot sing. Watching the casual exhumations of the gravedigger, Hamlet observes 'That skull had a tongue in it and could sing once' (V.1.71–72), and contemplating the skull of Yorick: 'Where be your gibes now? your gambols? your songs? Your flashes of merriment that were wont to set the table on a roar?'

(V.2.179–181). All the songs, all the courtly words – 'Good morrow sweet Lord: how dost thou good Lord?' (V.1.77–78) – all the legal niceties that sustained Polonius and are mocked by the gravediggers, all the quips and verbal punctilios: they are nothing. Silence.

Vocalizing is just one acoustic element in what, it has been noted, is a very noisy play (see for example Kinney 2006: 82). It begins with disembodied voices in the darkness. It ends with the noise of ordnance off-stage. Between these two sonic events, non-vocalized sound is pervasive. Cockcrow announces the morning and hautboys the dumbshow. There are around a dozen heraldic flourishes involving trumpets, drums and ordnance. The final scene is especially rowdy, with trumpets and drums announcing the king, trumpets signalling the beginning of the duel, flourishes and ordnance when Hamlet scores a hit, the sounds of shots and marching soldiers off-stage as Fortinbras approaches, drums to accompany his entrance, and the ordnance that closes the play. The sonic realm is so intrusive that that it can be regarded as a thematic as well as a theatrical device. A striking number of these sounds are acousmatic, that is, having no visible source. The disembodiedness of such sounds makes them deeply unsettling and disorienting. The uncertainty that is thematically pivotal in *Hamlet* is intensified by these pervasive acousmatic sounds, prompting the question: What may be known of a thing that is heard but not seen, or seen but not heard?

Several key scenes offer themselves as a mode of analysis which could constructively be applied to the whole play, and have relevance to the most frequent question that has come to be asked of the central character: why does he procrastinate in carrying out his act of revenge? It is provocative that the question itself only emerged historically at a later stage in the ascendancy of visual models in the analysis of culture. The image of Hamlet 'as a character hamstrung by over-intellectual analysis is very much a modern phenomenon. In the seventeenth century, Hamlet seems to have been associated more closely with frenetic movement and an antic disposition' (Tribble 2019: 140). We have inherited much of the Romantic fascination with the individual ego and the obsessive exploration of psychological states:

> The desire to explain what the play does by supplying the characters with motives and reactions on the model of our own is part of that demand for psychological realism which has dominated dramatic criticism since the eighteenth century, encouraged by the rise of the novel, which can trace the inner workings of its characters' minds to a degree that a play, presenting its persons through speech and action, cannot.
>
> Jenkins 1982: 124[3]

Hamlet himself shows no interest in many of the questions that exercised later commentators (Thompson and Taylor 2016: 138). For the moment, I suggest that while Hamlet's prevarication is essential to the suspense and forward thrust of the action, it might not have seemed so inexplicably perverse to a contemporary audience preoccupied with the socio-political questions associated with a fundamental 'in-between-ness' in the transition between knowledge systems.

The texts vary from edition to edition, as set out in Thompson and Taylor (2016: 76–96) in their Introduction to the edition I am quoting here. I believe that these textual variations don't necessarily have a bearing on my overview, which argues that the issues I draw attention to pervade the play, as they were pervasive in the society that produced it. The cake, we could say, tastes the same throughout, whichever slice we take. In the course of the discussion, the citation 'Notes' refers to the editorial commentary by Thompson and Taylor.

This is a play about uncertainty and the consequent difficulties of making decisions. It hinges on the question of what kind of testimony or evidence we can rely on before we act at this particular historical moment. The *in medias res* opening is not simply an explanatory *mise en scene*; rather to the contrary, it opens in darkness, with voices presenting a set of questions that are asked of the characters by each other, as well as raising questions for the audience: who are these people? Which king is referred to? Why is one speaker 'sick at heart'? Who is 'the Dane'? In establishing this interrogative mode, the relationship between sound and sight is central from the opening lines, and in particular in the way, the ghost is manifested, and what the men cry out to it as they demand to know its significance. It is not simply that the dialogue is about the uncertain relationship between these two sources of knowledge. The dramatic tension is actually generated by sudden shifts back and forth between sound and sight.

It is midnight; indeed, it is likely that the play opened with the sound of twelve chimes (Notes). It is dark.[4] Two men, as yet unidentified to the audience except by uncontextualized names, enter and conduct the following exchange:

BERNADO. Who's there?
FRANCISCO. Nay, answer me. Stand and unfold yourself.
BERNADO. Long live the King!
FRANCISCO. Bernardo?
BERNADO. He.
FRANCISCO. You come most carefully upon your hour.
BERNADO. 'Tis now struck twelve. Get thee to bed Francisco.
FRANCISCO. For this relief much thanks. 'Tis bitter cold,
   and I am sick at heart.
BERNADO. Have you had quiet guard?
FRANCISCO. Not a mouse stirring.
BERNADO. Well, good night.
   If you do meet Horatio and Marcellus,
   The rivals of my watch, bid them make haste.
Enter Horatio and Marcellus.

FRANCISCO. I think I hear them. Stand ho. Who is there?
I.i. lines 1–17[5]

This opening communicates an unease that would have resonated with an audience alive to the national anxieties of the day (Shapiro 2005: 211). It begins with a scenario of disembodied, acousmatic voices and, if the dialogue was preceded by chimes to signal the time, acousmatic sounds, a device exploited at several points in the play. In this opening, the characters can be only known by listening. Already the relationship between audition and vision is setting up ominous ambiguities.

Before anything else, this is a crime thriller of the sixteenth century, a piece of popular culture of the period, and indeed, it largely remained so until the nineteenth century, when it ascended into the realm of High Culture, significantly during the same period as Hamlet's procrastination became increasingly inscrutable.[6] The audiences came to be entertained with a tale of deception, passion, sex, murder and betrayal. It is a revenge play. A man has apparently been murdered by his brother, who has then married the widow. At the simplest level, the play is about how a son achieves his revenge. It is a straightforward and perennial genre, reappearing from biblical and secular mythologies to contemporary film.

But like any audience, the crowds seeking entertainment wanted it to be something that resonated with their own aspirations and anxieties, the issues of the day and of the epoch. There are larger resonances here. The father is a king, so there is a broader political relevance; in Horatio's words, the ghost's appearance '… bodes some strange eruption to our state' (I,i, line 68). The king was the supreme secular authority, with status approaching the divine-on-earth. When Hamlet seeks to know what is the will of the ghost of his father, this resonates with larger questions: what is the will of the supreme secular authority? What is the will of God-on-earth? What is the will of a secular god-figure who has died yet who continues to manifest himself? What is his will for us, the audience? And given that he is now dead, how are we to know?

This is not only about someone's father being murdered and betrayed, but it's also about the foundations of social and cosmic order. These issues are being debated in the larger context of profound changes in European society, which included an epistemological crisis: How do we know the world? How do we represent the world? And in that crisis, minds were obviously attuned to the status of the sensorium through which we gain our knowledge of the universe we inhabit. Sound is both technique of theatrical expressiveness, and a thematic motif. This is a sonically rich play, not simply in terms of the poetic force of the dialogue, but in the range of sounds exploited: song and instrumental music, brass fanfares, drums, sound effects on- and off-stage such as ordinance, and the deployment of the voice as sound in addition to the sense of what is said.

86 *Hamlet – The world is out of joint*

This is nowhere more apparent than in the case of the ghost. I have referred in general terms to the profound disorientation produced by the disembodied voice. Because the voice is so profoundly physical, to experience it without a body, or transposed from its body, has always been used to induce a sense of otherworldiness. I have used the term 'acousmatic', to refer to the voice that does not come from the visible action. Shakespeare uses this device in *Hamlet* to produce multiple levels of confusion about which order of reality the characters are occupying and we are witnessing. It is most striking in I,5, the 'voice under the stage' scene. He is playing very skilfully with the relationship between the different worlds that converge here: that of the court, that of Hamlet and that of the audience trying to make sense of the play. Hamlet has conducted a dialogue with the ghost of his father. It is significant that, while several have seen the ghost, only Hamlet has experienced it as an acoustic phenomenon. I express it thus very deliberately, since it remains arguable though, significantly, not certain that, in the absence of any independent corroboration of the conversation, it is an acoustic illusion on Hamlet's part, analogous to the 'voices' that accompany what we now think of as clinical schizophrenia. He then rejoins Horatio and Marcellus, and reports in very general terms what he has experienced. The use and role of sound in the ensuing exchange are, I suggest, pivotal to all that follow, and I therefore quote at length.

MARCELLUS. Lord Hamlet
HORATIO. Heaven secure him!
HAMLET. So be it.
MARCELLUS. Illo, ho, ho my lord!
HAMLET. Hillo, ho, ho, boy! Come, bird, come!
MARCELLUS. How is't, my noble lord?
HORATIO. What news, my lord?
MARCELLUS. O, wonderful![7]
HORATIO. Good my lord, tell it.
HAMLET. No, you will reveal it.
HORATIO. Not I, my lord, by heaven!
MARCELLUS. Nor I, my lord.
HAMLET. How say you then? Would heart of man once think it? -
    But you'll be secret?
MARCELLUS. *[with Horatio]* Ay, by heaven, my lord.
HAMLET. There's never a villain dwelling in all Denmark
    But he's an arrant knave.
HORATIO. There needs no ghost, my lord, come from the grave
    To tell us this.
HAMLET. Why, right! you are in the right!
    And so, without more circumstance at all,
    I hold it fit that we shake hands and part;
    You, as your business and desires shall point you,

> For every man hath business and desire,
> Such as it is; and for my own poor part,

HORATIO. These are but wild and whirling words, my lord.

HAMLET. I am sorry they offend you, heartily,
> Yes, faith, heartily.

HORATIO. There's no offence, my lord.

HAMLET. Yes, by Saint Patrick, but there is, Horatio,
> And much offence too. Touching this vision here,
> It is an honest ghost, that let me tell you.
> For your desire to know what is between us,
> O'ermaster't as you may. And now, good friends,
> As you are friends, scholars and soldiers,
> Give me one poor request.

HORATIO. What is't my lord? We will.

HAMLET. Never make known what you have seen tonight.

MARCELLUS. *[with Horatio]* My lord, we will not.

HAMLET. Nay, but swear't.

HORATIO. In faith,
> My lord, not I.

MARCELLUS. Nor I, my lord – in faith.

HAMLET. Upon my sword.

MARCELLUS. We have sworn, my lord, already.

HAMLET. Indeed, upon my sword, indeed.

Ghost cries under the stage.

Father's Ghost [beneath] Swear.

HAMLET. Aha boy, say'st thou so? Art thou there, truepenny?
> Come on! You hear this fellow in the cellarage?
> Consent to swear.

HORATIO. Propose the oath, my lord.

HAMLET. Never to speak of this that you have seen.
> Swear by my sword.

Father's Ghost. *[beneath]* Swear.

HAMLET. Hic et ubique? Then we'll shift our ground.
> Come hither, gentlemen,
> And lay your hands again upon my sword.
> Never to speak of this that you have heard.
> Swear by my sword.

Father's Ghost *[beneath]* Swear by his sword.

HAMLET. Well said, old mole! Canst work i'th' earth so fast?
> A worthy pioner! Once more remove, good friends.

HORATIO. O day and night, but this is wondrous strange."

HAMLET. And therefore as a stranger give it welcome.
> There are more things in heaven and earth, Horatio,
> Than are dreamt of in your philosophy.

> But come!
> Here, as before, never, so help you mercy,
> How strange or odd soe'er I bear myself
> (As I perchance hereafter shall think meet
> To put an antic disposition on),
> That you, at such times seeing me, never shall,
> With arms encumb'red thus, or this head-shake,
> Or by pronouncing of some doubtful phrase,
> As 'Well, well, we know,' or 'We could, an if we would,'
> Or 'If we list to speak,' or 'There be, an if they might,'
> Or such ambiguous giving out, to note
> That you know aught of me - this is not to do,[8]
> So grace and mercy at your most need help you.
> Swear.
>
> Father's Ghost *[beneath]* Swear.   *[They swear.]*
> HAMLET. Rest, rest, perturbed spirit! So, gentlemen,
> With all my love I do commend me to you;
> And what so poor a man as Hamlet is
> May do t'express his love and friending to you,
> God willing, shall not lack. Let us go in together;
> And still your fingers on your lips, I pray.
> The time is out of joint. O cursed spite
> That ever I was born to set it right!
> Nay, come, let's go together.   *Exeunt*
>
> 1.5 lines 852–945

This is immensely rich in its deployment of sound, and especially to what I have argued was the highly attuned Elizabethan ear. At the more obvious level of craft, it masterfully exploits the possibilities of dialogue, in variations of pace, rhythm, rhyme and in vocal textures, as in non-sense sounds, shouts and simultaneous utterance. It plays with the balance between speech and dumb-show (the 'swearing' is gestural), and sonic ambiguities and multiple meanings ('pioner' meant soldier, digger and miner).

This last takes us also into what is spoken of. The sonic jumble is not merely arresting theatre, but a parallel to the jostling of multiple orders of reality and ways of knowing. The contrasts between telling and showing, the juxtaposition of the 'business' of men's affairs and the otherworldliness of prayer, the deranged mix of levity and seriousness (which, with 'pioner' looks forward to the black comedy of the graveyard scene), the hypnotic emphasis on 'swearing', the implicit foreshadowing of feigned madness, the 'antic disposition', all cluster around the question of the ambiguity of experience and the veracity of testimony. All this ambiguity converges on the uncertain relationship between what is seen and what is heard, and in this scene, the disembodied voice of a 'disembodied' character – a now unseen ghost – is central, itself ontologically unstable.

The ghost orders Horatio and Marcellus to swear, and so they do. Yet it is by no means clear that they actually hear the ghost, or indeed that anyone apart from Hamlet hears it at any time in the play. What Hamlet discloses of the ghost's testimony is so oblique and generalized that, as Horatio says, it amounts to common knowledge that Hamlet himself was already in possession of before any supposed declaration by the ghost, who could therefore well be simply an image on whom Hamlet could project and legitimize his suspicions. That is, while many see it, its oral testimony may well be a delusion. In this scene, we may reasonably ask who actually hears this voice. The audience certainly does, but what status might they accord it? Is it verified by vision? Do the audience see it speak? The understage, from whence the voice is heard, would probably have been normally closed off. The actor playing the ghost would therefore be invisible to the audience, and the status of this voice ambiguous, a voice from an unseen source that might or not be objectively real as opposed to something merely imagined by Hamlet. Do Horatio and Marcellus hear it? They swear silence, but they have been insistently directed to do so at the point of a sword held by their Prince who, as it happens, is showing alarming signs of derangement, 'wild and whirling words'. Indeed, what may be taken to be their dismay at hearing the voice of the ghost ('but this is wondrous strange'), may with equal plausibility be caused by the spectacle of Hamlet apparently talking to himself.

And this too is plausible, that Hamlet is drifting on the borders of some delusional, schizophrenic state that he is 'hearing voices', which commission him to set the world at rights. I am suggesting in general that such liminality resonates with significant aspects of the Elizabethan consciousness. The play is about transition, instability, ambiguity and ambivalence. Hamlet is a microcosm of a society suspended between two orders of history and knowledge, between different ways of being certain, conflicting versions of the real. He says he feigns madness to draw out the truth. But one question that remains unresolved is: how far is he merely acting madness? The implied suggestion has particular plausibility within the world of the play also. Hamlet is young and introspective, at a stage in life often characterized by a cynicism and even disgust with the hypocrisy of social surfaces and established belief systems, and studying at a university internationally notorious for the encouragement of radical enquiry. His father has just died suddenly and mysteriously, and within a month, his mother has married his uncle. We know that before he hears the ghost, he is already deeply depressed, moody, dwelling on his loss, his disgust and loathing of the court in general and his mother and uncle in particular. It hardly requires the arcane skill of a psycho-analyst to expect and conclude that Hamlet is already on the edge. There is every reason for him to be susceptible to the most sinister of possibilities, and withdrawn into a world of obsessive speculations bordering on delusion, as is confirmed later when, in III, 4, having killed Polonius in a moment of what any bystander would regard as actual rather than feigned derangement, he begins to address a ghost which only he can see.

Among the many filmed productions of the play, the 1969 version directed by Tony Richardson is notably responsive to the play's acoustic dimensions in the evocation of the 'disruption of our state'. A particular example is worth noting for its proximity to Hamlet's first encounter with the ghost. As Marcellus and Horatio prepare the prince for the expected apparition of the ghost on the castle ramparts, a loud acousmatic noise suddenly breaks the midnight silence and the tense anticipation disclosed in Horatio's words:

> It then draws near the season
> Wherein the spirit held his wont to walk.
> *A flourish of trumpets, and two pieces [of ordnance] go off.*
> What does that mean, my lord?
> Hamlet. The King doth wake tonight and takes his rouse,
> Keeps wassail, and the swagg'ring upspring reels,
> And as he drains his draughts of Rhenish down
> The kettledrum and trumpet thus bray out
> The triumph of his pledge.
>
> I,iv, lines 631–639

This is an intensely dramatic effect, an acoustic shock through which is proclaimed a stepfather's tasteless usurpation, a King's debauchery and a state's decline – in Hamlet's words, a 'heavy-headed revel' which 'Makes us traduced and taxed of other nations' (lines 17–18). For the modern eye scanning the printed page, the stage direction is so innocuous as to be scarcely noted. Yet what we have here is the sound of trumpets, drums and ordnance suddenly blasting the cold, tense, midnight silence, as represented in the enclosed circle of the Elizabethan theatre. In the 1990 Franco Zeffirelli film, the shock is dispersed almost completely by the way the camera prepares us with a visual disclosure of the king's revels. In the Richardson production, the sound is a sudden, unexpected and deafening collision between two orders of reality and perception. While their anxious eyes scan the darkness for signals from the 'otherworld', the world of the Other, their ears are suddenly assaulted with the disordered raucousness of this one.

The disruption reinforces Hamlet's own increasing dislocation. The effect of the noise is as an alarm to a thief in the night. With darting eyes and an urgent, nervous vocal delivery, even before his conversation with the ghost, Nicol Williamson interprets Hamlet's dialogue as that of a man teetering on a breakdown, prey to obsessive but all too reasonable speculations, ready to believe anything and to trust nothing. When the voice is then heard from 'under the stage' (edited in the film to one interpolation), its disembodiedness is cinematically presented as audible only as a voice in Hamlet's head. This general suggestion that even the 'feigned' status of Hamlet's madness is ambiguous, is accentuated throughout the players' scene, where Hamlet's instructions as to how to 'feign' (to act), indicate a man shifting back and forth between different modes of consciousness and discourse. This is particularly so in his subsequent comments to the King and court. Williamson is doing no more than Shakespeare's dialogue warrants, with its abrupt shifts of tone, its bewilderingly rapid-fire double entendres, and the sallies in and out of apparent tastelessness and impertinence.

The ghost is witnessed by several, but its spoken testimonies and injunctions are arguably heard by only one individual, and he is in a state of deep psychological trauma and epistemological confusion. How can he be sure what he knows and how he knows it? What constitutes evidence? Which of the worlds in which we move is to be trusted? One of the most fundamental and pervasive ways the play pursues this question is through a shifting balance between sight and sound, which in turn reflects/echoes the tensions of an age in which print and orality, the visual and the aural, are in transitional contention. If Hamlet's prevarication is so mysterious to modern readers, perhaps it is because we are not exercised by the same kind of dilemma. We still have to make evidentiary decisions, but in general, they are between data that occupy the same secular information economy. That is, we have more or less agreed checks and measures. We have established ways of deciding. Hamlet prevaricates, largely because he has not. His era is balanced between not just conflicting information, but dissonant knowledge regimes. It is a condition of his life in that historical moment that he remains uncertain. If this helps demystify his procrastination, the word 'life' leads us to the moment of resolution and the final scene.

If I refer to it as what would now be called in cinema, 'the shootout', it is to try to bring to mind the chaotic play of emotions and actions that accompany such a cathartic moment of carnage. It is a scene which takes the action beyond the processes of agonized reflection, and it takes Hamlet beyond the mental 'life' that is hedged about with crippling doubts and puzzles, into something like the unequivocal consciousness of the berserker. Moments before this Hamlet and Laertes have wounded each other. The formal, ritualized passage at arms has become a 'grudge' match. 'Part them; they are incensed', orders the king (V,2.286). The Queen swoons, at the sight of their blood according to the King (line 293). As she dies, however, she declares that she has been poisoned, at which Hamlet cries 'Treachery! Seek it out' (line 297). But he is still missing a crucial piece of information, which is supplied by Laertes:

> It is here, Hamlet, thou art slain;
> No medicine in the world can do thee good.
> In thee there is not half an hour of life;
> The treacherous instrument is in thy hand,
> Unbated and envenom'd.

lines 3970–3977

What cuts the Gordian knot which all prior events have tied is the revelation that he, Hamlet, is 'slain'. He is released into action. He has been placed beyond the paralysing question of 'to be or not to be', beyond the choice, and the parallel question of to act or not to act is no longer of any significance. He is beyond the self-indulgent luxury of procrastination. He is a 'dead man walking'.

I want to use this key image to return to the role of sound, and conclude by drawing a long bow. I have suggested that the shifting relationship between sound and sight in the play has paralleled the liminality of the world of Hamlet and of Shakespeare and his time. The liminal, the not-quite-one-thing-nor-the-other, is a perennial site of traumatic disorientation. Of all of these, the most horrific is the undead dead. They exist as various archetypes which haunt our musings on mortality: from the zombie created by voodoo to the monster created by science, the prosthetic human being, as in Thomas Pynchon's novel *V*, or the android which continues to function even when dismembered as in Ridley Scott's 1979 film *Alien*.

Above all it is the 'ordinary' human being who is somewhere between the living and the dead who fills us with horror, and of these, none more so than the one who continues to utter in death. Thus, for example, nurses describe their shock at the first time they hear the exhalation of a corpse as they turn it over. It was because of such 'utterance' that the first casualty in the charge of the Light Brigade was also the one most vividly remembered. Within two hundred metres of the beginning of the advance Captain Louis Nolan (whose misinterpretation of the order played a pivotal role in the disaster), inexplicably broke ranks, and as he did so, had his chest torn open by a shell splinter. The contortion of his limbs twitched the bridle, turning the horse back through the ranks, and from the mounted corpse with the exposed heart came a sustained scream. In the words of a survivor, Private Wightman of the 17th Lancers, 'The weird shriek and the awful face as the rider and horse disappeared haunt me now to this day, the first horror of that ride of horrors' (Adkin 2000: 154). The sounding dead dismantles one of the most obdurate of all certainties: the distinction between life and death, the literal vitality of vocalization and the profound silence of the grave. The image haunts Shakespeare's 'rotten' Denmark, as the death of Hamlet's father awakens memories of the time 'ere the mightiest Julius fell', when

> The graves stood tenantless and the sheeted dead
> Did squeak and gibber in the Roman streets.
>
> Arden I,1, lines 114–115

For Hamlet himself, the ghost becomes a prime force of disequilibrium when it is supposedly heard to speak as well as merely appear.

With an appreciation of the impact of the vocalizing dead, let us turn to Hamlet's last utterance. The most usual version of Hamlet's final words is as printed in the Arden edition I am using for basic reference:

> O, I die, Horatio.
> The potent poison quite o'ercrows my spirit.
> I cannot live to hear the news from England,
> But I do prophesy th'election lights
> On Fortinbras: he has my dying voice.
> So tell him with th'occurrents more and less
> Which have solicited - the rest is silence.   *[Dies]*
>
> Arden V,2, 336–342

In the context of this argument about sound, there is particular resonance in these words, which are about hearing, speech and silence. Hamlet is now, indeed, dead. To be dead is to be silent.

But in some versions, as far as Hamlet is concerned, the rest is not yet silence. The first Folio gives the following lines:

> ... He has my dying voice.
> So tell him, with th'occurrents more or less
> Which have solicited - the rest is silence. O,o,o,o *Dyes*

This text has been retained in some modern editions but has been the subject of little comment, with the notable exception of Smith 1999, who even indirectly alludes to it in his running title: *Attending to the O-Factor*. I wish to repeat my acknowledgement of his study as the essential stimulus for what follows, and I briefly recapitulate some of his points in order to build further on them. These four exclamations, 'O,o,o,o', appear on the printed page as dispensable embellishments, standard vocal gestures in the same supposedly trivial category as 'Aaargh' of comic strips.

It is suggestive that in his Introduction to the earlier Arden edition, Jenkins includes them in his listing of additions found in the Folio which may well represent interpolations by actors (1982: 62). That is, they are generated out of performance rather than an earlier printed text, and Smith seeks to situate the sounds in the larger context of Elizabethan stage acoustics. In so doing, he reminds us of the power and importance of the sound 'O' in an era of relatively primitive stage technology, when attention and emphasis were not so easily focussed in the absence of the electric and electronically controlled stage lighting, or the close-up of the film camera. As the strongest of all phonemes, Smith argues that the physical intensity of the exclamation 'O' makes it an arresting marker in the Elizabethan playhouse (see for example Smith 1999:

8, 35, 225). I now want to develop this line of thought further, in relation to Hamlet, to give a final illustration of how sound (not just speech) underscores thematic issues.

We have noted the commonplace that in vocalization, sound can modify the lexical meaning of words. Furthermore, sound is often virtually all the meaning, and especially so at moments of greatest emotional intensity or crisis, as in a sigh, a scream, a sob. The 'meaning' is in the sound itself, and thus, all but disappears in print. What does 'O' *mean* in, for example, the sentence beginning, 'O that this too too sallied flesh would melt' (I.2.129)? In the grammar of print, it adds nothing to the sentence. But it is a very powerful sound. It announces itself, it proclaims, 'I am a vocalizing creature'. It signals something important about to be uttered, whether it is 'O what a feeling' to advertise a brand of car or 'O, I die'. It is the irreducible sonic assertion that I am, of ego.

Now, consider Hamlet's death. Where his last words are given as 'The rest is silence', he passes from words to silence (or, for a man who has been haunted by a voice, and in a play full of puns, to find that 'rest' is silence), as though there is no intermediate, ambiguous space between the two. But the play is about the uncertainty of such propositions, about not knowing and not knowing how we know. Hamlet the prince is situated ambiguously between a number of spaces. He is between two historical moments which may be simplistically described through a number of binaries: the medieval and the modern, the Christian and the secular. To recall the Marxist writer Lucien Goldmann: God is neither present nor dead, just in hiding and indistinct, 'The Hidden God' (Goldmann 1976). Hamlet is between two epistemologies, the oral and the textual. He thinks of himself as suspended between two states of reality – to be or not to be – and two states of mind: sanity and insanity. Hamlet's world, as created by Shakespeare for his audience, is not neatly constructed of mutually exclusive categories, like speech and silence.

'The rest is silence. O,o,o,o *Dyes*'. In this version, he passes not directly from speech to silence, but from speech, through which the mind projects itself acoustically, to pure sound, the projection of the body and finally to silence. 'O' is of course a common exclamation on the Elizabethan stage. Depending on which text we are referring to, over a dozen of the characters in *Hamlet* use it, each of them about two or three times (apart from the sound as embedded prominently in other words such as 'Ophelia' and 'obey'). Most frequently it draws attention to some mental or emotional disturbance, and is therefore used most frequently by characters thus afflicted – Ophelia and Laertes in their grief (about six times each), the Queen in her divided loyalty (about nine times), and the King in his moments of guilt (about eighteen times). But for Hamlet, the frequency (nearly fifty times) makes it something of an acoustic signature. It comes to seem more than a spontaneous exclamation, and something played with just out of a fascination with sound for its own sake:

> O heavens – die two months ago and not forgotten yet? Then there's hope a great man's memory may outlive his life half a year! But, by'r Lady, 'a must build churches then, or else shall 'a suffer not thinking on – with the hobby-horse, whose epitaph is 'For O! for O! the hobby-horse is forgot!'
>
> Arden III.2.123–128

The reference to the forgotten hobby horse is itself a message to the Elizabethan audience about social change, in particular a growing gap between high and low culture (see Lamb 2006: 15), but more immediately pertinent is the association between sound 'O', mental disorder and, here, death, especially in relation to the Folio's version of Hamlet's last sounds. If this discussion of a sound so apparently semiotically neutral seems some pointlessly fanciful piece of literary trainspotting, perhaps it is no more or less so than the exploration of motifs based on imagery, which sustains so much 'literary' analysis of Shakespeare. I am trying to gain a clearer appreciation of the fact that sound was a more primary medium than print. The audience was listening to, not reading, the dialogue. And if we try to 'audialize' that dialogue, we may begin to consider the cumulative impact of that motivic sound on alert ears. These last sounds Hamlet makes, as recorded in the Folio, refer back to his vocalized life but lead us also to his death. Consider how much of this play is about these two states overlapping in spite of our attempts to keep them separate. The courtiers, in particular as exemplified by Polonius, seek to do so by various acts of bad faith or false consciousness in which a corrupted court is rationalized. It could be said that they feign sanity, pretending that they live in a reasonable and orderly state, even while there is 'something rotten' in Denmark. But Hamlet moves in and out of both worlds, now mad, now sane, fighting in a grave, talking to a skull and to a ghost, suspended between two worlds, two historical epochs.

Let us think about how his final sounds, 'O,o,o,o', might impact on the ear in the context of the play's fixation on liminality, ambiguity and transition. How trivial this looks on the page. But consider how it might have been played, how deeply disturbing would be the inarticulate despair and agony of a body from which 'life', in the form of the speaking mind had departed – recall, this is the last utterance of a man who, it was widely believed, had in fact lost his reason. These final sounds he makes, apparently detachable 'afterthoughts' that some printers casually excised, could well have been one of the most horrifying moments in Hamlet's navigation of his liminal space. And it is irreducibly acoustic.

Notes

1. This discussion is a further development of an argument I first set out more briefly in 'Hamlet: voice, music, sound', in the journal *Popular Music* (2005), 24/2, 257–267, with whose kind permission I draw on it here.
2. A useful compendium of Shakespeare's use of music is Wilson and Calore 2005.

3 For an extended study in relation to this play, see for example Gottschalk 1972.
4 In Elizabethan theatre, in conjunction with the 'stage directions' embedded in the dialogue, the darkness would be presented visually in a stylised form, for example by the carrying of torches.
5 Although my point of reference for *Hamlet* is the The Arden Shakespeare, Third Series, ed. Ann Thompson and Neil Taylor, London: Bloomsbury (Shakespeare 2006), because of copyright restrictions, quotations of not more than one line, or as indicated by 'Arden', my extended quotations, act, scene and line numbers are taken from the 'Open Source' text at (Shakespeare 2022) where there are significant substantive variations they will be indicated by footnote.
6 On the 'sacralisation' of Shakespeare in the nineteenth century, see particularly Levine 1988.
7 In the Arden, this line is assigned to Hamlet.
8 The words 'this is not to do' are, in the Arden, 'This do swear'.

Reading

Adkin, Mark. 2000. *The Charge: The Real Reason Why the Light Brigade Was Lost*. London: Pimlico/Random House.

Crockett, Bryan. 1995. *The Play of Paradox: Stage and Sermon in Renaissance England*. Philadelphia, PA: University of Pennsylvania Press.

Folkerth, Wes. 2002. *The Sound of Shakespeare*. London and New York, NY: Routledge.

Fox, Adam. 2000. *Oral and Literate Culture in England 1500–1700*. Oxford: Clarendon Press.

Goldmann, Lucien. 1976 (first pub in English 1964). *The Hidden God: A Study of Tragic Vision in the Pensées of Pascal and the Tragedies of Racine* (Trans. Philip Thrody). London and Henley: Routledge & Kegan Paul.

Gottschalk, Paul. 1972. *The Meanings of Hamlet: Modes of Literary Interpretation Since Bradley*. Albuquerque, NM: University of New Mexico Press.

Gross, Kenneth. 2001. *Shakespeare's Noise*. Chicago, IL and London: University of Chicago Press.

Jenkins, Harold. 1982. 'Introduction' to William Shakespeare's Hamlet in The Arden Shakespeare Series. London and New York, NY: Methuen.

Johnson, Bruce. 2005. 'Hamlet: voice, music, sound', *Popular Music*, 24/2, 257–267.

Kinney, Arthur F. 2006. *Shakespeare and Cognition: Aristotle's Legacy and Shakespearean Drama*. New York, NY and London: Routledge.

Lamb, Mary Ellen. 2006. *The Popular Culture of Shakespeare, Spenser, and Jonson*. London and New York, NY: Routledge.

Levine, Lawrence. 1988. *Highbrow/Lowbrow: The Emergence of Cultural Hierarchy in America*. Cambridge, MA: Harvard University Press.

Shakespeare, William. 2006. *Hamlet*. The Arden Shakespeare, Third Series. Ann Thompson and Neil Taylor (eds). London: Bloomsbury.

Shakespeare, William. Open Source Shakespeare at https://www.opensourceshakespeare. org/views/plays/play_view.php?WorkID=hamlet&Scope=entire&pleasewait=1&msg= pl#a1,s4 accessed 3 October 2022.

Shapiro, James. 2005. *1599: A Year in the Life of William Shakespeare*. London: Faber and Faber.

Smith, Bruce. 1999. *The Acoustic World of Early Modern England*. Chicago, IL and London: University of Chicago Press.

Sternfeld, F.W. 1963. *Music in Shakespearean Tragedy*. London: Routledge and Kegan Paul.

Thompson, Anne and Neil Taylor. 2016 (Revised Edition). 'Introduction'. In Ann Thompson and Neil Taylor (eds), *Hamlet*. The Arden Shakespeare. London: Bloomsbury: 1–168.

Tribble, Evelyn. 2019 (first pub 2017). *Early Modern Actors and Shakespeare's Theatre: Thinking with the Body*. London: The Arden Shakespeare.

Trudell, Scott A. 2012. 'The Mediation of Poesie: Ophelia's Orphic Song'. *Shakespeare Quarterly*, 63 (Spring 1): 46–76.

Wilson, Christopher R. and Michela Calore. 2005. *Music in Shakespeare: A Dictionary*. London: Bloomsbury.

6
PRINT TRIUMPHANT

This chapter again illustrates an argument that has been exemplified throughout our discussion: that is, the often hidden root systems that connect apparently unrelated historical shifts. We have been exploring the transition towards a society in which literacy carries increasing authority over orality, visual channels – notably print – coming to dominate sonic networks. As citations have suggested, much has been written on the rise of literacy. Relative to that field of study, however, there is little written on its implications for the sonic environment. By the mid-eighteenth century, written records had permeated everyday life of the dominant classes. But what were the implications and effects on the cultures of the illiterate? Or, more broadly, how did the equation between literacy and power impact on the understanding of the role of sound in social dynamics?

As I wish to document in this chapter, 'how the change in those dynamics arcs over the early modern period'. To exemplify: Erasmus' essay 'On the Body', advised against immoderate public laughter, but described it primarily as a visible phenomenon, a distortion of the face (Parvulescu 2005: 118). This recalls the sixteenth-century advice against gentlemen playing the trumpet, because it distorts the features beyond recognition (Buxton 1964: 8). In neither case is it the sound that occupies the centre of attention. This is in the early sixteenth century. Just over two centuries later, Lord Chesterfield in his 1774 'Letters to His Son' advised against 'Frequent and loud laughter' … 'it is the manner in which the mob express their silly joy at silly things. In my mind there is nothing so illiberal, and so ill-bred, as audible laughter' (Parvulescu 2005: 118). He opposes the noisiness of laughter to refinement, true wit, reflection and reason. By the time we come to Chesterfield, the complaint against laughter is based on the fact that it is a noise, a site of ill-breeding and class antagonism. Unregulated noise is becoming increasingly vulgar, a marker of 'the other' to middle class manners and taste. This change is largely the subject of this chapter, that an examination of the 'underground' operations of cultural change will often disclose surprising connections. To dramatize this, I am going take as what might seem to be the unlikely entry point of the appearance in the eighteenth century of the celebrity criminal, and then trace its connections to the understanding of the social role of sound.

We have seen that the major transitions from the Elizabethan to the Jacobean period were accompanied by debates over the relative authority of information circulated acoustically and visually, of the spoken as opposed to the written word, over what is heard as opposed to what is seen. It was a debate that went to the heart of nothing less than the salvation of the soul. As the seventeenth century unfolded, the imbalance between the two 'information circuits' increased, with the visual in the ascendant. We now turn to that growing imbalance in the relationship between sight and sound and how that change functioned to 'silence' the underclasses produced by capitalism, emergent industrialization and growing urbanization. As the authority of the oral shifted to the written word, the new power balance favoured the literate and consigned those who were not to an underclass so disempowered as be to virtually and in some cases literally 'written out' of the community. By the later seventeenth century, illiteracy was regarded as a disqualification for public office (Fox 2000: 47). Through the seventeenth century, illiteracy came to be a marker of the vulgar. 'With the attainment of reading by all of the upper and any of the middle ranks in this period ... lack of the skill came to be confined to the lower orders and, in due course, to define them in altogether new ways' (Fox 2000: 46). As elaborated further below, it is a corollary to this that noisiness became a sign of vulgarity, disorder, even illegality, while silence advertised law-abiding self-improvement.[1]

The process was remorseless, if slow, and in fact so closely coincides with what we are referring to as the 'Early Modern' period that it could be seen as one of its defining features. The culture of literacy can be regarded as triumphant when everyday transactions were required to be in printed rather than spoken form: posters, theatre bills, newspapers, magazines, receipts, maps, diagrams, indentures, charters and contracts, tickets, bureaucratic, legal and commercial documents, scored music, treaties, and from the Napoleonic wars even paper money and later, transport timetables. It coincides with the rise of the novel, and of prose in general, of author's copyright, the writing of literary histories (Kernan 1989: 48–49). Even though print had become the dominant information economy by the mid-1700s, this still did not mean everyone was taught to read; that waited for the Elementary Education Act, 1870 which prescribed universal literacy. But the transition from a predominantly oral to a predominantly print culture took over two centuries, and was consolidated by around the mid-eighteenth century. Samuel Johnson's decision, referred to above, to include in his 1755 *Dictionary* only words that had appeared in print, declared in effect that the illiterate were excluded from the English language community.

Like the idea of a 'smoking gun', I suggest that other changes taking place over the same period which might at first seem unrelated are also signals of the transition from acoustic to visual authority. In any civil society, the site at which the relationship between authority and the subordinate is formally institutionalized is the written legal code, which overrides unwritten custom. We have already glimpsed this confrontation, and I shall now develop this as a case study: how written law became a weapon against the growing underclasses, who resisted with public volubility. It was a shift that transformed notions of crime and punishment, and which located unregulated sound as potential disorder, to the extent that from the eighteenth century there was a growing attempt by the powerful to impose silence upon the subordinate.

I am going to use as the entry point to this discussion the examples of two 'celebrity' criminals of the eighteenth century, because their celebrity status is highly instructive regarding the changing class dynamics between what is read and what is heard at a critical point in the rise of capitalism. The celebrity criminal is a very interesting phenomenon that burgeoned in England in the 1700s. And it runs parallel to a development in the cultural history of sound. Criminality has perennially been a significant presence in the heroes of the underclasses, as represented *par excellence* in Robin Hood. But what is notable is that in eighteenth-century England, there is a sudden increase in the public celebrity of certain criminals.

I begin with one whose name is still familiar centuries later. Dick Turpin was one of the celebrity criminals of his age and beyond. His popular image is perpetuated by William Harrison Ainsworth, whose 1834 novel, *Rookwood*, portrayed him as a likeable rogue who rode from London to York in one day on his horse, Black Bess. In reality, Turpin was a violent criminal. Baptised in Essex in 1705, he was a butcher who became involved with a gang of poachers and house breakers. When most of the gang were arrested in 1735, he became a highwayman. He was arrested in 1738. When evidence of his horse stealing came to light he was transferred to York Castle Prison. He was found guilty on two charges of horse stealing on 22 March 1739 and was hanged on 7 April. He was a thief and a murderer, yet he became a favourite folk figure among gypsies, and transported convicts and underclasses in the US and Australia. He was remembered in ballads and folk tales that placed emphasis on his remarkable mobility and evasiveness. Few if any remember his particular victims, but his supposed midnight ride to York, his clearing of the five-barred government turnpike gate at Hornsey while under pursuit, and the horse on which he achieved these feats, Black Bess, remain vivid in folk memory. He was equally romanticized for a Robin Hood social justice profile, as celebrated in the ballad, 'Turpin's appeal to the judge':

> He said, The Scriptures I fulfill'd,
> Though I this life did lead,
> For when the naked I beheld,
> I clothed them with speed:
> Sometimes in Cloth and Winter-frieze,
> Sometimes in Russet-gray;
> The Poor I fed, the Rich likewise
> I empty sent away.
>
> Linebaugh 2006: 203

Turpin was a 'star' in his own lifetime – common people came to see and admire him in prison, during his trial and execution for horse theft, and his passage through the streets of York to execution. He wore a new suit bought for the occasion, hired men to act as mourners, bowed to and addressed the crowd at length and chatted affably with his executioner Hadfield, who in fact had formerly been a member of the same gang. Rather than wait for Hadfield, he jumped from the ladder and technically deprived the state of the satisfaction of murdering him. The mob took forcible possession of his body, which would otherwise have gone to surgeons for dissection. They buried him deep to thwart bodysnatchers. Nonetheless, it was dug up the next day and the mob discovered that it had been deposited with one of the city surgeons. They repossessed it, 'laid it on a board, and having carried it through the streets in a kind of triumphal manner, they then filled the coffin with unslaked lime, and buried it in the grave where it had been before deposited' (Linnane 2004: 42; see further Linebaugh 2006: 203–204). Like Elvis nearly two centuries later, rumours immediately spread that he was still alive.

Why was it that a common criminal became a great hero to ordinary folk? The answer lies in that particular stage in the development of capitalism, and it is paralleled in the tension between the world of the ear and the world of the eye – between oral and written cultures. When the mob looked admiringly at the condemned in the tumbril and on the scaffold, what did they see? One thing they saw was a former butcher, a member of the labouring classes. In fact Turpin's crimes, methods and his 'patch' were all related to his former trade. He was active in the theft of livestock and poaching, in regions he knew to be profitable because of his former trade. He knew where to catch livestock, how to slaughter them and where to sell their hides and flesh. Indeed, it was his former trade that led him not only towards the physical terrain of his criminal career, but towards the cultural terrain also. Like other members of plebeian classes, the independence of a butcher depended upon being able to earn sufficient income within the political economy of his trade. Throughout this period, there were major changes in the butchering industry, of a kind that would serve to increase profit to capitalist middle men, the wholesalers and dealers. Their control over the market increased at the expense of workers who had traditionally been protected by the system of guilds and customary trading patterns including marketing sites and opening times (Linebaugh 2006: 196–202). The protections formerly enjoyed by apprentices were particularly hard hit. Indeed, one of the reasons industrial manufacturing was gradually relocated to the northern cities was because the London apprentices were so aggressively vocal in the face of these changes. Some forty percent of all those hanged during the first half of the eighteenth century had served apprenticeships (Linebaugh 2006: 101). The livelihood of those who had come through the traditional butcher's apprenticeship was reduced, and in many cases, to a point of crisis. Former butchers were very strongly represented among those executed in eighteenth-century England.

Let us consider another example of the celebrity criminal before drawing some conclusions. In his 1845 study of the English working class, Engels quoted from a commission into children's employment in England the assertion that while many children did not know the names Bonaparte, Wellington, Nelson, St Paul, Solomon, Moses or even the queen, the names Dick Turpin and Jack Sheppard were generally familiar (Linebaugh 2006: 7). Sheppard was in fact 'the single most well-known name from eighteenth-century England' and not just in his own country. Like Turpin, his celebrity was international, his name invoked in the nineteenth century in both Australia in connection with Ned Kelly, and in America the brothers Jesse and Frank James likened themselves to him (Linebaugh 2006: 7–8).

Sheppard lived in the labouring class district of Spitalfields, where he had entered into an apprenticeship as a carpenter, illegally leaving a few months short of the seven-year term. He began housebreaking and thieving, and in the process showed an expertise with locks that became the basis of his later celebrity. With his mistress, Edgeworth Bess, he embarked on a criminal career that included breaking her out of prison in 1723. She was ultimately transported to America. Jack was captured and imprisoned, and it was at this point that the basis of his fame was established. He broke out of jail within a few hours. Recaptured while picking a gentleman's pocket, he was confined in the most secure section of New Prison, and constrained with fetters weighing twenty-eight pounds. He cut through these with an implement probably smuggled in, then through an iron bar, through a nine-inch-thick oak beam, and with a female prisoner, made his way to freedom. For three months, he resumed housebreaking and highway robbery. He was turned in by the infamous fence Jonathan Wild, whose services Sheppard had contemptuously spurned. He was locked up in the condemned hold of Newgate Prison. On the day his sentence of death for robbery was warranted, he escaped yet again, with the assistance of visitors to the prison. Recaptured yet again after a robbery spree, he was manacled, fettered and regularly checked by the guards. Nonetheless, he managed to remove his handcuffs, to break one of the links in his fetters and to ease himself out of his chains. He removed an iron bar from inside the chimney, used this to break some of the chimney masonry and squeezed through it to the room above. In pitch blackness, he broke his way through four rooms, and finally reached the roof. Seeing that a jump would dislodge tiles, he retraced his path all the way back to his cell to retrieve his blanket, returned to the roof and used the blanket to lower himself gently to a neighbouring roof from whence, by two flights of stairs, he emerged into the street.[2]

His conduct next is of special interest. He might be expected to disappear, to flee the region if not the country. But in Drury Lane he stole a fine suit, sword, watches and jewellery. Finely decked out, he hired a coach in which he toured his local neighbourhood (including passing by Newgate Prison). For over two weeks, he presented himself openly in ale houses, regaling with his stories a huge and admiring audience, his 'fans'. In Linebaugh's words, he had achieved fame as an individual that 'united "the mob"' (Linebaugh 2006: 38). Inevitably he was again recaptured, drunk and revelling in a tavern. Confined in Newgate's most secure cell, pinioned with 300 pounds of shackles, this time there was no escape. His jailers charged hundreds of members of the public to view the prisoner. On the two-hour journey from Newgate to Tyburn, a vast crowd gathered to see him. Weeping women gave him flowers; men competed to shake his hand. The largest crowd in seventy-five years gathered at the scaffold, where he was hanged in November 1724 at the age of twenty-two. And like Turpin, the mob took possession of the corpse to keep it from the surgeons.

During these exploits, Sheppard became the subject of '"the Common Discourse of the whole Nation". The "common People" were "Mad about him"' (Linebaugh 2006: 32). Tradespeople stayed away from their workplaces to talk about his exploits in taverns. Ballad makers prospered. While he was in jail, women and children had kept the gallows under surveillance to warn of attempts to execute him secretly at night. He was visited in his cell by celebrities who probably included Daniel Defoe. In extensive interviews, he talked to journalists on the criminal justice system, the quality of locksmiths in London, on political economy and on the clergy who urged his improvement through study of the *Bible*: 'One File's worth all the Bibles in the world', was Sheppard's secular response (Linebaugh 2006: 33). His portrait was painted by James Thornhill, the official royal court painter, and he was the inspiration for Hogarth's series 'Industry and Idleness'. Following his death, the Sheppard memorial industry burgeoned, especially in popular culture. Two weeks after his execution, he was the subject of a popular opera – what we might today call a musical – that opened in Drury Lane, the first of nine plays inspired by him staged in one year (Cyriax 1996: 513). The most famous of the theatrical commemorations was John Gay's *The Beggar's Opera*. The general tenor of all these memorial events was anti-establishment, critiques of the hypocrisy of the political and economic system.

Here again we have a common criminal who becomes the most famous name in England, and loved by the common people. Why? Like Turpin and the numerous folk-hero criminals of this time, what enshrined them in the popular imagination was their of defiance of authority. The pivotal images and narratives underpinning their celebrity were, in Turpin's case, his bold escapes – the ride to York and the leaping of the turnpike gate, and in Sheppard's case, his magical gift for escapology.

Yet 'escape' is not quite the word. None of these heroes escaped, in the way that criminal absconders like Ronnie Biggs did in the twentieth century. They overcame the physical boundaries imposed upon them, *to return to their familiar community precincts*. It was this excarceration and return to their class that sustained the link with their 'fans' and which underpinned their romanticization.

It is to do with the recognition of something of ourselves in the celebrity. In the relatively unmediated world of eighteenth century London it was a spatial link, a literal return to and conversation with one's own people. This confirmed the continuing 'ordinariness' on which their reputation was built. Their celebrity status was based on breaking out of the prison of obscurity, overcoming the barriers of space to gain a public voice for local ordinariness. In Sheppard's case in particular, his ability to break free of his literal constraints – chains, fetters – was a triumph of the ordinary person over the capitalist mystique of the lock which symbolized the victory of private property over customary entitlements, fences over common land and binding labour contracts over flexible guild privileges.

This takes us to the point of Sheppard's apprenticeship as a carpenter. The London labouring classes of the eighteenth century made heroes of their criminals. But why did the underclasses not produce such heroes on such a scale earlier? And why do the criminal heroes largely disappear by the nineteenth century? I suggest that there is a clear link between the eighteenth-century criminal celebrity, and a specific stage in the development of capitalism, and that we understand that better if we think of the politics of sound as opposed to print.

Like butchering, the labouring trades underwent rapid transformation during the eighteenth-century phase of capitalism in England. The changes relate to production and distribution, governing such questions as: Who was able to compete in the market? Where might goods be sold and under what conditions? Who distributes and transports raw and manufactured goods? These are all associated with the emergence of a growing economic class: the mercantile entrepreneur, usually based in the growing middle classes. The effect was to abolish customary trade arrangements and entitlements. The barter system that operated in pre-urban local markets is being replaced by exchange based on written contracts, capital and a growing range of middlemen. This saw the decline of the rights that had protected the livelihoods of those who came through the old labour economy. That economy recognized, for example, customary rights to various forms of wastage at successive stages of production: timber offcuts in shipping yards, leftover fabric, offal from butchering and even the fine dust in the working of precious metals.

Over the eighteenth century, such unwritten customary rights, largely preserved as oral tradition, came into increasing conflict with a new phase of capitalism involving the fetishization of private as opposed to common property, enshrined in newly written laws. From the late sixteenth century, courts such as the Exchequer record the growing transition from unwritten local custom to the codification of written law (Fox 2000: 259–298), 'to a world defined by texts', putting 'an end to one of the last purely oral dimensions of economic life in England' (Fox 2000: 298, 412). Among the best known examples are the enclosures in England and the highland clearances in Scotland, the expropriation of common land by an emerging capitalist class in the interests of private profit. Originating as a rural phenomenon, it reverberated in cities in the massive influx of displaced rural labourers and artisans. The associated changes ranged from the introduction of new manufacturing technologies, to the criminalization of customary entitlements and agreements preserved and passed on by unwritten agreement. The new regulation of such rights, however, was inscribed in written law.

The relevant binary here, that produced the tension out of which the celebrity criminal emerged, is between unwritten custom and written law. The legal records of eighteenth-century England suggest a massive rise in crime. But this is not because the country suddenly saw a sudden shift to criminal activity. It is because of a significant transition from traditional customs to new laws in regulating social conduct. Central to this process was a legislative revolution in eighteenth-century England that put the 'ordinary' worker in opposition to the legal system with unprecedented brutality. In the difficult economic situation of subsistence labour, customary entitlements could be the difference between survival and penury. The right to leftover timber in shipyards, leftover cloth in tailors' workshops and leftover metal in silversmiths, goldsmiths, tinsmiths and coppersmiths frequently meant the difference between survival and penury. In the new capitalist economic environment, with its sanctification of private property, these traditional unwritten entitlements were abolished by new laws initiated by the emerging mercantile and industrial manufacturing classes for the protection of their property. These emerging economic and social classes had little place in the traditional economic systems of manual cottage production and face-to-face barter and exchange; the new laws created an economic space for them but obviously at the expense of unwritten traditions. So, the artisan producers were threatened by both the development of industrial manufacturing and the new laws designed to privilege the new system and its obsession with private (as opposed to common) property.

This led to increasing conflict between traditional labour groups and the new business entrepreneurs. From the 1690s, a series of 'capital acts' multiplied the number of crimes liable to the death penalty, including various forms of forgery and larceny, the former, be it noted, an offence against the written word (Linebaugh 2006: 54). The Combination Act of 1721 prohibited journeyman tailors from forming groups to discuss their deteriorating working conditions. This forerunner of anti-Union legislation was passed at the request of master tailors after about 15,000 journeyman tailors had struck for better pay and shorter hours (Linebaugh 2006: 17). The Riot Act of 1715 already denied them the right to assemble and protest volubly, to create public 'tumult', about the new restrictions. Part of the effect of such laws would be to force many individuals out of work, and, to support their families there was a strong motivation to turn to what was now defined as, in many cases, a capital crime. Regarding poaching, for example, the Waltham Black Act of 1723 created over 200 capital offences (Brooke and Brandon 2005: 72). The establishment of the forerunner of the UK police force emerged from this process. Thames shipping employed the largest labour force in London, which helps to explain why the first regular police force was the Thames River Police, proposed in 1797 with the backing of international merchant interests (Linebaugh 2006: 426). The establishment of the river police was one of the responses to the rising anxiety among the authorities regarding a crime rate that was rapidly increasing, largely because the legal definition of what was criminal was expanding.

The new laws ensured that both the customary conducts of the ordinary labourer was now likely to be criminal, and that in addition, he was out of necessity increasingly steered towards a life of crime. To illustrate: a lumper was a labourer who unloaded cargo on the Thames docks, shifting containers like barrels that might contain tobacco, sugar, spirits and other imported consumables. There was spillage from barrels damaged on the voyage or during their often long wait to be unloaded. The lumper had a traditional unwritten entitlement to sweep up and keep spillage, and doubtless this could be increased by some rough handling or 'accident'. On such low wages, these sweepings, and what they could be bartered or sold for, were essential to livelihood. As new labour relations and legislation abolished such customary privileges, a man could be hanged or transported for this offence against what was now strictly private property. At the very least, he would lose his job. Thus, if this 'ordinary' labourer continued his 'ordinary' labour customs, he was a criminal. If he desisted he would shortly be destitute, and crime his only salvation. In 1734, a Dutchman resident in London found that under current conditions it was impossible for such an individual to earn more than half what was necessary to support a wife and two children (Linebaugh 2006: 190). Impossible.

Yet most did survive, but to do so they constantly entered that changing and indeterminate space opening up between customary rights and written law. The timber workers in the shipping yards could survive with the perquisites of offcuts, but not legally so under newly written legislation. Under earlier labour conditions a cottage weaver kept some of the scraps for barter or sale, a customary entitlement for the self-employed. In the new framework of factory labour relations, this became theft from the boss. If you can imagine discovering that the pencils or writing paper that you took home from the office stationery cupboard suddenly made you liable to the death penalty, you may get some sense of the shock experienced by largely illiterate labourers under these rapidly changing conditions. A correspondent to the *Gentleman's Magazine* in 1757 noted that 'The persons most likely to offend against laws, more especially in criminal matters, are the low and illiterate part of the people'; this was because they could not read changes in laws that were proclaimed simply by being posted publicly (Fox 2000: 44–45).

Let us consider some of the social implications of all these developments. First, the ordinary labourer is increasingly excluded from the sense of belonging to society, partly because he is disappearing into the labouring urban masses. In a culture of growing individualism, he has no social 'individuation'. Second, he can no longer sustain himself and his family through unwritten customary entitlements, and is moved closer to the category of the criminal to survive. When he sees the criminal in the public procession from jail to scaffold, he is watching and hearing someone very like himself, but who has managed to achieve 'individuation', that is a kind of public voice. The criminals who lived in popular folklore all included one notable feature: at some point, they turned their criminal status into a form of voluble live public theatre: Turpin on his last journey through the streets, Sheppard parading himself in stolen finery while on the run.

The legal process itself created their celebrity and gave them their public theatre. Seventeenth-century highwayman, Francis Jackson advised novices to rehearse speeches for the courts. Next, there was the jail, made profitably accessible to visitors by the jail-keepers. On the night before execution, condemned prisoners held parties in their cell at which they made speeches and looked forward to the attention of the crowd (Babington 1971: 32). On the day of execution, there was the procession in the streets. Many took great pride in how they looked, often buying expensive new clothing for the two-hour parade from Newgate Prison to the gallows at Tyburn. And they made speeches and greeted the crowds as they proceeded. Highwayman Jack Rann had often been in the Tyburn audience and had declared to onlookers with pride that someday they would be looking at him up there. And so it came to pass when he was hanged in 1774, wearing an extravagant green suit with his trademark silk breeches with sixteen strings fastened at the knee, and a nosegay (Brooke and Brandon 2005: 144–145). On his final journey in 1765, a John Weskitt, wearing a striking blue and gold coat, drew applause as he casually ate oranges and threw the peel into the street; one criminal witness declared that the condemned were often dressed up like bridegrooms 'going to espouse old Mrs Tyburn' (Brooke and Brandon 2005: 141, 103).

But the great moment was the public execution. As Jimi Hendrix reportedly declared, 'Once you are dead, you are made for life'. The condemned were always given the opportunity to say some final words – an opportunity, the authorities hoped, for displays of remorse. But for most of the spectators a defiant or carefree manner was most appreciated, as in the case of Isaac Atkinson, who far from showing fear or remorse, stabbed the accompanying chaplain and announced to the crowd, 'There's nothing like a merry life and a short one' (Linnane 2004: xvi). Defiant comedy was especially enjoyed. One man pushed one of the officials out of the cart, and ostentatiously removed his own boots, declaring that thus he defied the proverb about dying with boots on. William Borwick drew loud applause as he elaborately checked the rope, saying he was worried it might break (Brooke and Brandon 2005: 188).

The public theatre of a procession to the gallows was one of the greatest occasions for a kind of proletarian festival (see especially Gatrell 1994: 29–105). They attracted buskers, street vendors and a range of entrepreneurs, trading franchises, 'cross-marketing' as hawkers sold mementoes (see Figure 6.1).

The execution was climactic for a number of reasons. First, it was the ultimate moment in the premodern version of what we now call 'Reality Television': real death as real life. But it also provided the largest possible audience in a

FIGURE 6.1   Execution of the Idle Apprentice. Wellcome Library, London. http://wellcomeimages.org engraving by T. Cook, 1795, after W. Hogarth, 1747. By: William Hogarth after: Thomas Cook. Published: 1 July 1795. Copyrighted work available under Creative Commons Attribution only licence CC BY 4.0 http://creativecommons.org/licenses/by/4.0/

pre-electronic media era. Instead of generating the sense of awe and terror intended by the authorities, an execution day was a great public carnival, with absenteeism from places of work commonplace (Babington 1971: 33; Brooke and Brandon 2005: 105). The Tyburn crowds ranged from estimates of 20,000 upwards, drawing the largest crowds of any public event (Brooke and Brandon 2005: 60, 105). If we add to these the crowds that thronged the route of the procession from Newgate, we have massive, highly voluble public assemblies, with an overwhelming preponderance of the lower orders, and especially as the century drew on (Brooke and Brandon 2005: 106). Contemporary accounts left by those who enjoyed the privilege of literacy identify the crowds lining the street and assembled around the Tyburn scaffold as predominantly plebeian. The 'mob', 'the vulgar', 'ragamuffins', 'rakewells', 'trollopes', 'Whores and Rogues of the meaner sort', 'rabble' (Brooke and Brandon 2005: 203–205). The cheering, the shouts of admiration, attempts to thwart the executioners (some were killed by the mob), and to retrieve the corpse from the representatives of authority, all suggest where their sympathies lay, particularly in contrast to their behaviour at the very occasional execution of members of the more privileged classes. They applauded the appearance and performance of the condemned, and as long as the condemned confirmed this link, their admiration was reinforced. John Aitken had tried to blow up one of the Royal Navy dockyards. His trial brought him the celebrity he had craved. The trial at the Winchester assizes attracted a crowd 'greater than ever was known' (Warner 2004: 188). On the Sunday before the trial, the crowd wanted Aitken to present himself before them, but he refused to leave his cell. It was this refusal, his silent absence – not his crimes which included rape and robbery – that prompted their belief that 'he ought to be hanged, or he would never have behaved so rudely to folk who came so far on purpose to pay him a visit' (Warner 2004: 189).

And they paid their visit to admire and listen to public individuations of their oppressed, suppressed ordinary selves, to see a defiant, unashamed voluble performance. The labour experiments of eighteenth capitalism inexorably drove the labouring classes towards criminality. What did the underclasses see on the scaffold? Themselves. The defiant stylish performances which the London proletariat enjoyed in their criminal heroes on the public stage of tumbril and scaffold were the spectacle of themselves as someone who had made it.

The gallows crowd was not uniformly plebeian, however. The prices charged for exhibiting the prisoner in his cell, and for a seat on the stands built at the gallows site, would have been beyond the means of most of the 'groundlings'. While written recollections suggest that the majority of the audience consisted of disaffected plebeians enjoying anti-authoritarian performances, those who wrote such accounts were privileged with literate access to the creation of the written public record. And among them, we find a very different attitude. In 1725, Bernard de Mandeville lamented that 'All the way from Newgate to Tyburn, is one continual Fair, for Whores and Rogues of the meaner sort' (Brooke and Brandon 2005: 2050). Henry Fielding declared in 1751 that

> The Day appointed by Law for the Thief's Shame is a Day of Glory in his own Opinion. His procession to Tyburn, and his last Moments there, are all triumphant; attended with the compassion of the meek and tender-hearted, and with the Applause, Admiration and Envy of all the bold and hardened.
>
> Babington 1971: 31–32

His comments reflect official dismay at the realization that the public theatre of judicial process did neither necessarily produce a sense of shame in the condemned criminal nor revulsion on the part of the public. He recounts the pride taken in the way they dressed for the gallows and the preceding parade through the streets, parties held on the night before at which the condemned and his guests were of good cheer, of the speeches they prepared and their gratification at the attentions of the crowds (Babington 1971: 32).

Through the public theatre of the criminal as visible and audible prisoner, in a procession intended as humiliation, and finally as executed victim of state power, the dominant classes hoped to construct the meaning of this theatre as a reminder of the wages of sin. But the proletariat audience inverted the meaning of the criminal celebrity into an inspirational reminder of the spectacular potential of their ordinariness. The 'bridge of meaning' across which dominant and subordinate classes negotiated hegemony collapsed. The parade of legal force actually gave the criminal representatives of the lower orders a forum for speeches that threatened disorder and riot. Far from being cowed by the theatres of state violence, during the Gordon Riots of June 1780, the biggest municipal uprising in the history of the city, the mob burned Newgate prison to the ground.

And so the authorities closed the public theatres of crime and silenced the speeches of the underclasses. In 1782, the City of London declared to the Secretary of State that the Tyburn procession hardened rather than chastened potential criminals (Linebaugh 2006: 363). The following year saw the last Tyburn hanging. The three mile procession of the condemned from Newgate to Tyburn was abandoned and a gallows built within the precincts of reconstructed Newgate, where crowds could be more effectively managed. The mobile theatre of the Tyburn rituals loudly proclaimed a celebration of ordinary people who had escaped the anonymity of the urban crowd, and opposed the oppression of the brutal new laws that deprived them of any place in capitalist society other than that of a proletarian labour force. When that theatre was shutdown, the criminal celebrity disappeared (Linnane 2004: 104). The last public Newgate hanging was in 1868 (Babington 1971: 156, 222, 227). The heroic celebrity criminal disappeared from London, and with it his capacity to mobilize the underclasses. In 1832 an article in *Fraser's Magazine* wrote about the underworld, 'Formerly the heroes of their party were fellows conspicuous and famed for daring acts of plunder, in which the whole body had a pride, and whom they all felt ambitious to imitate. ... All this kind of heroism has subsided' (Linnane 2004 104). The criminal was deprived of a public voice. As we shall shortly discover, this whole process is closely bound up with the politicization of sound, and the transition from a predominantly oral information economy to one that was primarily textual, from speaking to writing, from hearing to seeing.

The heroic celebrity criminals of the eighteenth century survived in the popular imagination, and also linked up to new sites of the phenomenon. Significantly, most of these new sites were to found in frontier spaces still undergoing the struggles between customary rights and new legal constraints characteristic of the earlier phase of capitalism exemplified in eighteenth-century London. In the American west, the tensions between the open range cattlemen and the barbed wire fenced sheepmen, between the defeated south and the victorious north, between goldrush adventurers and new mining rights legislation, all created new forms of criminal admired by the frontier underclasses. In Australia, the conflicts between customary common property entitlements (land, wandering livestock) and new property legislation produced folk heroes among transported Irish and later itinerant underclasses, like the swagman in the song 'Waltzing Matilda'. In the US, the James Brothers' invocation of Jack Sheppard and in Australia comparisons between Sheppard and Ned Kelly confirm the export of the celebrity criminal to earlier stages of capitalism, through networks that were primarily oral, such as popular balladry.

At the beginning of this chapter, I suggested that changes taking place over the period under discussion which might at first seem unrelated are also signals of the transition from acoustic to visual authority. Let us now draw out more explicitly the relationship between the developments in the legal system and its administration, and the cultural history of sound. Several relevant points have clearly emerged. One is that the apparent massive increase in the rate of crime in the eighteenth century was to a great extent the result of a collision between the unwritten customary rights preserved in a largely oral tradition and the proliferation of written legislation designed to secure and protect the property rights of an emergent capitalist class. Another is that the enforcement of this legislative revolution and its public rituals intended to demonstrate the power of the law, unexpectedly provided a forum that literally gave voice to the underclasses that potentially threatened that power. We have two historical records represented here: the oral testimony produced by the new underclasses created by capitalism, and the record created by the propertied classes who enjoyed its privileges. Closing down the public rituals was a recognition by the authorities of the alarming power of public tumult.

Where power was maintained by recourse to a written legal code, the sonic solidarity of the mob was a growing threat. The preservation of public order under the new hegemony came to be seen as requiring the regulation of public noise, and if necessary, its silencing.[3] This foreshadowed the shape of things to come in the penal system. Prison is a place of institutionalized violence by the state against the individual. And we can measure the growing power of the state by the violence of the conflict between sound and silence.

An account of the English prison system was published by reformer John Howard in 1777, and included a number of proposals for improving the institution: 'Solitude and silence are favourable to reflection, and may possibly lead to repentance' (Babington 1971: 109). Silence has come to be the signifier and the driver of civil obedience, deference to the rule of law. When prison reformer Elizabeth Fry visited Newgate Prison in 1813, she reported being shocked by the conditions, including 'the filth, the closeness of the rooms, the ferocious manners and expressions of the women towards each other .... And *her ears were offended* by the most terrible imprecations'. (Babington 1971: 153, my italics here and below). She later spoke of 'the dreadful proceedings that went forward on the female side of the prison; the begging, *swearing*, fighting, gaming, *singing*, dancing, dressing up in men's clothes – the scenes too bad to be described' (Babington 1971: 155). In April 1817, Fry formed The Association for the Improvement of Female Prisoners in Newgate, which passed rules of conduct calling for the women to be engaged in approved employment, and that there should be no '*begging, swearing*, gaming, card-playing, *quarrelling or immoral conversation*', and that at 9 am and 6 pm they should be gathered together to listen to readings from the Bible (Babington 1971: 156). These led to changes, described by a male visitor:

> On my approach no loud or dissonant sounds or angry voices indicated that I was about to enter a place, which ... had long had for one of its titles that of 'Hell above ground'. The courtyard into which I was admitted, instead of being peopled with beings scarcely human, blaspheming, fighting, tearing each others' hair, or gaming with a filthy pack of cards for the filthy clothes they wore, ... presented a scene where stillness and propriety reigned ... a lady from the Society of Friends ... was reading aloud to about sixteen women prisoners who were engaged in needle-work. ... They all rose on my entrance, curtsied respectfully and then at a signal resumed their seats and employments.
>
> Babington 1971: 157

Silence thus became the sign of obedience to the state. The Prison Act of 1865 enforced the 'separate system' throughout Britain, whereby prisoners shall be

> ... prevented from holding any communications with each other, either by every prisoner being kept in a separate cell by day and by night except when he is at chapel or taking exercise, or by every prisoner

being confined by night in his cell and being subject to such superintendence during the day as will prevent his communicating with any other prisoner.

Babington 1971: 222

The silent system was also imposed in German, Swiss, French, Italian and Irish prisons (Schwartz 2011: 202) and continued in some prisons well into the twentieth century, as in the case of Alcatraz, which was opened in 1934, 'and for the first five years operated the Silent System' (Cyriax 1996: 160).

Over the last 500 years, silence or regulated sound increasingly came to signify obedience, reverential submission to authority and the marker of secular moral and intellectual gravitas. Versions of a 'silent system', in the implementation of power relations, were not confined to the violently coercive context of prisons, but were emerging in other areas of social organization. The Bodleian Library, established in the early seventeenth century established the principle of silence, and in contrast to 'the noisy conviviality of the Renaissance court libraries', by 1711 'the rule of silence' had been generally imposed in European libraries (Pettegree and Der Weduwen 2021: 147). As compared with earlier audience conduct discussed above, by the nineteenth century, church congregations, 'art' theatre audiences, school rooms, galleries, museums, observed, and continue to observe, strict regimes controlling sound. As industrialization developed, codes of silence were also imposed upon factory workers. In offices, at least until the adoption of the typewriter, discussed below, silence was regarded as the sign of productivity and, contrarily, noisiness a sign of non-productivity. All places of study and improvement had sound tightly regulated. All places where there was no such regulation were regarded as threats to social order, characteristic of the vulgar lower orders. They make noise. In doing so, they manifest themselves as a threat to a hegemonic textuality.

The drive to sonic regulation was also manifest in the appearance of dedicated music performance venues, themselves associated with material, political and aesthetic changes. One John Banister is credited with 'inventing' the commercial concert in 1672, with the first dedicated room for public concerts opening in the York buildings in Villiers Street in the 1680s (Gouk 1999: 58–60). The process culminated in purpose built concert halls, a process which parallels the rise to authority of modern tablature in contrast to music transmitted 'by ear'. The first dedicated concert halls were built in the eighteenth century, in such centres as Oxford, London, Leipzig and Hanover; significantly, all with substantial and increasingly powerful middle class populations.

In their early history, however, the behaviour of concert and opera audiences 'was more like that of a soccer match. While the music was being played, people would talk to one another (both quietly and loudly), eat and drink, call upon the boxes of other patrons, and promenade in the hall', and interact volubly with performers (Müller 2017: 158). As the nineteenth century drew on, in Vienna and Paris from about 1830, then across Europe, audience rowdiness gradually subsided for a range of reasons including that, constrained by bourgeois notions of self-control, the 'educated middle classes ... began to attach a transcendental quality to music' (Müller 2017: 160). This change is also associated with the strengthening association between unregulated sound and the rising urban noise of the vulgar, distancing the middle classes by their own contrasting displays of sonic refinement and discipline.

By 1889, conductor Theodore Thomas wrote in *Modern Manners and Social Forms*, 'Perfect quiet should be maintained during the performance, and attention should be fixed on the stage. To whisper or do anything during the entertainment to disturb or distract the attention of others, is rude in the extreme' (Schwartz 2011: 226). Music in its most legitimate forms was both increasingly quarantined from 'noise', as in the protocols of the public concert hall where, even to applaud between movements of a symphony attracts a mixture of hostility and contempt, and the music is definitively quarantined in a visual text – the score (on this process of 'sacralisation' and the gradual 'silencing' of audiences as markers of bourgeois refinement see further for example Levine 1988; Kasson 1990; Johnson 1995). By the late nineteenth century, art music performance spaces had imposed their own version of the prison 'silent system'.

What of music performed outside the sanctified realm of the concert hall and opera house? This 'trajectory of acoustic politics', as I have called it, can be identified with particular clarity in the fate of street music since the medieval period.[4] Today, street music is rarely heard, except for annual sanctioned events like Australia's Anzac Day. At other times, it is associated with poverty or indigence, as in its scattered reappearance during the Great Depression, or, today, the occasional busker. This makes for a puzzling comparison with what we discussed above regarding the acoustic richness of Elizabethan street sound. These sounds included the cries of peripatetic street vendors, which were a form of music, to the extent that they could be incorporated into formal art music compositions and popular songs.[5] A great number of songs have been documented from the pre- or early-modern era, as in examples recorded by poet John Lydgate (ca. 1370 – ca. 1451) in his 'London Lackpenny'. Examples also include the cries of watchmen, also referred to as 'Waits', who used musical instruments as well as their voices to signal their activity. In many cases, these groups evolved into city bands employed by the local authorities to play in the streets.

In England, they are reported from as early as the thirteenth century, but they began to die out from the late eighteenth century, under the gathering weight of municipal legislation. The Metropolitan Police Act of 1864 explicitly legislated against street musicians in general. John Picker's benchmark study of Victorian soundscapes shows that by the mid-nineteenth century, this opposition had consolidated itself, literally with a vengeance, with street musicians characterized as alien enemies to native intellectual culture. Even that spokesman for the common man, Charles Dickens, subscribed to petitions against this democratic music experience (Picker 2003: 60–62). I believe that this process can be understood largely in terms of the history of modernity itself, and it illustrates a very simple idea: by studying the changing politics of sound in general, of which the disappearance of street music is one highly audible example, we understand more fully the history of emerging modernity. As obvious starting points: the watchman's cries were replaced by clocks and watches – also a product of the industrialized regulation of time; the town crier and ballad makers and sellers were replaced by the press. That is, the decline of street music is bound up with the material and intellectual culture of modernity.

It seems to be in the eighteenth century that the tipping point was reached, as in the famous Hogarth 1741 engraving, 'The Enraged Musician', beloved by sound historians (see Figure 6.2), and described by Henry Fielding as 'enough to make a man deaf to look at' (Cockayne 2007: 129). Cockayne's detailed summary identifies a parrot cawing next to a poster for Gay's *The Beggar's Opera*; a female ballad-seller with a crying baby, a girl with a rattle in her hand, a knife

FIGURE 6.2 Hogarth's 1741 engraving, 'The Enraged Musician'. William Hogarth 1741, CC0 1.0 Universal Public Domain Dedication via Wikimedia Commons, Gift of Sarah Lazarus, 1891

sharpener, a dustman ringing a bell, a sow-gelder on his horse and blowing a horn; a small coals seller, a street worker bashing the pavement, as well as potential sounds: a boy pissing into a hole will make a sound with the object attached by a rope to his waist, the flag on the church foreshadows that bells will shortly be rung, there is a sign advertising a pewterer, a notoriously noisy trade; the milkmaid's opening mouth suggests she is singing (Cockayne 2007: 129).

Represented here is the array of many of the conceptual binaries that summarize the historical tensions out of which modernity emerged: indoor music versus outdoor noise (albeit much of it also music); mobile versus 'stationed' cultural practices; propertied bourgeoisie versus the indigent underclasses; regulated versus unregulated sound.

Hogarth takes the trouble to show us that the violinist is reading from sheet music on a stand, while those outside are clearly sounding out 'by ear'. Thus, there is also here the tension between literacy and illiteracy that we have discussed above. As is suggested in Hogarth's engraving, this tension is also reflected in the difference between indoor and outdoor music, and those who produced and consumed it. We have a clear contrast between the 'propertied' violinist, and the peripatetic noisemakers in the street. Reflected here is the rapid expansion of the unpropertied urban underclasses. Two forces in particular drove this demographic: the displacements of populations from their rural homes by enclosures, discussed above, and the growing need for cheap labour in growing industrial centres. Together, these developments generated a large population of indigent wanderers and artisans with no stake in the system. This in turn set up a powerful political tension between the mobile and the stationary: that is, those with no apparent abode or fixed workplace, and those who owned property and worked from fixed bases. This mobility was accompanied by a suspicion of a general lack of fixity among underclasses: migrant labour, the homeless, the displaced, and information circuits that do not have written stability: such as, to point forward, the distinction between peripatetic musicians and those with fixed appointments in dedicated recreational sites. Likewise, music, oral forms, not written down, are regarded as low status and untrustworthy, rooted in the mobility of the body, not preserved in the permanent shrine of written ideas.

The idea of unpropertied or uncontracted wanderers became so threatening as to have given us the demonized abbreviation of the word mobile: the mob. At the same time, the word 'station' and its related forms, suggested order. This in itself arises from the developments I have been outlining. We have two words, stationery, referring to paper, and stationary, meaning fixed, still. They are connected in a way that discloses a significant force in our cultural history. Earlier we spoke of itinerant vendors. With the increasing industrialization of commerce, and the associated heavy equipment, places of business and manufacture became fixed, and one of the first of these was printing and publishing for the literate. It is necessary to conduct this new activity from a fixed location. Stationery can best be processed from a location that is stationary.

A fixed station became a modern sign of productive labour, a form of fixed property that indicated productive citizenship with a stake in the society, a person of station or, we can say, with status. Those who roamed the streets willy-nilly, on the other hand, were a threat to good order, as was traumatically demonstrated during the Gordon Riots of June 1780, referred to above, further confirmation of the need to regulate public behaviour by any means possible, and in particular, volatile voluble behaviour. All the forces of modernity converged in the increasingly severe regulation of public noise. Throughout the eighteenth century, unregulated sound and music were increasingly associated with the vulgar lower orders and the threat they presented to social order.

One of the great catalysts in the growing fear of the unregulated noise of the mob was of course the French Revolution. Originally inspired by its supposed emancipation of the common man, poet William Wordsworth came to despise the urban mass and its noise. In his perennial anthology piece, Wordsworth finds London beautiful when standing back from it in the silence of the morning on Westminster Bridge.

> Ne'er saw I, never felt, a calm so deep!
> The river glideth at his own sweet will:
> Dear God! the very houses seem asleep;
> And all that mighty heart is lying still![6]

Wordsworth has, however, removed one thing that gives a modern city a life of its own: people and their unruly noise.

In his famous poem in praise of Nature, *The Prelude*, in Book Seven he visits London again, and it becomes, instead, 'a monstrous ant hill' (line 149), full of the 'Babel din (line 151)'. Street music is unbearable noise, part of an oppressive 'roar' (line 168), a 'deafening din' (line 155), which includes 'a minstrel band' (line 178), an 'English Ballad-singer' (line 180), 'some female vendor's scream, … the shrillest of all London cries' (lines 182–83), all part of a 'thickening hubbub' (line 211). There are 'singers', not imagined as musicians, but as part of the 'uproar of the rabblement' (line 273), among which he hears 'for the first time in my life, The voice of woman utter blasphemy' (lines 384–85). The city confronts Wordsworth with the rising tide of modern mass culture, the actuality of the contemporary 'common man'. And it is demonized as an acoustic culture, its music experienced as part of the noise, summarized in microcosm at Bartholomew Fair:

> … what anarchy and din,
> Barbarian and infernall, …
> buffoons … screaming - him who grinds
> The hurdy-gurdy, at the fiddle weaves,
> Rattles the salt-box, thumps the kettledrum,

> And him who at the trumpet puffs his cheeks,
> The silver-collared Negro with his timbrel,
> ... Ventriloquists ...
> The bust that speaks ...
> ... far-fetched, perverted things, ...
> All jumbled up together, to compose
> A Parliament of Monsters
>
> From lines 686–718

Literally and metaphorically, the transition from rural folk to the modern urban industrial masses was understood in terms of noise: sound that is ugly and unintelligible. The masses do not invade the streets with music; they intrude upon the soundscape of the city with noise. For the aesthetic consolations of music, he looks to his countryside, where he can hear: 'A choir' of birds, 'minstrels from the distant woods' (lines 21–22), 'heartsome Choristers' (line 29) who 'chant together' with him (line 31) and 'warbled at my door' (line 41). Or he retreats to a classical pastoral of antiquity 'where the pipe was heard ... thrilling the rocks/ With tutelary music' (Book 8, lines 183–84). Wordsworth's advocacy for the common man was generally limited to the picturesque rural worker keeping his place by pursuing traditional forms and modes of labour.

The rise of the mob, the urban crowd, the embryonic working class or the proletariat, and those who were oppressed under capitalism are figured as the rise of noise. Elizabeth Gaskell's compassionate portrait of the industrial classes of Manchester in the novel *Mary Barton* was published in 1848. Notwithstanding her sympathies, she notes that among the city-dwellers enjoying a rural break, it was the factory girls who were 'loud-talking' (Gaskell 1996: 6; all quotations from this edition). The crowd that gathers to witness a factory fire is above all an acoustic entity: 'a murmur of many voices' (p. 50); 'A mighty shout ... a sound to wake the dead' (p. 52); 'louder than the blowing of the mighty wind' (p. 54). When the last worker is pulled safe from the flames,

> The multitude in the street absolutely danced with triumph, and huzzaed and yelled until you could have fancied their very throats would crack: and then, with all the fickleness of interest characteristic of a large body of people, pressed and stumbled, cursed and swore, in the hurry to get out of Dunham Street, and back to the immediate scene of the fire, the mighty diapason of whose roaring flames formed an awful accompaniment to the screams, and yells, and imprecations, of the struggling crowd. (p. 55)

The above account is intended as a particular case study in the politicization of sound throughout the early-modern era (see further Johnson 2006). In the meantime throughout the whole period, the larger context, literally the 'background noise', is a general rise in the volume of the soundscape. With denser urbanization, the sounds of the city streets became increasingly intrusive. By the mid-eighteenth century, in the Session House in Chelmsford, located in the market place, judges often found it necessary to halt proceedings because the voices of witnesses could not be heard over the sound of carts and carriages (Cockayne 2007: 106). While complaints about noise are as old as cities themselves, there were increasing echoes of Wordsworth's reactions, especially in rapidly growing urban centres. Apart from the sounds of voices and vehicles, intrusive sounds included those of pigs, dogs and night time revelry of drinkers and playgoers (Cockayne 2007: 107, 108). Communities would petition the authorities against public noise nuisances such as illicit alehouses, keeping a disorderly house and playhouses where coaches and crowds gathered. In 1743, a witness at an Old Bailey trial of a porter from the parish of St Bride's in London who kept a 'disorderly house', complained 'I have heard Noises all Night long; I have heard too much cursing and swearing, and everything that is obscene; I have it at my Door every Evening, as soon as it is dark; the house is like a Hogsty' (Cockayne 2007: 117).

In the wake of complaints came measures to suppress acoustic annoyance. There had been a 'Nuisance Assize' as far back as 1378 that occasionally ruled on noisy trades (Cockayne 2007: 115), but legislation regarding noise nuisance and its enforcement increased from the late sixteenth century, reflecting the acoustic problems created by growing urban congestion. *The Lawes of the Market* of 1595 ruled against 'affray, or beating hys Wife, or servant, or singing, or revyling in his house, in the Disturbance of his neighbours' after 9 pm; in 1610, a second-floor room for dancing instruction was forbidden such use between 2 and 5 pm; 1638, six alehouse keepers appeared before the Worcester Sessions of the Peace for noise that disturbed the neighbours at night (Cockayne 2007: 115, 116). In 1744, parishioners from Clerkenwell called for action against a number of local disorderly houses, each holding up to 500 patrons, sometimes until 4 am, and upon departing they 'frequently assembled in bodies, hallowing and knocking on doors, ringing bells and singing obscene songs' (Cockayne 2007: 117). In an increasingly literate urban society, street criers were first regulated by license in 1697 (Cockayne 2007: 126).

In all these complaints and associated legislation, we hear the consolidation of another dynamic particularly pertinent to my argument: the connection between public noise, disorder and vulgarity, a confrontation between the genteel sensibilities of a growing urban middle class and the culture of an urban proletariat. The period covered brought a

> clash of urban lifestyles and the increasing concern among the professional classes to control the sound environment saw attempts to take music off the streets and to place it indoors. ... It highlighted a growing gulf between polite and low society.
>
> Cockayne 2007: 124

It was the acoustic world of the poorest citizens that attracted the most complaints: street musicians with home-made or out of tune instruments, peripatetic traders like tinkers, alehouse drunks. In the early seventeenth century, Nicholas Breton noted that 'the cry of the poore is unpleasing to the rich' (Cockayne 2007: 126). And it was 'the rich' who were best placed to suppress these disagreeable sounds. Through the nineteenth century, the 'fight over rights to the soundscape, in keeping with the period, was a class struggle' (Blesser and Salter 2007: 106). As Picker's detailed study of the Victorian soundscape so comprehensively documents, those who complained most vociferously shared their privileged positions of entitlement and literacy with the authorities whom they petitioned against noise pollution. They were also able to afford various forms of acoustic insulation in the rebuilding that followed the great fire, when 'The Act for the Rebuilding of the City of London' (1667) made various stipulations about the construction of houses. The installation of glazing, panelling, draperies, the choice of building materials, of where they placed servants' quarters and access points, enabled the wealthy to construct a soundscape that increased their acoustic distance from the poor, preserving the peace and quiet in which they could read, reflect, entertain and attend to business (see further Cockayne 2007: 118–130).

There are several patterns here relating to the politicization of sound. The rise of print is connected with the ascendancy of the capitalist bourgeoisie, for whom the printed word in myriad forms is an essential embodiment of a capitalist hegemony. Confronting this network is an alternative information economy which is primarily sonic, a potential challenge to the print-based regime, especially as the labouring underclasses grow with urban industrialization. Acoustic regulation and silence signify approved social order, self-improvement, refinement and decorum; unregulated sound – noise – is a marker of plebeian vulgarity and potential social disorder. As we shall explore in more detail, the problem of sonic pollution is becoming an increasing nuisance not only because of growing urban congestion, to the changing soundscape, but also of the growing, literate urban bourgeoisie to whom noise is offensively vulgar. That trajectory will continue to rise throughout the nineteenth century, but will be intersected by another, as the profits from industrialization and the advent of sound technologies complicate the politics of sound.

Notes

1 By no means coincidentally, a process unfolded in parallel with this whereby particular speech habits and accents became markers of social differentiation (see Fox 2000: 101–109).
2 The information on Sheppard above and below and on executions in England is extrapolated from a range of sources, most notably Linebaugh 2006: 7–41; Brooke and Brandon 2005: 123–127; Linnane 2004: 9–17; Gatrell 1994. They do not always concur on factual material, but I have drawn only upon matters of agreement.

3 Much of the following account of the silencing of the underclasses is developed and adapted from Johnson and Cloonan 2008: 37–47.
4 The following account is set out in more detail in Johnson 2017.
5 The following account of Elizabethan street music is based on familiar and well-established texts, as exemplified by Scholes 1980: 986–990.
6 William Wordsworth, 'Composed upon Westminster Bridge, September 3, 1802': 214. All citations from Wordsworth are from the Oxford University Press 1959 edition.

Reading

Babington, Anthony. 1971. *The English Bastille: A History of Newgate Gaol and Prison Conditions in Britain 1188–1902*. London: Macdonald.
Blesser, Barry and Linda-Ruth Salter. 2007. *Spaces Speak, Are You Listening? Experiencing Aural Architecture*. Cambridge, MA and London: The MIT Press.
Brooke, Alan and David Brandon. 2005 (first pub 2004). *Tyburn: London's Fatal Tree*. Stroud Gloucestershire: Sutton.
Buxton, John. 1964. *Elizabethan Taste*. New York, NY: St Martin's Press.
Cockayne, Emily. 2007. *Hubbub: Filth, Noise & Stench in England 1600–1770*. New Haven, CT and London: Yale University Press.
Cyriax, Oliver. 1996. *The Penguin Encyclopedia of Crime*. Harmondsworth Middlesex: Penguin.
Fox, Adam. 2000. *Oral and Literate Culture in England 1500–1700*. Oxford: Clarendon Press.
Gaskell, Elizabeth. 1996 (first pub. 1848). *Mary Barton*. London: Everyman.
Gatrell, V.A.C. 1994. *The Hanging Tree: Execution and the English People 1770–1868*. Oxford: Oxford University Press.
Gouk, Penelope. 1999. *Music, Science and Natural Magic in Seventeenth-Century England*. New Haven, CT and London: Yale University Press.
Johnson, Bruce. 2006. 'Divided Loyalties: Literary Responses to the Rise of Oral Authority in the Modern Era'. *Textus,*, XIX (Spring): 285–304.
Johnson, Bruce. 2017 'From Music to Noise: The Decline of Street Music'. *Nineteenth-Century Music Review*, 15: 67–78. DOI: https://doi.org/10.1017/S147940981700009X published online: 06 February 2017: https://www.cambridge.org/core/journals/nineteenth-century-music-review/article/from-music-to-noise-the-decline-of-street-music/690653B23B54ABF8080362CBCD208A52
Johnson, Bruce and Martin Cloonan. 2008. *Dark Side of the Tune: Popular Music and Violence*. Aldershot: Ashgate.
Johnson, James H. 1995. *Listening in Paris: A Cultural History*. Berkeley, Los Angeles, CA and London: University of California Press.
Kasson, John F. 1990. *Rudeness and Civility: Manners in Nineteenth Century Urban America*. New York, NY: Hill and Wang.
Kernan, Alvin. 1989. *Samuel Johnson and the Impact of Print*. Princeton, NJ: Princeton University Press. Originally published as *Printing Technology, Letters, and Samuel Johnson*, 1987, same publisher.
Levine, Lawrence W. 1988. *Highbrow/Lowbrow: The Emergence of Cultural Hierarchy in America*. Cambridge, MA: Harvard University Press.
Linebaugh, Peter. 2006. *The London Hanged: Crime and Civil Society in the Eighteenth Century*. Second edition. London and New York, NY: Verso. First edition 2003.

Linnane, Fergus. 2004. *London's Underworld: Three Centuries of Vice and Crime*. London: Robson Books.
Müller, Sven Oliver. 2017 (first pub 2014). 'The Invention of Silence: Audience Behavior in Berlin and London in the Nineteenth Century'. In Daniel Morat (ed), *Sounds of Modern History: Auditory Cultures in 19th- and 20th-Century Europe*. New York, NY Oxford: Berghahn: 153–174.
Parvulescu, Anca. 2005. 'The Sound of Laughter'. *ASCA Conference Sonic Interventions: Pushing the Boundaries of Cultural Analysis, Reader for Panel 2: The Sonic in the 'Silent' Arts and Bring in the Noise*, Coordinator: Sylvia Mieszkowski: 117–119.
Pettegree, Andrew and Arthur Der Weduwen. 2021. *The Library: A Fragile History*. London: Profile Books.
Picker, John. 2003. *Victorian Soundscapes*. New York, NY: Oxford University Press.
Scholes, Percy A. 1980. *The Oxford Companion to Music*. 7th reprint ed. John Owen Ward (ed). London: Oxford University Press.
Schwartz, Hillel. 2011. *Making Noise: From Babel to the Big Bang & Beyond*. New York, NY: Zone Books.
Warner, Jessica. 2004. *John the Painter: The First Modern Terrorist*. London: Profile Books.
Wordsworth, William. 1959. *The Poetical Works*. London: Oxford University Press.

7
THE AURAL RENAISSANCE

Sound and modern technologies

For all its intensity and versatility, as a medium of social and political power, sound lacked one significant advantage enjoyed by print: the range of its circulation. The power of human utterance in particular was limited by its duration and the radius of 'earshot', so its power in any given situation was restricted to a few hundred yards. Print standardized commercial and legal discourses that underpinned international trade and politics and could mass-produce and circulate those discourses globally. We are now ready to ask this question: if sound is such an intensely powerful medium, but limited by 'earshot', what would then happen if its range and power were to be transformed by technology? And this is the question I now turn to.

As the industrial and technological revolutions from the late eighteenth to the nineteenth centuries gained momentum, a new soundscape also developed. Sounds never before heard were becoming so deeply embedded into the fabric of life and the circulation of information that we can begin to speak of an 'Aural Renaissance'. There were few sounds heard up to the late eighteenth century that would not have been familiar in antiquity, but subsequent developments introduced a soundscape that would have been unrecognizable even to the inhabitants of the most densely populated cities at the beginning of the early-modern period. We can think of these in two categories: the new technologies of sound storage and distribution, and the sounds of industrialization itself – technologized sonority and sonorous technology. The arrival of sound recording and then radio, amplification, portability and all the technologies that followed meant that sound could be preserved, stored and reproduced in infinite numbers of copies and circulated internationally on a mass level. In

DOI: 10.4324/9781003042662-8

due course, sound could also attain a volume and frequency range beyond the tolerance and capacities of the human ear and could be carried anywhere and delivered through a range of systems that almost anyone can now afford.

Technologized sonority

The use of mechanically enhanced sound goes back to antiquity, as in Greek theatre where the use of stage masks gave an otherworldly sound to actors' voices, and giant resonating vases, called 'echea' (Greek for 'sounders'), were used to amplify sound (Polychronopoulos et al. 2013). Later forerunners of loudspeakers included the Jesuit Athanasius Kircher's seventeenth-century proposal for enormous speaking trumpets (Schwartz 2011: 626). Apart from attempts at enhancement of natural sounds, mechanically generated sounding devices are equally ancient, evidence for which is to be found in the writing of the Greek Ctesibius (285–222 BC), who described his design for a mechanical singing bird (Chen et al. 2018: 273). Mechanical singing birds were only one of many pre-modern forms of automated sound, which included self-operating musical instruments (Leonardo da Vinci left sketches of automated drums), clocks with bells and drums and metal combs that foreshadowed the principle of the music box mechanism; these were driven by various means including clockwork, gravity and pullies, water and steam (see further Chen et al. 2018). And by the nineteenth century, as we have noted, mechanical hurdy-gurdies were so common in the streets of London that, far from attracting attention as a novelty, attempts were made to have them banned for disturbing the ponderings of 'brain workers'. Experiments in mechanically generated sound also included attempts to create machines which simulated the human voice, of which at least four such projects were being conducted in late eighteenth-century Europe (Schwartz 2011: 73).

None of these, however, would even begin to rival the outcomes and profound impact of the convergence of modern sound technology and information that gathered impetus throughout the nineteenth century. What that convergence added would be two of the main advantages that print had hitherto enjoyed over sound: range and storage. Probably the earliest form of sonic telegraphy was the use of 'talking drums' in, for example, Africa, Papua-New Guinea and tropical America, where European explorers were surprised to discover that their arrival had long before been announced as they slowly cut their way through barely penetrable jungle.

The range of information transmitted sonically was vastly extended with the advent of morse telegraphy from the 1830s. The first reference to the possibility of electric telegraphy was as early as a letter to the *Scot's Magazine* in 1753, but the first practical applications were in 1837 by William Cook and Charles Wheatstone, and in the same year by Samuel Morse, whose original patent application was for a visual readout system, whereby pressing the key would produce indentations on a tape, a system that was perfected by 1844

(Sterne 2003: 142, 144, 145). By the 1850s, rather than reading indentations on tape, 'listening to the telegraph became the favored method among operators'; the sound which had been a by-product of a visible medium had become its standard modality (Sterne 2003: 147). Like the talking drums, however, early morse telegraphy was in a sonic script that required a skilled decoder.

That specialized mediator was made superfluous by the advent of the telephone, the first conversation on which is usually given as taking place in 1876 between Thomas Watson and Alexander Graham Bell (whose father, Melville had inspired his son through his own experiments with 'speaking machines from the 1840s see further, Enns 2017: 52–57). Bell used a telephone to call his assistant Watson, downstairs: 'Mr. Watson – Come here – I want to see you'. This conversation did not become public knowledge until 1882, and in the meantime, the first public demonstration of the new technology was at the 1876 Philadelphia International Exposition in June (Sterne 2003: 247–248).

By then, the telephone was in global use both for person-to-person communication and in the form of the 'talking newspaper', a term that proclaims the shift from the visual to the aural, a forerunner of radio, providing news and entertainment from the late nineteenth century (Erhardt 2016: 105–107). The massive popularity of the telephone made it the subject of vigorous competition for patents until the Bell Telephone System 'absorbed its competitors, purchased the equipment manufacturer Western Electric, and eventually became the monopoly known as the American Telephone and Telegraph Company' (Thompson 2004: 91). Although originally a male profession, tele-operation became dominated by women, for various reasons including that not only they were cheaper to employ but also they were regarded as temperamentally better suited, with a 'quick ear', good at fine motions and had more soothing voices (Schwartz 2011: 329). The gender balance in switchboard telegraphy was so strong as to have given rise to the colloquial professional category of 'Hello girls', an early example of the complicity of gender and modern communications technology, to be taken up further below.

Much of this infrastructure gave way to other forms with the arrival of wire-less/wireless telegraphy that laid the foundations for radio transmission. Guglielmo Marconi began experimenting with Hertzian waves to transmit messages without the wires that were essential to earlier forms of electrical telegraphy and by 1901 he was able to achieve trans-Atlantic transmission. The potential benefits of wireless radio transmission were given wide publicity by the role it played in rescuing survivors of the sinking of the *Titanic* (1912) and the *Lusitania* (1915). The path to the development of the more general use of the technology was then opened when David Sarnoff, later to found RCA, sent a memo to the Marconi company in 1915 outlining the possibilities of domestic radio (Bodanis 2006: 113).

Among the significant developments presented by wireless is that, rather than one to one encoded communication by wire, radio waves could *broadcast* sounds that did not require specialist decoding knowledge, making it a major technology of mass communications, with a profound impact on the public imagination. In the wake of the slaughter of World War I and the accompanying interest in spiritualism, it was even speculated that 'the radio would eventually allow for communication with the dead since it picks up vibrations in the ether and the dead "simply vibrate at a slower rate than the living"'(Sterne 2003: 289).

There was an ancient tradition associating contact with other worlds with sound. In the Bible, messages from divinity are almost without exception communicated by voice (excepting for Exodus 33:20-23, when God declares to Moses that while no man may see His face and live, He will reveal His 'back parts'). In ancient Egypt, ghosts entered into human consciousness through the ear (see further Finkel 2022). The voices of the dead were also implicated with the other category of sonic technologies emerging in the late nineteenth century: sound recordings, which made the connection literal. While radio telegraphy increased the range of sonic transmissions, the sound recording enabled the unprecedented direct storage of sound, preserving sounds beyond the lifespan of their sources. The dead could now speak. In 1890, on the first anniversary of the death of poet Robert Browning, the London Browning Society gathered to listen to a cylinder recording of him reading his poetry, to the chagrin of his sister, who described it as an 'indecent séance … Poor Robert's dead voice to be made interesting amusement … God forgive them all. I find it difficult'. The event was publicized as 'the actual voice of a dead man' (Picker 2017: 35).

Like radio, the earliest devices for recording and storing sounds were far narrower in their application than later became the case. In the 1840s, Carl Ludwig invented the kymograph, which was able to inscribe vibrations with a stylus on a revolving cylinder; its primary function was to record such bodily processes as blood and lung pressure, and shortly thereafter the imprint from a vibrating tuning fork was added to the inscription to indicate the speed of the turning cylinder (Kursell 2012: 179–180). The purpose of the Kymograph was not only to produce a recording for sonic playback but also to transduce sounds into a visual form for medical diagnosis. Likewise, the earliest recordings of the human voice, on a device called the phonautograph, were invented in 1857 by Édouard-léon Scott de Mandeville. Like its predecessor, it transcribed sound into visible tracings on a surface like paper, and was never intended to be played back as sound. As such, this innovation in the recording of sound was a further example of the visual bias that we have traced in earlier chapters. It was intended to be seen rather than heard, part of the 'boom in nineteenth century devices that rendered visible the otherwise invisible aspects of the natural world' in the belief that 'to see sound was better to know it' (Sterne and Akiyama 2012: 546). Even so, with the development of appropriate technology, the sound of the phonautograph was retrieved in 2008, and we can now enjoy the rather eerie experience of hearing a voice from 1860 of a man whose life overlapped with Napoleon's at, for example, https://www.youtube.com/watch?v=YABES_D9xfE (accessed 14 July 2021).

It is, however, the patent taken out on sound recordings, first demonstrated in 1877 and patented in 1878 (Sterne and Akiyama 2012: 544), which marks the moment, unprecedented in human history, at which sound, notably music and voice, could be stored, played back and circulated without symbolic mediation (such as in a score or morse code): that is, that sound could be detached from its source and experienced repeatedly beyond 'earshot'. The sound recording thus represented two revolutionary advances over the earlier technologies we have noted. Unlike morse and telephone, it both directly rather than symbolically transmitted as well as stored sounds. It also formed the foundation for most if not all subsequent sound media. Without the means to record and store sound in some form, there would have been no growth in the musical repertoire of radio, no film soundtrack, no television, no Walkman, iPod and internet music shareware. It was in its recorded form that sound thus began to emerge as a potential equivalent site of power as print.

The earliest form taken by the sound recording was cylindrical, echoing the kymograph and the phonautograph, but now providing audible playback; Bell heard his own words, 'Mary had a little lamb', from a cylinder in 1878. These early sound recording devices had the double function of being able both to record and to playback, and in fact sometimes this is the distinction drawn between a phonograph and the gramophone, which was only a playback device (Sterne 2003: 303; Gauß 2017: 78). Because the phonograph could thus function like a dictaphone, Edison originally conceived it as an office accessory, and while Emil Berliner saw its future of playback in entertainment, Edison disapproved of the use of the technology as a public and domestic amenity, signalled with the advent of coin-in-the-slot music machines in 1890 (Gauß 2017: 77). These were installed in various public venues like hotel lobbies and train stations, forerunners of what from the late 1920s became known as the jukebox (Sterne 2003: 201). Credit for the invention of what became the standard physical format of the sound recording – the gramophone disc – is usually accorded to Emil Berliner in 1888, a choice at least in part dictated by his wish to avoid appearing to violate existing patents on cylindrical recordings (Sterne 2003: 77). First marketed in 1895, they also enjoyed the very significant advantage over cylinders of using masters that could be mass produced (Sterne 2003: 203).

The sound recording conferred a new status on sonic information, which, since the advent of print, had been demeaned through such terms as 'rumour', 'gossip' and 'hearsay'. The shift was reflected during the trial of famous US attorney Clarence Darrow who, in 1912 was charged with perjury and attempting to bribe a juror. An officer of the National Erectors' Association (aligned with the prosecution) was interviewed by a reporter for Hearst's *Examiner*. Among all the matters that could have been headlined, and the general text of the interview, the headline sentence was: 'I shall convict Darrow with my dictaphone' (Stone 1961: 197). The sound recording not only enabled sound to be circulated as widely as print, but to become as permanent a record, with authority as evidence in the court of law.

With radio and the mass production and circulation of sound recordings, the role of sound in relations of power was globally expanded. With the increasing diversification and sophistication of acoustic technologies, the voice became an instrument of power that outflanked a medium based on the specialized skills of reading, and the ear again challenged the eye as the source of information. The case of radio amplifies the point. Coming into general public use in anglophone societies through the 1920s, already by 1931, a radio was owned by fifty per cent of urban families in the US where, by 1940, radio news had overtaken the press as the primary source of information and political news (Cashman 1989: 320, 334, 336). The importance of radio to political debate changed the personal profile of the successful politician. During the US elections of 1928, Democrat candidate Al Smith lost to Herbert Hoover, in spite of the fact that in person, Smith was by far the more visually arresting speaker than his stolid opponent. One reason was radio. Smith

> … could not be persuaded to stand still before a radio microphone and the effect of his voice, with its pronounced East Side accent, moving in and out of earshot, was grotesque and his words unintelligible to many in the South and West. By comparison, Hoover, who was a dull speaker, disciplined himself to talk directly into the microphone, have his shyness mistaken for modesty, and give a general impression of Midwestern sobriety.
>
> Cashman 1989: 107

It is likely that Orson Welles' notorious 1938 radio broadcast of *War of the Worlds* would not have had the impact it did, were it not for the authority in disaster reportage gained from the broadcast of the Hindenburg disaster in the previous year; indeed, Welles made the actor playing the role of the reporter repeatedly listen to Herbert Morrison's emotional report of the destruction of the Hindenburg as a model for his accounts of the invasion (Rankin 2008: 421). The power of radio was recognized by the more far-seeing – or far-hearing – politicians. One of F.D. Roosevelt's first priorities on gaining office was to set up a committee of enquiry into the role of government in the regulation of wireless broadcasting, and he became one of the most effective pioneers of political broadcasting (Cashman 1989: 325, 336).

Finally, however, let us recognize the ambiguity of the power of the mediated voice. Roosevelt mobilized the energy of Americans against the Great Depression through his celebrated 'fireside chat' broadcasts. It is less easy to applaud the agenda of the great pioneer of twentieth-century vocalized demagoguery, Adolph Hitler. He first became aware of his own political destiny through his voice. He later wrote of how, as an education officer at a Reichswehr camp near Augsburg in 1919,

> ... all at once I was offered the opportunity of speaking before a large audience; and the thing that I had always presumed from pure feeling without knowing it was now corroborated; I could speak ... in the course of my lectures I led many hundreds, indeed, thousands, back to their people and fatherland. I 'nationalised' the troops.
>
> Kershaw 2001: 124

What makes Hitler so 'modern' is not simply his oratorical power, but, along with Goebbels, the effectiveness with which he grafted this to possibilities for mass mediation. In the elections of 1932, through technologized mobility – the aircraft – his energetic 'Hitler over Germany' schedule enabled him to deliver speeches personally across Germany (Kershaw 2001: 363, 364, 369). But it was *sound* technology that was crucial. Through sound film and the distribution of over 50,000 recordings of his 'Appeal to the Nation' speech, Hitler flooded the country with that disturbingly electrified and electrifying voice (Kershaw 2001: 369). Supplemented by rented *Lautsprecherwagons* – vans equipped with external loud speakers – to fill the streets with Nazi speeches and songs (Birdsall 2012: 39, 48, 74, 127–128, 137, 187 fn 33), his voice became the basis of his connection with the German people, and would reach an estimated twenty million citizens as acoustic theatre through the new facility of state radio (Kershaw 2001: 433, 440, 453). The careful stage management of these broadcasts explicitly politicized a paradox that crooners like Bing Crosby had stumbled upon: through the radio voice, it was possible to reconcile the mass with the individual, to speak to everyone as though speaking directly to each (Johnson 2000: 100–101). No one demonstrated more effectively than Hitler the re-uniting of sound and power in the era of modernity.

The shift in that balance was epitomized in the case of music, at the aesthetic apex of which was Western art music. This could only be circulated either by the very limited migration of its practitioners, or by a score, the impact of which was limited by class factors such as education. The case of jazz upended this dynamic. Within only months of what are regarded as its first recordings in 1917, it was being spoken of as far afield as Australia and by the early 1920s was being played around the world, the most rapid globalization of music in history (Johnson and Cloonan 2008: 58). Jazz was, in fact, so closely allied with the new technology as to be implicitly equated with it: an advertisement for the Melola record player in the Australian journal *Graphic*, 20 January 1921, declared its product to be 'as effective as a full jazz band' (Johnson 2000: 9). Jazz emanated from the US (it was later referred to as America's 'secret sonic weapon') and was circulated through a technology largely controlled by the US. The invention of the sound recording thus made of music a literal instrument of global imperialism. In the way they impacted materially on the production, circulation and consumption of music, sound technologies enlarged the range of sound as an instrument of power, and through, for example, digitization, altered the nature of its capabilities. These material changes redefined the ways in which sound and music could be deployed in confrontations over place, identity, class, territory and community.

The subsequent history of recorded sound is marked by an increasing breadth of application and the pursuit of playback quality. Regarding the former, apart from the jukebox, recorded sound is now ubiquitous, essential to radio, film, television, both in the home and in public spaces including background music in malls, restaurants, supermarkets and airports. Recording technology has saturated contemporary life to the extent that I suggest it was not mere hyperbole when I referred above to the transduction of information into sound as marking an 'Aural Renaissance' in technology, culture and society from the late nineteenth century. This 'era' has also been characterized by a continuing development of the quality and character of recorded sound. The term 'fidelity' was first applied to recorded sound in 1878 (Sterne 2003: 221), and is implicit also in the HMV logo, in which it is suggested that a dog (itself an emblem of fidelity) appears to believe that it is actually hearing 'his master's voice'. A major milestone in the quest for sound fidelity was the invention of the 'audion' by Lee de Forest in 1906, which enabled the amplification of electrical signals without distortion, and was called by historian Hugh Aitken 'one of the pivotal inventions of the twentieth century' (Thompson 2004: 92). It opened the path to the successful transition from acoustic to electrical recording technology, and all that followed from the mid-1920s.

Sonorous technology

The modern soundscape was not only transformed by the technological processing of sounds, technologized sonority – radio, TV, record players – but also by the industrial revolution, which introduced a range of technologies that produced their own categories of sound, sonorous technologies. The locations of these sounds were both public and domestic. The former included industrial, military and everyday technologies such as motor vehicles, factory and construction site machinery, rail and air transport. And the domestic soundscape was transformed by the sounds of refrigerators, vacuum cleaners, alarm clocks, radios, washing machines and driers. Industrialization produced a greatly enlarged spectrum of sounds in terms of timbre, tempo and pitch, such as the sounds of electric lathes, internal combustion engines, machine guns and teletype machines, all of which operated a speed hitherto unimaginable. They also made the world louder. In the pre-industrial era, the loudest of everyday sounds were from the blacksmith's forge and church bells, both sonically dwarfed by natural sounds such as thunder. But post-industrialization, the loudest sounds are now human constructions – anthropogenic – including jack hammers, steam forges, mechanical presses and transport systems, especially aircraft.

As we have noted, throughout the early-modern period, urban spaces were rich with a distinctive range of noises, such as pedestrian conversation and the cries of street pedlars, and sounds related to the tools of craftsmen ranging from the grinding of blade sharpeners to various kinds of smithy. In the late sixteenth century, contemporary chronicler and antiquary William Camden reported that the streets of Birmingham were 'resounding with hammers and anvils, for most of them [the inhabitants of the streets] are Smiths', and still, one hundred and fifty years later, a German visitor observed that 'almost everyone is busy hammering, pounding, rubbing and chiselling' (Cockayne 2007: 7). As demand for copper goods increased in the eighteenth century, the constant hammering led to early reports of a form of what later became known as Boilermakers' Disease (Cockayne 2007: 110–112), later subsumed under the more general heading of industrial deafness (see further Schwartz 2011: 363–374).

The development of the steam engine, however, was a major forerunner of 'the shape of sounds to come'. Although various forms of rudimentary steam-driven engines were reported as far back as the first-century AD by the Greek engineer Hero of Alexandria, the first ones that could be deployed on a commercial scale began to appear from the early eighteenth century. Their efficiency was much increased when James Watt invented a separate condenser for a steam engine on which he took out a patent in 1769, a major step on the road to the industrial revolution. By the late eighteenth century, the contemporary soundscape had been transformed. The sonic profile of London at the end of the seventeenth century would have been recognizable to a citizen of ancient Rome, albeit amplified. But industrial technology – railways, rock borers, steam whistles, various forms of factory production, the building of iron ships – brought into existence an unprecedented soundscape and its meanings.

This transformation of the soundscape has been amply documented, and it also entered the literary imagination, most famously perhaps in the work of Charles Dickens. Trains were not the only source of the sound of the steam engine, however. The idyllic rural soundscape and its leisurely sense of time and pace to which Wordsworth had turned for auditory solace were transformed by farming machinery like steam-driven threshing machines, as is illustrated by comparing a pre-industrial account of harvesting with an industrialized version. Although both these examples are from the late nineteenth century, the first is drawn from Russia, and while the steam train (which ultimately kills the eponymous heroine) is a recurring feature of the novel, the country is still a basically feudal and pre-industrial rural economy. In Tolstoy's *Anna Karenina*, first published in book form in 1878, the enlightened

132 The aural renaissance

aristocratic land owner, Konstantin Dmitrievich Levin, Count Vronsky, wishes to embrace land reform and joins his muzhiks, his peasant workers, in the harvest.[1]

> Levin lost all awareness of time ... A change now began to take place in his work which gave him enormous pleasure. In the midst of his work, moments came to him when he forgot what he was doing and began to feel light (251).
>
> In this hottest time the mowing did not seem so hard to him. ... These were happy moments.
>
> ... And right after that came a blissfully slow walk with scythe in hand, during which he could wipe off the streaming sweat, fill his lungs with air, look at the whole stretched out line of mowers and at what was going on around him in the woods and fields (252).

The mowers continue mowing as the sun goes down and the dew begins to fall.

> The work was in full swing.
>
> Sliced down with a succulent sound and smelling of spice, the grass lay in high swaths. Crowding on all sides in the short swaths, their whetstone boxes clanking, to the noise of scythes clashing, of a whetstone swishing along a sharpening blade, and of merry shouts, the mowers urged each other on (255).

Before proceeding to our second example, it is useful to note certain features of this account. Although Vronsky finds the unaccustomed labour tiring, he also finds pleasure as it absorbs him completely. Its pace is determined by the capacities of a human collective in charge of their tools and in mutual consultation. Indeed, the work is punctuated by conversation, and 'merry shouts', audible in a pre-industrial soundscape consisting also of the noise of scythes and their rustling through the grass, the sharpening of blades and the clanking of whetstone boxes. It is helpful to 'audialize' this soundscape as we now turn to our other example.

This is also an account of harvesting, from Thomas Hardy's *Tess of the d'Urbervilles*, first published in 1891 (all citations are from the Macmillan edition of 1965). Like *Anna Karenina*, Hardy's novel is centred on a female protagonist in a time of significant change, but in this case the change is to industrialization. Much of the traditional rural culture and its sounds survive. The milkmaids in the local dairies, for example, often sing to encourage the cows to give milk (130). But the shift to a more secular modernity is penetrating even this remote rural region in southwest England. Tessa herself is described as expressing feelings 'which might have been called those of the age – the ache of modernism' (147). The tension between rural tradition and encroaching modernity is made explicit as Tessa and Angel deliver newly filled milk cans to the railway station, where 'Modern life stretched out its steam feeler to this point three or four times a day, touched the native existences, and quickly withdrew its feeler again, as if what it touched had been uncongenial' (214).

It is against this background that Hardy describes the harvest, pervaded by an instructively contrasting atmosphere and soundscape from Tolstoy's, for it will be dominated by a steam thresher owned, not by the farmer, but by a stranger who rents out his services throughout the region with his machine, an embodiment of alienation. The thresher itself is 'the red tyrant that the women had come to serve … a despotic demand upon the endurance of their muscles and nerves', and its operator 'was in the agricultural world but not of it. He served fire and smoke' (365, 366).

It is now the steam-driven thresher that determines the pace of labour and dominates the soundscape, suppressing human conversation:

> the perspiring ones at the machine, including Tess, could not lighten their duties by the exchange of many words. It was the ceaselessness of the work which tried her so severely. … The hum of the thresher, which prevented speech, increased to a//raving whenever the supply of corn fell short of the regular quantity. … Tess and the man who fed could never turn their heads' (367//368).

The machine, 'the insatiable swallower' (374), and its sound dominate the harvesting. The workers are weary, aching and silenced as they try to keep up with the machine, and Tessa was 'shaken bodily by its spinning … The incessant quivering' reduced her to 'a stupefied reverie in which her arms worked on independently of her consciousness. She hardly knew where she was', and the workers become robotic, zombie-like slaves, 'cadaverous and saucer-eyed' (375).

The development of the steam engine over the eighteenth century would become one of the most pervasive auditory markers of the new industrial soundscape, and already the embodiment of one of its paradoxes. If industrial noise introduced a new form of pollution to the early-modern soundscape, it was simultaneously a signal of power and productivity (Thompson 2004: 120). The perceived link between industrial noise and power was so strong that James Watt had deliberately to increase the noise level of his steam engine (Schwartz 2011: 160). This recognition of the importance of the sonic environment in defining power relations recalls the history of reverberation, discussed above. The ambiguous status of industrial noise – both an overbearing sonic pollutant, yet a sign of power and capital – was inscribed in ubiquitous steam power, in such manifestations as the factory whistle, steam-driven machinery and the railways which enabled the rapid national distribution of commodities. As Tess and Angel leave the railway station after delivering the fresh milk, she reflects that the fruit of their labour will be consumed by total strangers throughout the country, who know nothing of those who produced it (215).

Apart from the railway system which carried Tess's produce beyond her ken, which depersonalized the relation between the producer and consumer of primary products, the steam engine became a ubiquitous source of grievance at industrial noise. In 1872, a complaint against the noise of a steam engine in a mill came before the courts under Lord Selborne (Cockayne 2007: 114). But, with its networks spreading rapidly across the land, the sound of trains was particularly intrusive. In the words of an unnamed writer in 1873:

> Whenever I arrive at, or depart from, the London Bridge terminus of the South-Eastern, and of the London, Brighton and South Coast railways, my ears are perpetually assailed – I might, without exaggeration, say pierced – by the short, sharp, sudden shriek of the steam-whistle, notifying the egress or ingress of a train. The sensation sends a pang through my nervous system; my teeth jar, and my hands involuntarily rise to my ears to deaden the excruciating sound.
>
> Mansell 2017a: 139

In relation to the ambiguous status of the sounds of modernity, referred to above, it is worth noting as an aside that, without these sonic shocks, the writer would not have habitually arrived from Brighton with anything like the same speed, ease and predictability; one innovation brought by the railways was the timetable.

Steam trains were just one of the more prominent elements in a growing array of previously unheard sounds and their unforeseen consequences emerging in the modern era. The modern noise problem can be distinguished by a constellation of sounds associated with industrialization and its related technologies, from the factory whistle to the electric streetcar, the honking of automobile horns, the increasing ubiquity of electrically and electronically amplified sounds, and from the early twentieth century, aircraft. The growing number of zoning laws, discussed in further detail below, responded to the distinctive character of modern industrial noise. The New York Department of Health used sanitary inspectors and co-opted a special unit of the police force, a 'health squad' that would be sent out to follow up on noise complaints. In 1912, they divided these into two categories, one of which, 'dogs, horses and animals', would have been familiar throughout the history of urbanization. The other, 'machinery, motor boats and pumps', reflected the distinctive profile of the modern soundscape (Thompson 2004: 127).

The Industrial Revolution brought noise that was both louder and in some cases so different in kind as to have been unimaginable in previous centuries, including, as mentioned above, machinery operating at hundreds of revolutions per minute. 'Flat line' sounds of technology have so widely proliferated that they now subliminally pervade domestic space, coming from refrigerators, air conditioners, light fittings, microwave ovens and computers. The industrial revolution disrupted traditional labour patterns and relations, not only economically, demographically and politically but also sonically, as factory sirens gained authority over the chiming of town clocks and church bells, and the rhythms of labour based on nature, such as sunrise and sunset.

In addition to the physiological phenomenon of industrial deafness, the soundscape of modernity also presented new threats to mental welfare. In 1869, George M. Beard identified a new affliction which he called neurasthenia, which he described as 'the most frequent, the most important, the most interesting nervous disease of our time' (Schwartz 2011: 282; see also Mansell 2017b: 282). He listed its causes as 'steam-power, the periodical press, the telegraph, the sciences, and the mental activity of women' (Schwartz 2011: 283). It is not clear what he meant by the last, but it was increasingly recognized that the noise of industrialized urbanization was potentially if not actually pathological in its effects. A writer in 1880 declared that 'The strongest man, after days spent amidst noise and clatter, longs for relief, though he may not know from what'. Noise is 'the most unnatural feature of modern life. In our cities and commercial towns the ear is never at rest' (Schwartz 2011: 307). And in the case of cities like New York, street noises were amplified by the resonating canyons of urban architecture; Boston physician Robert Hastings pointed out that 'these noises are intensified and repeated by the high walls which they strike and from which they rebound again and again' (Schwartz 2011: 309). This problem is further exacerbated by the fact that an increasing proportion of these reverberations is Low-Frequency Noise, which as we have remarked, generates distinctive pathologies. Their sources lie in a range of sound-generating features of everyday urban life, including fan and ventilation systems, compressors, pumps, traffic, factories and commercial premises, amplified music (Johnson 2009a: 189).

Given the interest here in the shifting relationship between the visual and the aural, it is relevant to note a parallel development from the nineteenth century in the conceptualization of sprawling urban space. As the city came to be increasingly identified with audibility, it also came to be regarded as illegible, as being impervious to visual comprehension. By the end of the nineteenth century, seventy-five percent of the population of England was urban, both by internal migration and national population increase (Williams 1973: 217). The number of houses in outer west London (Acton, Chiswick, Ealing, Hanwell) increased from fewer than three thousand in 1851 to more than thirty-three thousand by 1911 (Carey 1992: 46). The northern manufacturing industrial cities like Manchester, Leeds, Bradford, Birmingham and Liverpool, expanded at the greatest rate, between 1820 and 1850, and some by more than forty per cent in a decade (Williams 1973: 220). These cities were swelling beyond the capacity of 'visualization'. This last word applies figuratively and literally. Such cities stretched geographically and conceptually beyond the possibilities of panoramic representation (Carey 1992: 57–58). They were illegible cities. The modern city and its masses became unreadable, visual mysteries. Its alley ways and labyrinthine streets, its shadows, blind windows and blank brickwork, its inscrutable crowds, its sheer extent, make the city and its inhabitants unreadable. It is the scenario for Wordsworth's streets full of unreadable faces, Dickens's fogs, Stevenson's Jekyll and Hyde, Poe's illegible 'Man of the Crowd', Melville's (1987) inexplicable Bartleby, T.S. Eliot's 'unreal' city, and for the emerging detective narrative in which it takes the superhuman skill of Sherlock Holmes to 'read' people and places (see further Williams 1973: 58–60, 64, 70; Carey 1992: 32, 57–58, 94; Johnson 2009b). For ordinary mortals, the visible order becomes meaningless. In Elizabeth Gaskell's novel *Mary Barton*, the character John Barton looks at the crowds in the streets and is mystified:

> But he could not, you cannot read the lot of those who daily pass you by in the street. How do you know the wild romances of their lives; the trials, the temptations they are even now enduring, resisting, sinking under. You may be elbowed one instant by the girl desperate in her abandonment, laughing in mad merriment in her outward gesture, while her soul is longing for the rest of the dead, and bringing itself to think of the cold-flowing river as the only mercy of God remaining to her here. You may pass the criminal, meditating crimes at which you will tomorrow shudder with horror as you read them. You may push against one, humble and unnoticed, the last upon earth, who in Heaven will forever be in the immediate light of God's countenance. Errands of mercy – errands of sin – did you ever think where all the thousands of people you daily meet are bound?
>
> Gaskell 1996: 63

Visually, the city is incomprehensible. The city discloses itself sonically. The emerging shape of the modern is not spectral but acoustic (see further Johnson 2006). The impacts of the 'Aural Renaissance' from the late nineteenth century, however, were profoundly ambiguous in the way they transformed our relationship with sound.

World War I

All these changes converged in the soundscape of the cataclysm that both summarized political and technological developments throughout the nineteenth century, and foreshadowed their impact on the twentieth: the 'Great War' of 1914–1918. The conflict brought with it a new sensory hierarchy, a new soundscape, new forms of acoustic alertness and new acoustic technologies. War has always been an arena of acoustic mayhem, and versions of what later became known as 'shell shock' were recorded as early as the Battle of Marston Moor in 1644 (Schwartz 2011: 66–67). The loudest sounds at the Battle of Waterloo were cannonades, described as deafening, but they did not drown out the sounds of men, animals and music. One soldier recalled the sound of fire from the British squares striking the enemy's cuirasses as 'the noise of a violent hailstorm beating on panes of glass' (Barbero 2005: 291). Those present also recall organic noises: the men preparing for battle like 'the distant murmur of the waves of the sea', cheering, shouts, shrieks of anger and pain, commands, music including drums, pipers in the squares. There was also the noise of horses – neighing, galloping and screaming when wounded (Keegan 2004: 141–142). Acoustically, this was warfare on a human scale, and as in ancient times, troops could still inspire their comrades on the battlefield with rallying cries and music.

But the volume of military technology was being remorselessly turned up. The experience of those serving in the US Civil War was often recorded and remembered in terms of acoustic violence: 'The thunder of cannon was awful' (Smith 2001: 202). The Battle of Gettysburg, fought over three days in July 1863, was compared to an earthquake (Smith 2001: 309 note 28). A third of Union soldiers finished the war with hearing loss that, for the first time, was recognized as a service-related disability. A doctor who treated Union infantryman Dixon Irwin reported symptoms that foreshadow shell shock of World War I; 'Whenever he spoke of the cause of his trouble he said it was the constant roar of the guns in the service' (Keizer 2010: 110). Similar reports came out of the Boer War (Schwartz 2011: 559), but it was the acoustics of World War I that gave birth to the actual term 'shell shock', first proposed by Charles Myers, of the Royal Army Medical Corps in France, in 1915 (Schwartz 2011: 571).

Even so, and notwithstanding the overwhelming noise of the US Civil War, it remained, in the words of Mark Smith 'premodern' (Smith 2001: 200). It is the sound of modern technologized violence that pervades the traumatized accounts of the participants in World War I. All branches of the military were affected by the sounds of military modernity, even beneath the sea; German submarine crews complained of the 'nightmare' of a fourteen-day patrol, oppressed by 'alarms, sounds of explosions, depth charges, and propellor noises' (Jean 2012: 55). But it was the land battles that produced the most widespread sonic trauma. We have read the testimony of Rowland Feilding who, after watching silent film footage of the Somme battle, declared that the 'most unpleasant' part of the experience – the noise – was absent. Above all was the sound of artillery (much of the primary material on shell shock below is gathered together in Johnson and Cloonan 2008: 50–56; Schwartz 2011: 571–605).

War diaries and memoirs are pervaded by horrified recollections of the overpowering noise of modern military technology. Rowland Feilding wrote of the opening barrage on 1 July:

> Between 6.30 and 7.30 a.m. our bombardment was intensified. Major Watkins, a Coldstream officer, told me that on his corps frontage alone (about 3,600 yards), 42,000 shells were sent over by our artillery in sixty-five minutes, or nearly 650 shells per minute. I hear we have 360 guns on this sector, including 8-inch, 12-inch, and 15-inch howitzers'.
>
> Foley and McCartney 2006: 70

This massive weight of ordinance was accompanied by a hitherto unimaginable acoustic profile. 'It was rapid fire by every gun and noise was like hell let loose. As the shells passed over our heads the air hummed like a swarm of a hundred million hornets' (Foley and McCartney 2006: 72). At Ypres in 1915, an infantryman described a 420 mm shell as: 'such a sound as one might hear if hanging by the arms from a high railway trestle while an express train passed at full speed overhead, its emergency brakes set and all wheels locked'; an English Captain described a bombardment 'as if on some overhead platform ten thousand carters were tipping loads of pointed steel bricks that burst in the air, all with a fiendish, devastating, ear-splitting roar' (Schwartz 2011: 572). Author and poet Robert Graves of the Royal Welch Fusiliers: 'you can't communicate noise, noise never stopped for one moment – ever'; and fellow writer Guy Thorne: 'After months of blood and mud, hunger and cold, [it was] noise which thrust itself between the skull and brain and bear out thought' (Schwartz 2011: 572, 573). A Canadian at Vimy Ridge reported: 'I felt that if I lifted a finger I should touch a solid ceiling of sound, it now had the attribute of solidity' (Schwartz 2011: 577). During the sustained bombardment at Verdun 'the men of a crack French unit were weeping; not that they had been hit or hurt, but the sound had gotten to them, a vortex of concussed air that shook them to their depths, as if caught up in a "loudening tornado"' (Schwartz 2011: 577).

It was the magnitude and remorselessness of this new regime of noise that had the most profound impact on mind and body. Of the opening of the German offensive in March 1918, an officer in the British front line wrote, 'Think of the loudest clap of thunder you have ever heard, then imagine what it would be like if it continued without stopping. That was the noise that woke us on Thursday, 21 March. I have never before or since heard anything like it'; even deep in a dugout well behind the front, another officer 'awoke with a tremendous start, conscious of noise, incessant and almost musical, so intense that it seemed as if a hundred devils were hammering in my brain. Everything seemed to be vibrating – the ground, my dugout, my bed' (Holmes 2005: 405). Because of the all-enveloping nature of sound, both sides in the conflict were equally victims. From the German side at the Somme, from Ernst Jünger: 'There was nothing but one terrific tornado of noise ... Head and ears ached violently, and we could only make ourselves understood by shouting a word at a time. The power of logical thought and the force of gravity seemed alike to be suspended. ... A N.C.O. of No. 3 platoon went mad' (Schwartz 2011: 572–573). Sound itself is the adversary, attacking both body and mind. The sounds were typically described as organically destructive: 'The noise was terrific, one's ear-drums felt as though they would burst, when, by chance, we passed close to a battery, firing rapid. We staggered like drunkards with the concussion' (Foley and McCartney 2006: 71). The 'sonic effect' was part of an interconnected array of potentially lethal factors, including 'over-pressures or vacuums in the body's organs, rupturing the lungs and producing haemorrhages in the brain and spinal cord', with fatal effects (Keegan 2004: 264).

As discussed earlier, the distinction between organic and cognitive distress generated by sound is an uncertain one. This ambiguity underpinned continuing debate among the medical profession as to whether shell shock was 'neurological, somatic or psychosomatic' (Schwartz 2011: 581). Exposed for the first time to the sound of the barrage, young men wept: 'They cried and one kept calling "mother" and who could blame him, such HELL makes weaklings of the strongest and no human nerves or body were ever built to stand such torture, noise, horror and mental pain' (Holmes 2005: 66). At Third Ypres in 1917, a patient in a hospital marquee which had a shell-shock ward, reported the effect of the continuing sound of the bombardments:

> The bombs were very near, and in the ward I was in some of the patients went berserk. They were very, very bad cases of shellshock, much worse than I was, and two of them in particular got up and ran amok in the ward with their hands over their heads, screaming and screaming and screaming. It was shocking as it was all in the dark, for they'd had to put the lights out because of the air raid, and they were charging around banging into things and this dreadful screaming going on all the time.
> Macdonald 1993:158–159

The effect of the continuous noise of barrages was to obliterate identity, to render human sonority meaningless, reducing human scale to the infinitesimal. The 'shrapnel and high explosives were falling so fast you could hardly hear yourself speak'; 'You couldn't speak, the gunfire was so terrific'; if a soldier fell into the mud, 'There was no good shouting for help because there was so much racket going on and shells bursting all around that no one would have heard you' (Johnson and Cloonan 2008: 54).

The war was experienced and remembered as an acoustic phenomenon, and not surprisingly the truce of 11 November 1918 was most strikingly recalled as the end of noise, as in the words of a Captain Charles Douie, '... a soldier's abiding memory of the armistice was of silence free from gunfire; another soldier wrote, 'To me, the most remarkable feature of that day and night was the uncanny silence that pervaded ... No rumbling of guns, no staccato of machine guns, nor did the roar of exploding dumps break into the night as it had so often done. The war was over' (Johnson and Cloonan 2008: 54–55).

Even as it deafened and drove men mad, the war brought new kinds of attentiveness to sound. Ernst Jünger recorded in his diary that 'When you have been in the field long enough, then you get to know all kinds of strange noises. Experience is important in this respect; you learn to distinguish who has fired, where it went, what sort of projectile it was, etc. Even the rifle bullets that can be heard whistling through the air and the artillery shot that thunders into the ear from a long way can tell a lot' (Volmar 2017: 252, fn 38). In the post-war period, accounts of the soundscape were published, as in the collection in 1925 by Dietrich Behrens and Magdalene Karstien, *Geschütz und und Geschosslaute im Weltkrieg* (*Noises of Shells and Projectiles in the World War*), and Ernst Jünger, referred to above, created an extensive acoustic inventory in *Geräusche der Projektile* (*Sounds of the Projectiles*) (Volmar 2017: 237).

Paradoxically, as the 'sonorous technologies' were inflicting irreparable damage to frontline soldiers, at the other end of the sonic spectrum, the war was awakening increased acoustic alertness through developments in 'technologized sonority' that were driving new listening practices and awareness. Apart from the surprising number of record players that soldiers lugged into the trenches for entertainment, the modern topographies and technologies of war, such as static trench lines and massive artillery barrages, changed the sensory balance of battle. In the desolate, defoliated landscapes of the Western Front trench lines extending nearly five hundred miles from the English Channel to the Switzerland, concealment became a basic tactic for survival. As early as 1899, German military strategist Alfred von Schlieffen had predicted a wartime scenario in which 'the customary methods of visual orientation proved to be of only limited use'; Futurist spokesman Luigi Russolo made explicit the consequences for the balance between sight and sound in the year before the outbreak of the war that proved the point: 'In modern warfare, mechanical and metallic, the element of sight is almost zero. The sense, the significance, and the expressiveness of noises, however, are infinite' (Volmar 2017: 229, 238).

Thus, not only did the war introduce a new technologized soundscape, it also drove new forms and technologies of aural attentiveness. Research into wireless and telephone communications was driven by the reliance upon long range artillery for which visual location triangulation was of limited usefulness, and by the installation of 'listening posts' extending even into no man's land (Volmar 2017: 228, 232, 233). Other military listening devices included hydrophones for tracking submarine traffic, huge trumpet-shaped devices for locating aircraft (Jean 2012: 56; Volmar 2017: 234). At the same time, for sappers, a combination of sonic technologies and learned active listening was essential in the subterranean war for locating trench activity and placing massive mines. Stethoscopes were originally used, until the development of the sound detector, 'a microphone fitted in a solid metal casing, [which] transmits the sounds via cables to the telephone set' (Volmar 2017: 234).

By 1915/1916, radio technology had become an 'essential telecommunications method' during the war (Volmar 2017: 235), and by war's end, the sonic imagination was irrevocably transformed; there was a 'shift in the hierarchy of the senses' (Volmar 2017: 232). The war had added the noise of technology to the expressive repertoire of the modern condition. In the lead-up to the Passchendaele offensive, a soldier reported that one of his colleagues had developed

> ... an irritating habit of imitating the noise of approaching shells, a bellicose parlour trick which he had perfected to a fine art. He was doing it now as they trudged towards the line – as if there weren't enough shells coming over and noise going on without Alf joining in. 'Why don't you shut it just for a change?' said Tom wearily. 'Whizz-z-z-z-z-z BANG!' replied Alf'.
>
> Macdonald 1993: 38

This expressive tic is referred to as a 'bellicose parlour trick', disclosing the degree of internalization of such noise into the public imagination. After the First World War, we thought about sound in new ways. The 'Aural Renaissance' was multi-dimensional and ambiguous in its impact. It democratized not only access to music but also created a new threat to welfare. It changed attitudes to the dead (whose numbers had been violently increased by World War I), who could now be listened to. And it cast an enveloping acoustic shadow over the twentieth century.

Note

1 All citations are from the Penguin edition of 2006. Ideally, I would cite larger sections from pp. 251–255, but am unable to because of copyright constraints; likewise in the references to Hardy's *Tess of the d'Urbevilles* below.

Reading

Barbero, Alessandro. 2005. *The Battle: A History of the Battle of Waterloo* (trans. John Cullen). London: Atlantic Books.
Birdsall, Carolyn. 2012. *Nazi Soundscapes: Sound, Technology and Urban Space in Germany: 1933–1945*. Amsterdam: Amsterdam University Press.
Bodanis, David. 2006 (first pub 2005). *Electric Universe: How Electricity Switched On the Modern World*. London: Abacus.

Carey, John. 1992. *The Intellectuals and the Masses: Pride and Prejudice among the Literary Intelligentsia 1880–1939*. London and Boston, MA: Faber and Faber.

Cashman, Sean Dennis. 1989. *America in the Twenties and Thirties: The Olympian Age of Franklin Delano Roosevelt*. New York, NY and London: New York University Press.

Chen, Yu-Hsun, Marco Ceccarelli and Hong-Sen Yan (2018): 'A Historical Study and Mechanical Classification of Ancient Music-Playing automata'. *Mechanism and Machine Theory*, 121: 273–285, https://doi.org/10.1016/j.mechmachtheory.2017.10.015.

Cockayne, Emily. 2007. *Hubbub: Filth, Noise & Stench in England 1600–1770*. New Haven, CT and London: Yale University Press.

Enns, Anthony. 2017 (first pub 2014). 'The Human Telephone: Physiology, Neurology, and Sound Technologies'. In Daniel Morat (ed), *Sounds of Modern History: Auditory Cultures in 19th- and 20th-Century Europe*. New York, NY, Oxford: Berghahn: 46–68.

Erhardt, Christine. 2016 (first pub 2014). 'Phones, Horns, and "Audio Hoods" as Media of Attraction: Early Sound Histories in Vienna between 1833 and 1933'. In Daniel Morat (ed), *Sounds of Modern History: Auditory Cultures in 19th- and 20th-Century Europe*. New York, NY and Oxford: Berghahn: 101–125.

Finkel, Irving. 2022. *The First Ghosts: Most Ancient of Legacies*. Great Britain: Hodder and Stoughton.

Foley, Robert and Helen McCartney. 2006. *The Somme: an Eyewitness History*. London: The Folio Society.

Gaskell, Elizabeth. 1996 (first pub 1848). *Mary Barton: A Tale of Manchester Life*. London: Everyman.

Gauß, Stefan. 2017 (first pub 2014). 'Listening to the Horn: On the Cultural History of the Phonograph and the Gramophone'. In Daniel Morat (ed), *Sounds of Modern History: Auditory Cultures in 19th- and 20th-Century Europe*. New York, NY and Oxford: Berghahn: 71–100.

Hardy, Thomas. 1965 (first pub. In book form 1891). *Tess of the d'Urbevilles*. London: Macmillan & Co Ltd.

Holmes, Richard. 2005. *Tommy: The British Soldier on the Western Front 1914–1918*. London: Harper Perennial.

Jean, Yaron. 2012. 'The Sonic Mindedness of the Great War: Viewing History through Auditory Lenses'. In Feiereisen, Florence and Akexandra Merley Hill (eds), *Germany in the Loud Twentieth Century: An Introduction*. Oxford: Oxford University Press: 51–62.

Johnson, Bruce. 2000. *The Inaudible Music: Jazz, Gender and Australian Modernity*. Sydney: Currency Press.

Johnson, Bruce. 2006. 'Divided Loyalties: Literary Responses to the Rise of Oral Authority in the Modern Era'. *Textus*, XIX (Spring): 285–304.

Johnson, Bruce. 2009a. 'Low Frequency Noise and Urban Space'. *Popular Music History*, 4 2): 177–195.

Johnson, Bruce. 2009b. 'Sites of Sound'. *Oral Tradition*, 24 (2): 455–470.

Johnson, Bruce and Martin Cloonan. 2008. *Dark Side of the Tune: Popular Music and Violence*. Aldershot: Ashgate.

Keegan, John. 2004. *The Face of Battle: A Study of Agincourt, Waterloo and the Somme*. London: Pimlico.

Keizer, Garret. 2010. *The Unwanted Sound of Everything We Want: A Book About Noise*. New York, NY: Public Affairs.

Kershaw, Ian. 2001. *Hitler*. 2 Volumes. London: Penguin. first published 1998.

Kursell, Julia. 2012. 'A Gray Box: The Phonograph in Laboratory Experiments and Fieldwork, 1900–1920'. In Trevor Finch and Karen Bijsterveld (eds), *The Oxford Handbook of Sound Studies*. Oxford and New York, NY: Oxford University Press: 176–197.

Macdonald, Lyn. 1993 (first pub. 1978). *They Called it Passchendaele: The Story of the Third Battle of Ypres and of the Men who Fought in it*. Harmondsworth: Penguin.

Mansell, James G. 2017a. *The Age of Noise in Britain: Hearing Modernity*. Urbana, Chicago, IL and Springfield: University of Illinois Press.

Mansell, James G. 2017b (first pub 2014). 'Neurasthenia, Civilization, and the Sounds of Modern Life: Narratives of Nervous Illness in the Interwar Campaign against Noise'. In Daniel Morat (ed), *Sounds of Modern History: Auditory Cultures in 19th- and 20th-Century Europe*. New York, NY and Oxford: Berghahn: 278–302.

Melville, Herman. 1987. 'Bartleby, the Scrivener: A Story of Wall Street'. In Harrison Hayford, Hershel Parker, and G. Thomas Tanselle (eds), *The Piazza Tales, and Other Prose Pieces 1839–1860*, Vol. 9 of The Writings of Herman Melville. Evanston and Chicago, IL: Northwestern University Press and The Newberry Library.

Picker, John M. 2017 (first pub 2014). 'English Beat: The Stethoscopic Era's Sonic Traces'. In Daniel Morat (ed), *Sounds of Modern History: Auditory Cultures in 19th- and 20th-Century Europe*. New York, Oxford: Berghahn: 25–45.

Polychronopoulos, Spyros, Dimitris Kougias, Polykarpos Polykarpou and Dimitris Skarlatos. 2013. 'The Use of Resonators in Ancient Greek Theatres'. *Acta Acustica United with Acustica*, 99: 64–69.

Rankin, Nicholas. 2008. *Churchill's Wizards: The British Genius for Deception 1914–1945*. London: Faber and Faber.

Schwartz, Hillel. 2011. *Making Noise: From Babel to the Big Bang & Beyond*. New York, NY: Zone Books.

Smith, Mark M. 2001. *Listening to Nineteenth-Century America*. Chapel Hill, NC and London: University of North Carolina Press.

Sterne, Jonathan. 2003. *The Audible Past: Cultural Origins of Sound Reproduction*. Durham, NC and, London: Duke University Press.

Sterne, Jonathan and Mitchell Akiyama. 2012. 'The Recording That Never Wanted to Be Heard and Other Stories of Sonification'. In Trevor Finch and Karen Bijsterveld (eds), *The Oxford Handbook of Sound Studies*. Oxford and New York, NY: Oxford University Press: 544–560.

Stone, Irving. 1961. *Clarence Darrow for the Defense*. New York, NY: Doubleday.

Thompson, Emily. 2004. *The Soundscape of Modernity: Architectural Acoustics and the Culture of Listening in America, 1900–1933*. Cambridge, MA and London: MIT Press.

Tolstoy, Leo. 2006 (first pub in book form 1878). *Anna Karenina: A Novel in Eight Parts*. London: Penguin Books.

Volmar, Axel. 2017 (first pub 2014). 'In Storms of Steel: The Soundscape of World War I and its Impact on Auditory Media Culture during the Weimar Period'. In Daniel Morat (ed), *Sounds of Modern History: Auditory Cultures in 19th- and 20th-Century Europe*. New York, NY and Oxford: Berghahn: 227–255.

Williams, Raymond. 1973. *The Country and the City*. London: Chatto & Windus.

8
THE AURAL RENAISSANCE AND CULTURAL CHANGE

A new sonic imaginary

The soundscape of World War I identified a spectrum of auditory experience running from a new attentiveness to sonic nuance, to an unbearable sonic avalanche capable of destroying mind and body. This chapter takes as its point of departure the former – new forms and functions of listening – and traces their larger cultural implications. This will take us to unexpected places. Changes in the soundscape saturate every aspect of our material existence and the ways we use and understanding sound. The diversity of the cases we consider in this chapter is intended to illustrate that ubiquity. All the cases concern changes associated with modernity, and in spite of their heterogeneity, they are linked by the centrality of sound and how we understand it.

In an age of new sounds and sound technologies, it became necessary to cultivate new listening skills, what Sterne calls 'audile technique' (Sterne 2003: 96, 98; see also for example Blesser and Salter 2007: 103–105). As a formal science, acoustics emerged as 'a recognizably independent branch of natural philosophy in the course of the seventeenth century', notably in Newton's *Principia Mathematica* of 1687 (Gouk 1999: 157–158). Hermann von Helmholtz pioneered the scientific study of 'sympathetic vibration, or resonance, in *On the Sensations of Tone* in 1863' (Jasen 2017: 67). The subject of hearing as a distinct field of scientific study culminated in a 'new branch of medical science: otology (or ear medicine)' (Gouk 1999: 51). Although at first relatively marginalized, otology began to flourish through the second half of the nineteenth century (Gouk 1999: 55). Unsurprisingly, this coincided with the enlargement of the auditory realm, including 'the detection of sound waves both below and above the normal hearing ranges of humans – infra and ultrasounds' and

DOI: 10.4324/9781003042662-9

more recently 'capacities that stem from various computer processes' (Ihde 2007: xv).

It was not only the content of the new auditory realm that was studied; audition became a major method of study, perhaps most dramatically exemplified in the development of the instrument that has come to be emblematic of the physician: the most widely recognized image of a medical doctor is a man with a stethoscope. As noted above, in addition to ancient writers like Aristotle and Galen, since the fifteenth century the way to access knowledge of the human body had been for visual inspection. In 1816 Dr. René Théophile Hyancinthe Laennec listened to the noises of a body through a tube of paper, using what Régis Buisson had called 'active hearing', or auscultation (Schwartz 2011: 202, 206; see further 201–221). According to Picker, 'modern aurality begins with the stethoscope', and he cites Stanley Joel Reiser: 'The effects of the stethoscope on physicians were analogous to the effects of printing on Western culture' (Picker 2017: 26). The stethoscope 'gained acceptance in Britain and the United States over the second quarter of the nineteenth century' (Picker 2017: 26).

The sonic technologies we reviewed above – wireless telegraphy, telephone, sound recording, radio and the stethoscope – have both enabled and imposed new protocols of listening as well as new technologies for doing so. Electronics have made us aware that what were previously regarded as realms of silence are in fact sonically active, from the interstellar, with radio waves emanating from almost inconceivable distances, to the terrestrial, as in marine noises, such as whale song and the percussive sounds of shrimps as they click their claws together (Ihde 2007: 4; see further below). Between the macro and the micro there opened up what Thompson refers to as '"the listening habit"' as an important new element of ... "Modern life"'. In particular, at the everyday level, the development of the talkies in the 1920s, according to the journal *American Architect* in 1931 had made people 'sound conscious' (Thompson 2004: 247 and 401 fn. 56).

If the new forms of listening expanded some aspects of sonic experience, they reduced others. Experiments on the acoustics of performance spaces and the reduction of reverberation, discussed in Chapter One, focused attention on what one of the major figures in the later history of acoustics, Vern Knudsen, described as 'percent articulation', that is, the intelligibility of speech (Thompson 2004: 252). While this is obviously a primary criterion in such technologies as the telephone and the sound movie, it centralizes just one aspect of speech as the measure of effectiveness. I shall call this 'denotative intelligibility', by which I mean simply understanding what the uttered words mean; the telephone 'was subjected to the pursuit rather of intelligibility than expressivity' (Schwartz 2011: 700). As noted in the earlier discussion of reverberation, this does not take into account why there is such an ancient tradition of deliberately enhancing resonance in auditory 'performance' spaces, nor consider other possible aspects of music and speech that were so valued since antiquity. Archaeoacoustic studies have found that many megalithic structures have distinctive sonic 'signatures' that can be made audible by the voice or even the prevailing wind; they are in effect 'giant Helmholtz resonators', with dominant frequencies clustering around the range of 95–120 Hz. Early church organs were more important for their emotional impact than their specifically musical articulation, and intelligibility of the liturgical voice only became important as the language of the mass changed from Latin to the local vernacular, as late as the second Vatican Council in the 1960s (Jasen 2017: 111, 234 fn 165, 186–187; see further Cirillio and Martellotta 2006).

Knudsen's 'percent articulation' seeks to render the 'medium' invisible (or inaudible), that is to reduce 'noise' as a form of interference with the verbal content of a message. We don't want to hear the telephone, only the voice coming through it. New technologies also required new ways of discriminated or filtered listening that were specific to particular occupations and interests. Handbooks for car owners 'often included sections on how to listen to their cars' in order to identify and diagnose problems (Bijsterveld 2008: 77). Trained ears were required to monitor various forms of technology, such as factory machinery, and the importance of this specialized auditory alertness was one of the reasons factory workers tended to ignore medical advice to wear earplugs while operating noisy machinery (Bijsterveld 2008: 72, 80).

Such changes in listening habits, the soundscape and the meanings attached to it, have been particularly dramatic in rural areas where the process of modernization has been telescoped into short time spans, presenting a 'time-lapse' succession of sonic photographs. Finland provides useful case studies in the development of new listening habits because modernization arrived so late and rapidly, in many cases well within a single lifetime. In 1959, on 1,816 dairy farms working around 4,000 cows, there were only 73 mechanical milking machines and two milk coolers; within a decade the figures for 1,387 farms holding roughly the same number of stock were 325 and 191, respectively (Pöyskö 1994: 75). Other new technologized sounds in dairies were those of dung shifters and ventilators. The transformation of the soundscape required very different auditory attitudes to the new sounds of productivity, both on the part of the farmers and of the dairy cattle. The stress the animals initially experienced in the transition to milking machines was managed by a further change to the soundscape – that is, the introduction of music from radios – and the dairy farmers also had to attune their attitudes to the new sonic environment. The sound of the mechanical dung shifter, for example, was 'deafening', and yet one female farmer described it as a 'blessed noise' (Pöyskö 1994: 86).

The collision between pre-industrial and modern listening was documented by Canadian R. Murray Schafer and by Finnish researcher Helmi Järviluoma (now Järviluoma-Mäkelä) when she and her team revisited the villages studied by Schafer as recorded in his 1977 *Five Village Soundscapes*. One of the locations was Lesconil, a fishing village on the coast of Brittany, France.

The life of the village was particularly sensitive to 'an onshore-offshore wind cycle known as *les vents solaires*. These winds affected the acoustic horizon of the community and brought villagers vital information about the environment beyond' (Schafer et al. 1977/2009: 324). The sequence of sounds carried on *les vents solaires* defined the daily fishing rhythm central to the village economy and therefore 'the routine of the whole village' (Schafer et al. 1977/2009: 364). The pivot of daily life was the return of the fleet and the fish auction, signalled by two long air horn blasts. 'Once over, the villagers go home, and little evening activity occurs' (Schafer et al. 1977/2009: 326).

From the late twentieth century the definition of these rhythms by this pre-modern listening regime came under threat from the acoustics of modernity. The rising level of traffic noise from the highways outside the village, including motorized trucks carrying the catch to inland cities, threatened to drown out the acoustic nuances that had been listened to as a way of defining the diurnal cycle (Schafer et al. 1977/2009: 335, 391). When Järviluoma's research team was conducting their follow-up work over the years 1998–2000 and with subsequent visits (Järviluoma et al. 2009: 13), much of the soundscape recorded by Schafer decades earlier survived only in memory – of milking (177; all page numbers refer to Järviluoma et al. 2009), of the smithy, of street chatter (179), of horses' hooves and pedestrians' *sabots* on cobbles (181, 183) of the sounds of ship building (181). Many of these sounds were of activities now gone, or replaced and overwhelmed by motorized traffic (178). Such changes brought a new listening regime. During a visit in 2004, Järviluoma asked some of the remaining fishermen 'about this old habit of listening to the sounds brought by the wind – I asked if it still had an effect on whether they would go fishing or not – they said: "No, we listen to the weather forecast in the radio"' (Personal communication 27 October 2021).

The often unforeseeable complexity of the influence of modern sonorities both on what we hear and how we hear it can be demonstrated through a technology that is so taken for granted as to seem to be a simple and straightforward addition to the soundscape: sound recording. The relationship between recorded sound and the original was more complex than a simple model of acoustic reproduction discloses. It is widely understood that in the earliest acoustic recordings, changes had to be made to the music itself in order not to disrupt the technological process. Performers had to be grouped in certain ways around the recording bell, certain instruments had to be muted or even omitted or replaced (Gauß 2017: 80).

In the process, for those encountering music on recordings the understanding of what it sounded like did not in fact conform to the sound of live performance. Jazz, the first new music to be globally dispersed by recordings, is the pre-eminent example, particularly with regard to instrumentation. A banjo cut through on a recording better than the guitar that photographic evidence suggests was as widely used in early performance (see for example Keepnews and Grauer 1968: 6, 7, 14, 20). The drum kits had to be assembled and used with more discretion than in live performance so as not to throw the cutting needle out of its groove. And overall dynamic range was limited; when Australian audiences first heard the black US band Sonny Clay's Plantation Orchestra in 1928, reviewers were surprised to discover that jazz did not have to be noisy (Egan 2020: 158; see further on jazz recordings as interventionist rather than simply replicative Johnson 2020: 126–128).

Ironically, these adaptations to the recording process were conducted in the name of 'fidelity', which became the Holy Grail of recording technology. In the teens of the twentieth century the Edison company arranged 'demonstration recitals' in which a recorded performance would alternate with a live performance by the same performer, in order to demonstrate the fidelity of the recording; but the live performers 'were encouraged to conform their voices to match the sounds generated by the phonograph' (Hui 2017: 142). There are two striking features in these experiments which are particularly relevant to the arguments set forth here. One is that the singers were encouraged to adapt their performance to the sound of the recording rather than the reverse. The other relates to newly learned listening habits. Hearing, today, early acoustic recordings, it is scarcely credible that listeners could persuade themselves that they could not distinguish the live from the recorded versions. In persuading themselves of the fidelity of the phonograph recording, audiences developed a new listening habit, of simply blocking out the noise of the recording itself (Hui 2017: 146). Modern sonic technologies were changing our capacities for discrimination and our criteria for listening.

By the 1950s, that change in criteria had come full circle, particularly with the advent of stereophonic sound reproduction. The history of this recording technology dramatizes the point that the search for 'High Fidelity' to live performance entailed changes to the music itself, the listening habits of audiences and even domestic interior design. By 1931, musicians were composing and performing for recording rather than for live performance. Duke Ellington's composition 'Creole Rhapsody' was timed to occupy two sides of a ten inch 78 rpm disc. From the late 1920s, Ellington and Leopold Stokowski were among a growing cohort of musicians experimenting with stereo recording and – most pertinent just here – developing compositional and performance practices specifically adapted to these purposes. Recording 'Black Beauty' in 1927, Ellington discovered that microphones responded to some notes and tones with 'sympathetic vibrations', which he then went on to deliberately exploit in, for example, 'Mood Indigo' (see further Johnson 2000: 85–86).

Sound recordings were thus not simply frictionless conduits of music in live performance, but filters, enhancers and modifiers that changed listening habits and expectations. Recorded sound in many cases became the reference point for quality rather than the live original, generating new ways of listening and new expectations of what was heard. While early sound recordings proudly advertised the difficulty of distinguishing their output from the live music situation, advances in the technology produced a new sonic regime in which it was the recorded/playback sound that became fetishized. With the advent and steady improvement of recording technology, 'the parlor was, not an alternative to the concert hall, but rather the preferred listening space' (Blesser and Salter 2007: 113). A critic for the *New York Times* wrote of a Mantovani concert in Carnegie Hall in 1966, 'as the sumptuous sounds filled the auditorium you could almost close your eyes and imagine yourself back home listening to the hi-fi' (Lanza 2007: 85). And 'back home' itself was being materially transformed by the criterion of 'fidelity'. The development of high fidelity sound and stereo affected the spatial arrangement of the home and expectations of the soundscape and newly learned modes of listening (Peterson 2021: 142, 143, 145).

The changes in listening habits, expectations and functions of sound, however, were not simply related to changing criteria of fidelity. More broadly they reflected an intensified interest in sound itself, which in turn gave impetus and status to auditory evidence. It enabled and coincided with, for example, the more comprehensive development of anthropology, the study and preservation of cultures at risk of extinction, and the complementary establishment of sound archives (Sterne 2003: 311–325, 328–333). Bela Bartok discussed these advantages in his preface to *Romanian Folk Songs from Bihor County,* published in 1913, and in several essays on methods and problems in collecting folk songs (Hui 2017: 149 fn. 36). In Bartok's opinion, it was the ability to record and replay field material that made ethnomusicology into a scientific enterprise (Hui 2017: 140).

This supposedly ideology-neutral 'scientific enterprise', however, also points us towards the less obvious, but no less significant, political implications of the modern soundscape. An enormous proportion of early sound recording was devoted to, and therefore did much to encourage, the development of modern ethnomusicology and also broader public (mis)understandings of the so-called 'primitive' cultures, ranging from American-Indian to African, Asian and Oceanic. From Germany, for example, Beka-Record, established in 1903, recorded 1400 titles in Turkey, Egypt, India, Burma, Thailand, Java, Singapore and China, advertising material from these countries in its 1906 catalogues (Gronow 1996: 96). All this record production was in the hands of a few Anglo/US/European companies so virtually none of this massive catalogue was owned or controlled by the communities whose culture was being recorded. Germany produced ethnological recordings from Dahomey, but Dahomey never produced ethnological recordings of Germans. Western ethnographic sound recordings (later supplemented by film) thus established standards of 'authenticity' in the definition of the cultures of the 'Other'. In presentations by Western comparative musicologists much was made of authenticity, that the field recordings were uncontaminated by any outside, modern, influences, 'conserved pure and orthodox' (Garcia 2017: 90).

In fact, this conception of the authentic, uncontaminated 'Other' was increasingly misleading, ironically because the very sonic technologies that were recording the supposedly 'authentic' local sounds were also ensuring that few cultures escaped the influences of globalization. The idea of remote and therefore authentically uncontaminated music ignores the fact that even in, for example, 'out-of-the-way' Cuba, people bought 78 rpm records, watched Mexican films, listened to the radio and indeed often 'incorporated some of these tunes into their performances for anthropologists, folklorists and comparative musicologists' (Garcia 2017: 115).

Sound recordings thus played a political as well as a scientific role by setting the standards of 'authentic' folk cultures and at the same time locating them as primitive 'Other' and excluding them from modernity. This spilled over into commercial record production of 'exotic' music and their promotion through links between the 'commercial record industry and folklore, anthropology, and comparative musicology' (Garcia 2017: 111). Later supplemented by the imagery and notes on record covers, these links influenced ways of listening, or what Garcia calls 'listening dispositions', which encouraged the listener to hear the music (for example Cuban or Caribbean) as 'emanating from a distant and often dangerous place' (Garcia 2017: 80). In a parallel dynamic, African-American bands between the wars were deeply disappointed at not being given opportunities to record the waltzes and sweet non-jazz material that was in fact a significant component of their performance repertoire, because they were identified as exclusively jazz orchestras (Wald 2007: 135). The recording industry thus played a decisive role in shaping the perception of the identities of their subjects, as for example in the belief that 'only black musicians could play jazz and that black musicians could play only jazz' (Johnson 2020: 127). The modern soundscape invited particular ways of sounding and listening that helped politicize what might have appeared to be politically innocent projects. In the case of ethnomusicology, for example, it set up misleading standards of 'authenticity', with far-reaching consequences for the way 'the West' imagined and represented 'the Rest'.

We don't have to imaginatively travel to distant and exotic locations, however, to discover the way the modern soundscape transformed power relations between the dominant centre and the subordinate margins. This distinction pervades everyday life through such fields as ethnicity, generation, profession, physical location and gender. I want to conclude this exploration of the pervasive influence of modern sonicity by considering two cases of power dynamics in everyday life that are so taken for granted as to seem politically innocuous, yet which profoundly changed the politics of gender relations. As we have noted, the 'Aural Renaissance' could function to reinforce 'Otherness' and its exclusion from modernity. But it could also function to reverse power imbalances, and there are many ways in which this played out in gender relations, giving access to forms of cultural experience hitherto denied to those suffering various forms of marginalization including through socio-economic status and education, converging on the politics of gender.

To frame the outlines of the following argument, some context needs to be sketched. In broad terms, the impact of World War I was very different for the male and female populace. Apart from the pain of losing loved ones, for women, war brought considerable benefits, accelerating their entry into public space that had begun in the late nineteenth century. The male experience of modernity was most likely to be traumatic in the face of military technology and its soundscape. One in three British soldiers became casualties during the War, ranging from death to serious wounding. Those who returned were often maimed physically and even more so mentally and emotionally, suffering trauma leading to neurosis, alcoholism and social dysfunction. Modernity and its technologies as experienced by the millions of men at war was a profoundly negative experience. With fewer men and a smaller sperm bank, a larger number of women were competing for a reduced number of often now crippled and socially dysfunctional men. It changed the balance of sexual initiative, as in the Australian film from 1926, *Should a Girl Propose?* (now lost), the poster for which proclaimed: 'The modern girl jazzes, smokes, indulges in athletes [sic], enters law and politics, and, in short, does most things a man does, and in most things does better. WHY SHOULD SHE NOT PROPOSE?' (Pike and Cooper 1998: 131). This was just one of scores of post-war films that were plotted around the enlarged horizons now available to the 'modern girl'. In Australia, by 1921, more people went to movies than all other forms of theatre combined. And seventy per cent of those attending were women, enjoying a very high proportion of films centred on the expanded life-style possibilities for young women. These will take her into an imaginary realm that, like *The Sheik* (dir. George Melford from 1921), involves a massive expansion of sexual and erotic options and initiatives, of private and public agency.

Men returning from war, damaged and traumatized, were often radically politicized, but at another level generally nostalgic for the life they had left behind and fought for, to return to an Edwardian order. But women had been liberated by the technologies of modernity, which brought labour saving commodities. The spreading option of gas and electricity increasingly saved women the trouble of having to light a wood, coke or coal stove. Their new leisure time was further increased by access to an expanding range of cheap canned, powdered and otherwise preserved foods, so there was no need to go to market every day for fresh food. And, as the century unfolded, modern technologies announced themselves in a changing domestic soundscape. In 1889 Nobel Prize winner Bertha von Suttner wrote in 'Lectures from the Future':

> The prospects of the immediate future already offer a lot of pleasure: the phonograph, which records and reproduces both our words and our voices; the telephone, which broadcasts those same voices across vast distances ... indeed, all those marvelous valves and channels that carry everything imaginable into our homes
>
> Erhardt 2017: 101

All these 'marvelous' innovations she lists are sonic; this is a woman expressing gratification at technologies for providing 'pleasure', and its locus is the home. And with the twentieth century, the sounds of these recreational devices were augmented by others associated with domestic comfort and the saving of labour, including over time the often almost subliminal hum of refrigerators, washing machines, electric fans, air conditioners and fluorescent lights.

Apart from domestic life, her public and economic space has expanded with new employment possibilities. As noted below for example, the arrival of the telephone created a vast labour market for sections of society whose education in literacy might not be as well developed as men. As a woman, and especially a young one, she is a member of the biggest single consumer group of mass culture from the mid nineteenth century. An abundance of cheap mass-produced goods enabled her to buy, out of her own income, commodities, and services, and with electric/gas light, extra hours of leisure time to enjoy them. She could enjoy music on the new gramophone and the wireless; she could telephone friends to arrange social events.

In a collection republished in 1983 as *Backless Betty From Bondi* of poems he had written in the interwar period, Australian poet Kenneth Slessor's recognition of the 'New Woman' who emerged after World War I was summarized in a series of profiles that included cinema usherettes in 'Firefly' 6 (all page references to the collection cited), aviatrices ('Butterflies' 9 and 'The Moth and the Candle' 29) – a girl flying a Tiger Moth is compared to a moth, a frequent metaphor for the Modern Girl – modern nurses ('Nightingale 1930', 14); she outshines men in ski-ing ('Skis and Shes' 11), hiking ('She Keeps on Walking' 12) and surfing ('She Shoots to Conquer' 13). She travels ('Streamer's End' 17); she wears revealing lingerie ('Pantette' 31) and skimpy bathing costumes ('Backless Betty from Bondi' 32). In a particularly telling mixed metaphor in the present context, Slessor says of Backless Betty that 'her eyes are full of wireless' (32). 'Silence' (25) was an elegy for the rural soundscape, free of the sounds of banjos, ocarinas, popular music ('Blue Heaven') 'riff-raff with a phonograph', mandolins and steel guitars (25). And chief among the modern dance was the new American import, jazz. The association of the liberated young woman, the 'flapper', with jazz and jazz dancing was pervasive in social practice, in cinema, in lifestyle journals. Its loud and brassy sounds were integral to the rising volume of urban modernity, as in the sonic collage of Australian Jean Curlewis's prose poem 'The City': 'Jazz. Traffic. Noise. Trams ... Sirens. Steel Hammers clanging' (Matthews 2005: 46). The young modern girl was 'the incarnation of the Jazz Age' (Matthews 2005: 65).

The modern woman can also attend the movies which, with the advent of talkies, expose mass audiences to an accent which abolishes the class markers that have plagued the Anglo-Celtic accent. She can also participate in and hear about an enlarged range of outdoor sports and recreations, with opportunities to cycle, drive, explore and literally fly, as in the 1926 song 'Flappers in the Sky', whose lyrics spoke of the freedom of women to outsoar mere men. The sheet music illustration showed women aloft in an aeroplane called the 'Sky Pirate', indulging in various (semi)transgressive activities like drinking, smoking and homo-eroticism. That is, in every way such songs modelled an emancipative violation of standards of Victorian femininity and declared that a range of sexual pleasures was available as part of everyday life.

Significant in her enlarged cultural horizons was sound. She could participate in music more actively at one of the increasing numbers of public dance halls, where she may also eat, drink, smoke, apply makeup as well as dance with an abandonment unrestrained by convention or bulky clothing. Indeed, much to the outrage of conservatives, she may find a 'corset check room', where she can leave a constraining item of underclothing while she shimmies or charlestons or does the tickle toe, the turkey trot, the black bottom. She can also find work in the popular music industry. Many women, having been trained as pianists to adorn the Edwardian domestic space, became bandleaders (including the Australia's first jazz band advertised as such). In Australia the majority of silent movie improvisational pianists were women, who were also prominent in the cutting of player piano rolls, as Musical Directors in radio and recording, and as dancing teachers in the latest styles (see further for example, on the Australian case, on cinema Whiteoak 1999: 61–70; Johnson 2000: 59–76, on life-style journals see Mackay 1994; Moore 2012: 121, 134).

Let us consider a much more subtle example of how gender politics were redefined by changes in sound technology. The case study underpinning the following discussion is, again, Australian but the conclusions which relate to new styles of singing are I believe as broadly applicable as internationally as the phenomenon called 'crooning' from the 1930s (the following is a condensation of a discussion set out at length in Johnson 2000: 81–135, where all the following arguments are documented). Until around that time, popular music vocalizing as preserved on sound recordings was characterized by a version of the 'Bel Canto' tradition: open throat, massive projection and timbral purity, an approach calculated to fill a large and unamplified auditorium, whether opera house or music hall.

These conditions favoured big, 'masculine' voices, while women were forced into higher registers to project most effectively. The difference between male and female singers, with all the implications that we have noted earlier about the relationship between low frequency and power, was dramatic. As vernacular performance spaces for popular music, like dance palais, became larger, along with the bands required to fill the space and override audience noise, even the most powerful of voices were overstraining to be heard. Softer performers began to experiment with ways of bringing their sound up to a competitive level, particularly acoustic guitars, basses and vocalists.

US singer and saxophonist Rudy Vallée is widely credited with the introduction of the microphone in live performance to address this problem of rising ambient sound. The innovation introduced to live performance the singing style generally known as crooning, that was of particular suitability to singers with 'smaller' voices. There were unforeseen consequences of the use of the microphone in vocal performance: men could project adequately in a higher register, leading to the derisive accusation from pre-microphone male vocalists that the style was emasculated and effeminate, an accusation with particular force in highly masculinist cultures such as Australia. The charge of feminization, however, was no discouragement for women, who therefore were under no peer pressure to avoid experimenting with vocal 'microphone technique'.

The most famous of the dance palais singers in Australia from the 1930s was Barbara James, who sang nightly in the vast new Trocadero dance palais that opened in Sydney in 1936, with a big fourteen piece dance orchestra. A study of her recordings from her first in 1933, before she began using the microphone in live performance, through to the 1950s, discloses several interesting changes: a significant extension of her register downward, and the extension of her timbral palette to more conversational as well as more closed throat glottal effects. In interviews with the author she attributed the changes in her style to nightly experimentation with the microphone. And in general, the same patterns are evident in popular music vocalization internationally.

For the purposes of the present argument about sound and gender politics, there are two points to be made about the impact of the microphone. First, the register disparity between male and female singers was reduced, which in turn reduced the disparity in perceptions of power between men and women. And the second point is that the microphone enabled women to express themselves convincingly in a more natural and comfortable vocal register, rather like being able to dispense with tight dresses and stiletto heels, finding a voice 'that could articulate the anxieties, ironies and ambiguities of heterosexual modernity' (Johnson 2000: 133). Together, these changes pointed towards two of the major streams in twentieth-century popular music vocalizing: the thick, clotted closed throat styles associated with, for example, Little Richard through to Tom Waits, and the conversational ease of singers exemplified by singers from Doris Day to Nora Jones. And they also changed the balance of power in gender politics, as refracted through popular music.

It is notable how many of these liberating developments associated with modernity are related to changes in the soundscape: recordings, radio, talkies, music and public dancing. The 'Aural Renaissance' was simultaneously a sign of female emancipation and a threat to many male-dominated power blocs and elites, a new instrument of political power playing a significant role in the liberation of the 'New Woman' during the 1920s. As such, she was the subject or suspicion and opprobrium. In 1925 the conservative

Australian newspaper *Truth* published a poem called 'Recipe for a Flapper', which included the lines:

> Take a handful of girl of about seventeen ...
> Soak in the foetid atmosphere of a City until all Modesty and Rationality disappears.
> Cover the face with a thick, double or triple layer of Cosmetic, and stain two fingers of the right hand brown ...
> Fill with the notion that Jazz is the noblest work of God and garnish with a trifle of slinky dress and considerable legs. Overall sprinkle the dust of Complete Conceit.
>
> Matthews 2005: 66

To lead to our concluding case study of '*un*usual suspects' in sound and gender politics, I want to refer to another information technology that became involved in the change in both the material and symbolic power of sound. In the early modern period in which the circulation of information came to be dominated by the printed word, those with limited educational opportunities were placed at a disadvantage. In economic terms, this meant the lower, labouring classes. In gender terms it meant women, whose opportunities for formal education and participation in the public sphere were far more limited overall than for men. The increasing circulation of information by sound media rather than just the printed word enabled women to participate more actively in the public information economy. You didn't need to be able to read or write to enjoy a sound recording, a radio programme and a telephone conversation. As we have noted, the modern soundscape also created and sent messages about the increased opportunities for women to participate in the public sphere. You didn't have to have achieved a high degree of literacy to operate a telephone switchboard or listen to an office dictaphone, nor did you need a high degree of manual handwriting fluency to copy what you heard onto a typewriter. The female protagonist of the 1897 novel *The Type-Writer Girl*, credited to Olive Pratt Rayner and discussed at greater length below, encounters a young woman with whom she had casually crossed paths earlier, and strikes up a conversation: 'I found she could type fairly well, though quite unintelligently, like a well-trained Chinaman. ... given a copy, she could reproduce each word with mechanical fidelity' (Rayner 2004: 93).

The typewriter is a complex case study in the political implications of the modern soundscape, since it is an example of the 'sonification' of information technology – the typewriter was a noisy modern machine – but this was a side effect of its function, and leads our attention forward also to sonorous technology, technology that made noise. Like the stethoscope, the typewriter reconfigured the relationship between information, the eye and the ear.

Nonetheless, although incidental to its function, it was the *sound* of the typewriter that came to be the major marker of its cultural impact, as a revolution in information technology and the transformation of gender politics.

The first commercially successful typewriter model was produced in 1873. The first typewritten novel was *Tom Sawyer* by Mark Twain (who had bought a Remington in 1874); interestingly he instructed his publishers not to disclose that fact (Kittler 1999: 192). This reticence complemented a more general anxiety associated with modern technologies in domestic and recreational spaces for a range of reasons. Martin Heidegger recorded that to write a letter to someone on a typewriter was 'a breach of good manners' (Kittler 1999: 199). The impact of the typewriter, however, was far deeper than a violation of genteel courtesies. Apart from transforming the auditory metaphor of office productivity, the earliest typewriters broke the connection between vision and information. Indeed, as inventions originally intended to aid the blind, that was their intention (Kittler 1999: 187). In early models of the typewriter, the words as they were typed were hidden within the machine. The philosopher Nietzsche turned to the typewriter as his sight failed, and enthused, 'The eyes no longer have to do their work' (Kittler 1999: 202). It was not until Underwood's design in 1897, that the typist could see the script appearing on the paper (Kittler 1999: 203, 210). That is, the typewriter immediately destabilized the dominant position of the visual in a print culture. Even for those without visual impairment, their skilled touch typing, often from a dictaphone, reinforced the growing connection between sound and the recording and storage of information in the commercial workplace. My own mother and aunts recalled that when learning to touch type in the 1930s, they were prevented from seeing the keyboard by a screen, a practice that certainly continued until the 1960s (if not longer). In 2022, professional editor Jo-Ann Wallace recalled that 'Typing class meant a room full of women working heavy manual typewriters with pieces of paper taped to the machines so that you couldn't see the keyboard' (Wallace 2022: 22).

The typewriter did not become successful until its production was made profitable by growing demand, which involved changes in the modern economy, in particular, a massive increase in the rate and quantity of information circulating in a modern capitalist bureaucracy. The scribal hand could not cope with this proliferation of information. In 1985, however, a typing speed of 773 letters/minute was recorded over a period of thirty minutes. The growing demand for the typewriter was complemented by the advent of the office dictaphone, which had originally served the original purpose of the phonograph.

Apart from achieving its breakthrough in the same decade as the sound recording was patented, however, it is instructive to explore how a machine that (re)produces visual print is connected to the meaning of sound and came to be associated with class and gender relations. Let us consider several literary examples of the representation of sound in a commercial environment. The first is Herman Melville's short story 'Bartleby the Scrivener: a Story of Wall Street', published in 1853 (Melville 1987: 13–45). Bartleby is a scrivener who comes to work for a law firm (all male). A significant feature of the workspace is its silence, signifying quiet, focused productivity. All that can be heard normally is the scrape of pen on paper. The most valued employee, around sixty years old, has one flaw. His work in the mornings is exemplary, but it is hinted that he tipples at lunch. It is not this in itself that is held against him, however, but the change it produces in his sonic conduct.

> The afternoon brought with it occasional blots on the page, ... but some days he went further and was rather noisy. ... He made an unpleasant racket with his chair; spilled his sand-box; in mending his pens, impatiently split them all to pieces, and threw them on the floor in a sudden passion; stood up, and leaned over his table, boxing his papers about in a most indecorous manner
>
> Melville 1987: 15

At the centre of this tale is Bartleby's unexplained decision not to carry out certain tasks, because he 'prefers not to'. The point here, however, is the regime of silence that accompanies the processing of information.

From the beginning to the late twentieth century, when the softer mutter of digital keyboards became standard, however, the sonic representation of stenographic productivity was completely reversed, to become noise. And at the same time, this noise became gendered, so much so that in the late nineteenth century, the word typewriter denoted not only the machine but also a female typist (Kittler 1999: 183). If you are an office worker transcribing by hand, a high level of writing skill is necessary, but if you are pressing keys on a typewriter as you follow the original script or listen to a dictaphone, then the same level of skill is not required. Classes of worker previously excluded from the labour force because they could not shape words easily, because their education was less adequate, could now find a place in the economy. This is a radical transformation of the relationship between gender and the labour force, a parallel to the domination of women in telephone switchboards referred to above. Put simply, women became central to the information economy. Among Australian poet Kenneth Slessor's cameos of the modern girl in the collection *Backless Betty from Bondi*, discussed above, is 'Underwood Ann'. It is not the boss or the Board of Directors, but the typist, who 'runs the whole show ... Napoleon in laces,//General Manager//Underwood Ann' (Slessor 1983: 10). The close association between the typist and the machine help strengthen a gendered distinction between the masculinity of intellectual labour and the feminization of the mechanical (Suranyi 2004: 13; see further on labour and gender over this period Zimmeck 1986; Lewis 1988). Not coincidentally, then, early mass-produced typewriters were developed by sewing and knitting machine companies (Kittler 1999: 187). Kittler cites census statistics that indicate an extraordinary gender shift in stenography. In 1870, only 4.5% of stenographers and typists in the US were women. By 1930, the figure was 95.6% (Kittler 1999: 184).

In general, women were not professionally required to write and the teaching of writing to women was erratic. Accordingly their handwriting was notoriously uneven, ungrammatical and illegible. At the same time, there was an enormous pool of unemployed women – that is, women excluded from the labour force, and in particular the information economy. As Kittler argues, the typewriter transformed this situation. In 1895 two German economists noted a connection between the digital dexterity developed by young women taught to play the piano, and their ubiquity as typists, who have 'evolved into a kind of type: she is generally very high in demand and is the ruling queen in this domain, not only in America but in Germany as well' (Kittler 1999: 194).

Unsurprisingly, given the growing ubiquity of the female stenographer, young female readers could enjoy a fashion for popular stories about 'typewriter girls' in the late nineteenth century (Suranyi 2004: 9). One such example is Grant Allen's 1897 novel *The Type-Writer Girl*, referred to above and republished in 2004; the page references below refer to this edition. It is a sign of the changing readership demographic and its interests that, in a significant reversal of a tradition of early women novelists writing under a male pseudonym, he chose to adopt the female *nom de plume* of Olive Pratt Rayner. For it is a narrative of female liberation and independence.

The protagonist, Juliet Appleton is an early example of the New Woman: 'I am all for equation of the sexes' (53). Should anyone wish to object to a story lacking a romantic love interest, she defiantly invokes the legion of her young independent peers who are similarly lacking: the 'Ten thousand type-writer girls [who] crowd London today' (73–74). She is rescued from unemployment by competing successfully for a position as 'Shorthand and Type-writer (female)' (32). Just as the word 'typewriter' denoted both the machine and its female operator, Juliet merges herself with this stenographic technology, and through its sound. She describes her new workplace in sonic terms: 'the anteroom where I clicked' (33); 'I was seated at my table, clicking away at some letters' (88); engaged in conversation she replies without looking up and 'went on clicking' (101). It is the sound of the typewriter that identifies her and proclaims her entry into the public sphere.

The independence that she enjoys is extended by other influential technologies emerging from the late nineteenth century. On leisure evenings she retires 'at odd moments' to 'the hospitable electric light of the British Museum' (94–95). And, sonically signalling her progress through the wider world is the bicycle, fitted with its distinctive warning bell following the patent taken out in 1877. Juliet's ticket to freedom is her 'faithful bicycle': 'How light and free I felt! … A woman on a bicycle has all the world before her where to choose; she can go where she will, no man hindering' (42–43). As a cyclist, she 'owns' the land, its streams, skies, roads, fields, flora and fauna 'by virtue of my freehold in the saddle of my bicycle' (109).

Her entry into the commercial world, however, is marked by the sound of the typewriter with which she identifies herself, and which she uses as a weapon of defence against the inane chatter of her male colleagues. Surrounded by male clerks who talked incessantly of sport and female music hall stars, 'my typewriter continued to go click, click, click, till I was grateful for its sound as a counter-irritant to their inanity' (34); 'I continued to click, click, click, like a machine that I was, and to listen to as little as possible to the calculated odds upon King Arthur for the Ascot Cup' (35). The word 'weapon' is used advisedly. It did not go un-noticed that the noise made by an accomplished typist resembled that of another modern technological development, the machine gun. Jean Cocteau wrote a play in 1941, called *The Typewriter*. It is about a detective trying to track down a woman who has been terrorizing the community, causing a number of suicides, with anonymous typewritten letters, signed 'The typewriter'. He is fascinated by the fact that whenever the letter 'm' appears, it is a capital; unaware that it is a woman, he visualizes the writer:

> Can't you picture him, typing and firing away these capital 'M's' like a Maniac at a Machine-gun. Can't you hear the bell ring at the end of every line? Ping. This'll Muddle them. Ping. This will Make them Mad. Ping. They're after Me... Yes, yes, I can just imagine him. The other night walking home I came through one of those little back streets. A window was open. I heard someone typing. My heart stopped and I wondered if it were the murderer.
>
> Cocteau 1947: 33–34

Kittler cites the first sentence, paralleling the typewriter with the speed of delivery of information with that of the machine gun. But the rest of the quote makes the connection also, and more insistently, a matter of sound. It is sounds that signal and punctuate the delivery of information

Finally the perpetrator confesses:

> But I writhed in malice against this whole town with its fake piety – its bogus respectability and its false charity. And I ran my head blindly against the whole egoistical, avaricious, invincible bourgeois pack of them. ... So I chose the filthiest, most despicable of human weapons to beat them with – a typewriter.
>
> Cocteau 1947: 33

In light of the comments I made earlier about the assault on the established order by the acoustic renaissance, it is significant that her target is bourgeois society.

I wish to pursue another point here, however. I repeat with emphasis the importance of modern technological noise. Luigi Russolo transcribes a poem included in a letter written to him from the trenches in Ariadnople by the Futurist writer Filippo Tommaso Emilio Marinetti describing 'the orchestra of a great battle':

> 1 2 3 4 5 seconds the siege canons gut the silence by a chordTamtoumb! Immediately echoes, echoes, echoes, all echoes-quick! take-it-crumble it-spread it-infinite distance to hell. In the center, center of these flattened TAMTOUMBS-width 50 square kilometers-leap 2 3 6 8 splinters-fisticuffs-headrammings-rapid fire//batteries Violence, ferocity, regularity, pendulum game, fatalitythis grave bass apparent slowness-scan the strange madmen very young-very mad mad mad-very agitated altos of the battle Fury anguish breathless ears My ears open nasals! beware! such joy is yours o my people to sense see ear scent drink everything everything everything taratatatata the machineguns shouting twisting under a thousand bites ...
>
> Russolo 2004: 7–8

And so on for twenty more lines. The rapid, intermittent staccato of modernity infiltrates modern life from urban street noise to the rhythm of modern literature and the new soundscape of the commercial office under the fingers of the 'Napoleons in laces'. The typewriter transformed the acoustics of scribal sites; its noise became the inescapable and constant reminder of the technologization of knowledge. Women with informational machine guns replaced the old male scribes with their slow silent weapons. Writing had been a silent regime that established ascendancy over sounded utterance. The typewriter and keyboard restored sound to letters – and a technological sound at that. It is notable how many descriptions of modern offices in literature and film up to the 1980s, foreground typewriter noise as the primary metonym of the work it produced.

The entire sonic transition I have been exploring, from the silent office regime of pre-modern male domains to the technological 'chatter' of the twentieth century female stenographic space, is summarized in a film whose title makes explicit the transition in terms of gender conflict: *Battle of the Sexes* (1959, dir. Charles Crichton, available online at https://www.youtube.com/watch?v=5i1yw5IRjI4).

It is perhaps no coincidence that the story on which it was based was by the almost blind writer James Thurber. Set in a Scottish tweed manufacturing and export business in Edinburgh, the accounts department is headed by a long-time employee played by Peter Sellers. The opening scenes recall Bartleby's workplace, of handwritten ledgers and silence broken in this case only by the sound of the tea lady rattling her tray to the consternation of the ageing all-male staff. The narrative that ensues centres on the arrival of an 'Industrial

Consultant', significantly a garrulous and overbearing American woman (played by Constance Cummings), who regards the business as 'something out of Dickens ... a museum piece', and proceeds to modernize its operations. The first sign of her influence is the installation of mechanical adding machines, the noise of which overwhelms the soundscape, becoming a weapon in the conflict between the Old World pre-modern and the New World modern.

The impacts of the Aural Renaissance thus went deeper than a transformation of the modern soundscape. These new information technologies destabilized the foundations of cultural capital, and most fundamentally in democratizing access to information by bringing it back to the realm of the acoustic. It should not therefore be surprising that traditional power blocs were frequently suspicious of and felt under threat from these new information circuits, as Cocteau's 'typewriter' made explicit. The Aural Renaissance from the late nineteenth century both generated and signalled fundamental social cleavages that accompanied modernity, and introduced new weapons, both symbolic and literal, that could be deployed both individually and collectively. It is to these that we now turn.

Reading

Allen, Grant. 1897. *The Type-Writer Girl*. Clarissa J. Suranyi (ed). Toronto: Broadview Reprint Edition.

Bijsterveld, Karin. 2008. *Mechanical Sound: Technology, Culture, and Public Problems of Noise in the Twentieth Century*. Cambridge, MA and London: MIT Press.

Blesser, Barry and Linda-Ruth Salter. 2007. *Spaces Speak, Are You Listening? Experiencing Aural Architecture*. Cambridge, MA and London: MIT Press.

Cirillio, Ettore and Francesco Martellotta. 2006. *Worship, Acoustics and Architecture*. Brentwood, Essex: Multi-Science Publishing.

Cocteau, Jean. 1947. *The Typewriter: A Play in Three Acts* (trans. Ronald Duncan). London: Dennis Dobson.

Egan, Bill. 2020. *African American Entertainers in Australia and New Zealand: A History, 1788–1941*. Jefferson, NC: McFarland and Co. Inc. Publishers.

Erhardt, Christine. 2017 (first pub 2014). 'Phones, Horns, and "Audio Hoods"as Media of Attraction: Early Sound Histories in Vienna between 1833 and 1933'. In Daniel Morat (ed), *Sounds of Modern History: Auditory Cultures in 19th- and 20th-Century Europe*. New York, NY and Oxford: Berghahn: 101–125.

Garcia, David. 2017. *Listening for Africa: Freedom, Modernity, and the Logic of Back Music's Origins*. Durham, NC and London: Duke University Press.

Gauß, Stefan. 2017 (first pub 2014). 'Listening to the Horn: On the Cultural History of the Phonograph and the Gramophone'. In Daniel Morat (ed), *Sounds of Modern History: Auditory Cultures in 19th- and 20th-Century Europe*. New York, NY and Oxford: Berghahn: 71–100

Gouk, Penelope. 1999. *Music, Science and Natural Magic in Seventeenth-Century England*. New Haven, CT and London: Yale University Press.

Gronow, Pekka. 1996. *The Recording Industry: An Ethnomusicological Approach*. Tampere: University of Tampere.

Hui, Aexander E. 2017 (first pub 2014). 'From the Piano Pestilence to the Phonograph Solo: Four Case Studies of Musical Expertise in the Laboratory and on the City Street'. In Daniel Morat (ed), *Sounds of Modern History: Auditory Cultures in 19th- and 20th-Century Europe*. New York, NY and Oxford: Berghahn: 129–152.

Ihde, Don. 2007. *Listening and Voice: Phenomenologies of Sound*. Albany, NY: State University of New York Press.

Järviluoma, Helmi, Meri Kytö, Barry Truax, Heikki Uimonen and Noora Vikman (eds). 2009. *Acoustic Environments in Change*. Tampere: Tampereen Ammattikoekeakoulu.

Jasen, Paul C. 2017 (first pub 2016). *Low End Theory: Bass, Bodies and the Materiality of Sonic Experience*. New York, NY and London: Bloomsbury.

Johnson, Bruce. 2000. *The Inaudible Music: Jazz, Gender and Australian Modernity*. Sydney: Currency Press.

Johnson, Bruce. 2020. *Jazz Diaspora: Music and Globalisation*. New York, NY and London: Routledge.

Keepnews, Orrin and Bill Grauer Jr. 1968 (first pub 1955). *A Pictorial History of Jazz*. Middlesex: Spring Books/Hamlyn House.

Kittler, Friedrich. 1999 (originally published in German, 1986). *Gramophone, Film, Typewriter* (trans. Geoffrey Winthrop-Young and Michael Wutz). Stanford, CA: Stanford University Press.

Lanza, Joseph. 2007. *Elevator Music: A Surreal History of Muzak, Easy-Listening, and Other Moodsong*. Revised and Expanded Edition. Ann Arbor, MI: University of Michigan Press.

Lewis, Jane E. 1988. 'Women Clerical Workers in the Late Nineteenth and Early Twentieth Centuries'. In Gegory Anderson (ed), *The White Blouse Revolution: Female Office Workers Since 1870*. Manchester: Manchester University Press: 27–47.

Mackay, Mary. 1994. 'Almost Dancing: Thea Proctor and the Modern Woman'. In Maryanne Dever (ed), *Wallflowers and Witches: Women and Culture in Australia 1910–1945*. St. Lucia: University of Queensland Press: 26–37.

Matthews, Jill Julius. 2005. *Dance Hall and Picture Palace: Sydney's Romance with Modernity*. Sydney: Currency Press.

Melville, Herman. 1987. 'Bartleby, the Scrivener: A Story of Wall-Street'. In Harrison Hayford, Alma A. MacDougall, G. Thomas Tanselle et al. (eds), *The Piazza Tales and Other Prose Pieces 1839–1860*, Vol. 9 of *The Writings of Herman Melville*. Evanston and Chicago, IL: Northwestern University Press and The Newberry Library, 1987: 13–45. Available online at http://moglen.law.columbia.edu/LCS/bartleby.pdf accessed 22 August 2021.

Moore, Tony. 2012. *Dancing with Empty Pockets: Australia's Bohemians Since 1860*. Sydney and London: Murdoch Books.

Peterson, Marina. 2021. *Atmospheric Noise: The Indefinite Urbanism of Los Angeles*. Durham, NC and London: Duke University Press.

Picker, John M. 2017 (first pub 2014). 'English Beat: The Stethoscopic Era's Sonic Traces'. In Morat, Daniel (ed), *Sounds of Modern History: Auditory Cultures in 19th- and 20th-Century Europe*. New York, NY and Oxford: Berghahn: 25–45.

Pike, Andrew and Ross Cooper. 1998 (revised edn.). *Australian Film 1900–1977: A Guide to Feature Film Production*. Melbourne: Oxford University Press.

Pöyskö, Maru. 1994. 'The Blessed Noise and Little Moo – Asects of Soundscape in Cowsheds'. In Helmi Järviluoma (ed), *Soundscapes: Essays on Vroom and Moo*. Tampere: Department of Folk Tradition and Instutute of Rhythm Music: 71–89.

Rayner, Olive Pratt. 2004. *The Type-Writer Girl*. Clarissa J. Suranyi (ed). Toronto: Broadview Reprint Edition.

Russolo, Luigi. 2004 (first pub 1913). *The Art of Noise* (trans. Robert Filliou). Ubu Classics, online at file:///C:/Users/brujo/Desktop/CURRENT%20PROJECTS/Cult%20Hist%20Sound/Not%20incorporated%20yet/russolo_noise.pdf

Schafer, R. Murray, Helmi Järviluoma, Meri Kytö, Barry Truax, Heikki Uimonen and Noora Vikman (eds). 2009 (first pub 1977). *Five Village Soundscapes*. *Acoustic Environments in Change*. Tampere: Tampereen Ammattikoekeakoulu: 283–421. (Reprinted).

Schwartz, Hillel. 2011. *Making Noise: From Babel to the Big Bang & Beyond*. New York, NY: Zone Books.

Slessor, Kenneth. 1983. *Backless Betty from Bondi*. London, Sydney and Melbourne: Angus & Robertson.

Sterne, Jonathan. 2003. *The Audible Past: Cultural Origins of Sound Reproduction*. Durham, NC and London: Duke University Press.

Suranyi, Clarissa J. 2004. 'Introduction'. In Clarissa J. Suranyi (ed), *The Type-Writer Girl*. Toronto: Broadview Reprint Edition: 9–16.

Thompson, Emily. 2004. *The Soundscape of Modernity: Architectural Acoustics and the Culture of Listening in America, 1900–1933*. Cambridge, MA and London: MIT Press.

Wald, Elijah. 2007. 'Louis Armstrong Loves Guy Lombardo: Acknowledging the Smoother Roots of Jazz'. *Jazz Research Journal*, 1 (1): 129–145.

Wallace, Jo-Ann. 2022. 'On Typing'. *London Review of Books* 44: 2.

Whiteoak, John. 1999. *Playing Ad Lib: Improvisatory Music in Australia 1836–1970*. Sydney: Currency Press.

Zimmeck, Meta. 1986. 'Jobs for the Girls: The Expansion of Clerical Work for Women, 1850–1914'. In Angela V. John (ed), *Unequal Opportunities: Women's Employment in England 1800–1918*. Oxford: Blackwell: 153–177.

9
SOUND IN THE CONTEMPORARY WORLD

There is the widest divergence of opinion among the massive and transdisciplinary body of academic literature on the distinctive character of modernity. But there is one assertion that can be made that is beyond contention: the modern era can be absolutely distinguished from the pre-modern by its soundscape: 'Sound, hearing and listening are central to the cultural life of modernity' (Sterne 2003: 2; similarly, Thompson 2004: 2; for a useful literature review see Mansell 2017: 8–11, 192[1]). And throughout the industrialized world, we live with a permanent and mysterious low frequency sound known as 'The Hum', wave energies first identified in the 1940s and reaching a peak in the 1970s, probably at between 4 and 80 Hz, causing sleep deprivation, depression, nausea, headaches, ear pain and chronic anxiety; its cause could be related to radio waves, or mechanical vibrations associated with gas and water reticulation systems (Jasen 2017: 58–61).[2] Modern city dwellers 'swim, always, within a sea of low-pitched noise' that penetrates at least a km into the earth (Haskell 2022: 326).

As early as his 1913 Futurist manifesto *The Art of Noise*, Luigo Russolo declared that 'Today noise reigns supreme over human sensibility' (Russolo 2004: 4). The noise about noise reverberated throughout the twentieth century. In 1928, 'The Age of Noise', was the title of a lecture given by W.S. Tucker to the Royal Aeronautical Society (Mansell 2017: 1). In the early 1940s the Health Organization of the League of Nations produced a Report on Noise and Housing, on 'the growing "environmental problem" of noise from radios, motorized traffic, and the acoustic conductivity of cheap housing materials' (Schwartz 2011: 671). The changing soundscape was not simply the arrival of sounds unprecedented in volume, pitch, intensity, frequency and timbre but also their saturation of increasingly congested communities that

DOI: 10.4324/9781003042662-10

both caused and complained of them. London's population increased from about 200,000 in 1600 to 900,000 in 1800 (Goldsmith 2012: 77). By the 1860s, Manhattan's Tenth Ward had '196,000 people to the square mile and fourteen to a tenement room' (Schwartz 2011: 274). With growing urbanization and proliferating professional specializations, 'mental workers' found themselves in tension with the rising flood of modern noise. Early motorized traffic noise was increased by ordinances requiring drivers to sound their horns at frequent intervals, being quieter than the horse-drawn traffic they replaced; in the early years of the twentieth century, one listener recorded sixty-seven horn blasts per minute in the 5 minutes between 7.50 and 7.55 pm on an 'otherwise quiet' street in London's Mayfair (Schwartz 2011: 478, 479). Complaints about traffic noise rose to a peak in 1936, with 12,480 complaints (Goldsmith 2012: 169). In 1913, Luigi Russolo had anticipated R. Murray Schafer's 'soundwalks' by about half a century:

> Let's walk together through a great modern capital, with the ear more attentive than the eye, and we will vary the pleasures of our sensibilities by distinguishing among the gurglings of water, air and gas inside metallic pipes, the rumblings and rattlings of engines breathing with obvious animal spirits, the rising and falling of pistons, the stridency of mechanical saws, the loud jumping of trolleys on their rails, the snapping of whips, the whipping of flags. We will have fun imagining our orchestration of department stores' sliding doors, the hubbub of the crowds, the different roars of railroad stations, iron foundries, textile mills, printing houses, power plants and subways
>
> Russolo 2004: 7

Traffic noise today mingles with the sounds of rail transport, construction sites with jackhammers and pile drivers, factories and their whistles and sirens, and recorded music spilling from shopfronts and malls. Among the most intrusive of such sounds is aircraft noise, a problem so distinctive that I take it up in further detail in the next chapter in the discussion of noise abatement programmes.

Apart from the soundscape within factories, we have noted the transition of white collar office spaces from silence to the clatter of typewriters, to which we can add telephones and intercoms, boilers, ventilators and air conditioning systems, many of them Low Frequency Noise (LFN) with its own pathologies. The soundscape of modern domestic interiors was also transformed. Apart from the intrusion of many of the street sounds referred to above, in high-density communities, globally, neighbours acoustically intrude upon each other, and the modern home produces sonic clutter of its own. The sources of some of this are intended to increase domestic sound levels: radio, TV, stereo systems, telephones, computers and various alarms ranging from clocks and timers to smoke detectors. In other cases, the sound is a side effect of function:

household appliances, including dishwashers, electric jugs, garbage disposal units, refrigerators, vacuum cleaners and floor polishers, blenders, mixers, electric can openers and knife sharpeners, extraction fans and air conditioning systems, all underpinned by low level mains hum. While this sonic transformation generally signalled technological progress, productivity, and the comforts of modern life, the sonic overload also brought high levels of stress; a report from the University of Wisconsin estimated that domestic noise could cause 'all the symptoms of combat fatigue' (Schwartz 2011: 831).

We have also become dangerously 'noisy neighbours' to marine life. Sound travels four times faster through salt water than air (Haskell 2022: 12; see further on modern submarine noise, 291–319.). Much submarine acoustic activity is the work of marine denizens, from the clicking of shrimps' claws (up to 189 dB – fatal to small fish on which they prey) to sounds made by whales which can reach up to 243 dB (Goldsmith 2012: 184). The loudest animal sound known is made by groups of sperm whales (Haskell 2022: 296). Modern human activity, however, has proliferated submarine acoustic mayhem in a range of ways. From the mid-nineteenth-century military action has introduced the sound of submarines. Through World War II, experiments with radar echolocation (Goldsmith 2012: 182–186) generated increasingly sophisticated technologies involving the deployment of sound. The SOFAR (Sound Fixing and Ranging) project was launched in 1960 and is now used to measure sea temperature variations, emitting low frequency signals (75 Hz) around the globe. Its activities have included explosions off the Australian coast which were heard 20,000 kilometres away in Bermuda (Goldsmith 2012: 185). The noisiness of oceans is also increased by motorized shipping (a 200,000-tonne supertanker emits noises of 232 dB, audible for 'a full day before they appear on the horizon'), dynamiting for construction of piers, at 296 dB, enough 'to crush a whale's earbones' (Schwartz 2011: 736). In 2022, Haskell reported that the US Navy plans exercises across the northwest Pacific, involving the use of loud sonar and explosives which, by its own estimates, 'will kill or injure close to three thousand marine mammals and disrupt feeding, breeding, movements and nursing of 1.75 million more' (Haskell 2022: 308). The seismic surveys conducted by fossil fuel (oil and gas) companies can be heard up to 4,000 kms away. The airgun blasts, as loud as 260 dBs, are arranged in batteries of up to four dozen, each battery going off every 10 to 20 seconds. The survey tracks back and forth and each survey can run for months (Haskell 2022: 310).

While generally and conveniently inaudible to us, all this intervention in the submarine soundscape causes serious ecological damage, particularly given the importance of echolocation in communication among and beyond species, and the migratory, feeding and breeding cycles of marine life. And the damage is also more direct. In 2000, an exercise in the Caribbean involving projecting sound, equivalent in intensity to the blast of 2,000 jet engines, was followed by the stranding of thirteen whales on the sands of the Bahamas, bleeding around their brains and ears (Schwartz 2011: 738). A single airgun used off the Tasmanian coast killed 'every krill larva – a key prey animal in the food web of southern oceans – within more than a kilometer and wiped out most other plankton' (Haskell 2022: 311).

Among the most prominent categories in the contemporary sound deluge is music, and this is primarily because of modern technological mediations. Live pop music is almost invariably amplified to the max irrespective of the size of the venue. But it is what is generally thought of as recorded background music that is most pervasive. Sources include radio, sound systems both domestic and in transport, TV, film and music from personal stereos and iPhones consumed through earbuds which also expose the user to dangers that require less distracted aural attentiveness, such as the risk of traffic accidents or physical assaults. Music is piped into so many public spaces it is almost inescapable: various forms of background music fill supermarkets, specialized shops and boutiques, malls, cafes and restaurants, sporting events, election campaigns, waiting rooms, hotel reception areas, airports and ferry embarkation points.

The so-called 'background music' is generally accepted as a form of harmless sonic wallpaper, but in many cases its purpose is to regulate conduct and belief systems, generally in an apparently benign way. The ideological function of background music in shops and supermarkets to encourage purchasing by customers is by now well known (see for example DeNora 2000; Lanza 2007). But let us consider more subtle forms of the sonic reinforcement of ideologies in the home, using the example of the dominance of vinyl recordings from the 1950s to the late twentieth century. This manifested itself especially in the politics of gender. We have already made reference to the emergence of the 'New Woman' from the late nineteenth century, and her progressive invasion of hitherto male spaces. This faltered in the parlous years of the Great Depression, followed by World War II which for six years had stolen the youth of yet another generation. In its wake came a period of conservative reaction, part of the attempt to restore comforting value systems and lifestyles. Women's couture, grooming, body shape and demeanour moved away from the aggressive, quasi-androgynous image of the 1920s to an image of a child bearer and household nurturer. Films like *Mildred Pierce* (1945, dir. Michael Curtiz) dramatized the dysfunctional results of a woman venturing into the world of public commerce, and sci-fi movies like *Cat-Women of the Moon* (1953, dir. Arthur Hilton) and *The Attack of the 50 Foot Woman* (1958, dir. Nathan H. Juran) turned the woman whose place was not in the home into an alien feral grotesque. The man resumed his role as the breadwinner out in the public space; the member of the nuclear family who carried final authority: *Father Knows Best*, declared the title of a popular postwar sitcom beginning on radio in 1949 before becoming a TV series from 1954 to 1960.

In league with all this, the vinyl LP recording, with its multiple tracks, liner notes and design, became a sonic site of gender politics. The LP offered the possibility of themed programmes that had not been possible on earlier, discrete 78 rpm recordings. One of the most successful was the 1956 release on Capitol, 44 minutes of music whose theme was proclaimed explicitly in the title *Songs For Swingin' Lovers*, sung by Frank Sinatra with the Nelson Riddle Orchestra. Massively successful, in 2000, the album was inducted into the Grammy Hall of Fame, and ranked number 306 on *Rolling Stone* magazine's list of the 500 greatest albums of all time in 2003. The total package – repertoire, liner notes and design – was virtually a manifesto of the gender politics summarized above, a soundtrack to parties, dinners and seductions, as well as to daily leisure and housework performed by the wife. Many bands prospered from such themed collections which reinforced traditional gender relations. Consider these liner notes from a Frank Chacksfield album, presented as background music for a dinner party:

> The musically aware hostess no longer allows the butler, or her husband, to sling records on to the turntable in a haphazard way. She no longer risks the soup being spilled by 56 Haydn's 'Surprise' Symphony, of Mrs Alias-Jones choking over the fish because an ill-timed bit of jazz trumpet has frightened her. She now supplies a ready-made background of elegant and suitable music to smooth the evening into one long feat of pleasure and unshattered nerves
>
> Connell and Gibson 2003: 200

Although apparently innocuous, this is heavily loaded with gender and class politics. Obviously, it assigns to the woman total control of the leisure domestic space; the husband has no more rights here than a butler. Her supposed management of the auditory environment happens also to be ironic, given that advertising that featured sound systems invariably foregrounded male control, with women, if appearing at all, ornamental accessories in the background.[3] Apart from the masculinized technology of Hi-Fi sound systems, the man's natural realm is out in the world, the economic hunter–gatherer, while the woman is house-bound; the reference to the butler, and to a guest with a hyphenated name, creates the comfortable impression of wealth and refinement in the buyer of the recording – even suggested in the reference to fish rather than steak. At the same time the buyer is not narrowly niched into either high or low culture (Haydn or jazz). And the duty of the woman is to provide pleasure, an elegant surface to life. The home is her place; her place is in the home.

In other manipulations of the sonic space, the coercive function of music is more overt. My own files record that from the late twentieth century, piped music has increasingly been deliberately deployed to deter 'undesirables' from occupying various public spaces. From the UK, Europe as well as Australasia, there are reports of its use in such locations as shopping malls, fast food chains, like McDonalds, car parks, church precincts, funfairs and railway stations.

Most frequently, the music used to restore and maintain order seems to have been from the 'classical' canon, including Vivaldi, Bach, Handel, Mozart, Rachmaninov, Rimsky-Korsakof and Delius, but forms of popular music, golden oldies and 'uncool' MOR have proven equally effective. In the earliest example that I have on file, from 1998 in Wollongong, New South Wales, Bing Crosby records were the weapon of coercion (Johnson and Cloonan 2008: 184). What one Local Government Area in the UK called the 'Manilow Method' has produced its own 'chartbuster list' of twenty songs that would deter teenagers. Top of the list was 'Release Me', by Englebert Humperdinck, with Cliff Richard's 'Mistletoe and Wine' listed at number nineteen (Johnson and Cloonan 2008: 185).

This sonic tactic has succeeded in reducing antisocial disorder by over thirty per cent, and at first glance seems to be an unexceptionable way of maintaining public order. But as in all the cases of sonic power relations that we have noted, there is a political dynamic operating here which is not so innocent. The same music that encourages big spenders in supermarkets and restaurants is the music that drives out those who cannot spend, who do not fit the model of citizen as paying consumer. The Manilow Method was not only applied against potential assault and vandalism but also homeless street sleepers, drug addicts and unemployed youth just 'hanging out'. Residents of luxury apartments in Salamanca Square in Hobart (Australia) requested the piping of Bing Crosby into the Square to deter loitering youth, a clear example of a class-based musically controlled differentiation of occupancy of public space (Johnson and Cloonan 2008: 185). At issue here are questions of who has the right to occupy what is *public* space. Sound has been crucial in defining community identity. In a tactic analogous to Samuel Johnson's exclusion of the illiterate from the anglophone linguistic community, in this modern sonic equivalent, a very specific form of musical 'literacy' and taste becomes a condition of community membership (for an extended discussion of this use of music, see Johnson and Cloonan 2008: 181–187).

The modern advent of portable recorded sound and its full spectrum has introduced increasingly aggressive deployments of sound. Music has perennially thematically drawn upon and accompanied conflict, from national anthems to 'pump-up' recorded arousal music that increases risk-taking in battle, as in recent and contemporary war zones (on sound as weaponry see further for example Pettan 1998; Cusick 2008; Johnson and Cloonan 2008; Pieslak 2009; Daughtrey 2015). Debate continues over whether or not popular music actually causes violence (Johnson and Cloonan 2008: 65–146). But less problematic is the role clearly played by sound in constituting, *in itself*, a form of violence. In our discussion of the history of sound the images of conflict and weaponry have constantly recurred, from war cries to early modern class antagonisms. But the modern technological mediation of sound has made it literally a weapon. In 1989 Panamanian dictator, opera-loving General Noriega was driven out of his refuge in the Vatican embassy by US troops continuously playing pop music; similar sonic assault was used at Waco against the Branch Davidian sect in 1993 (Johnson and Cloonan 2008: 150–151).

Since at least 1997 when the Defence Department created Joint Non-Lethal Weapons Task Force, the US along with contracted private companies has experimented with and deployed a diverse arsenal of sonic weaponry. Perhaps most famous is the Long Range Acoustic Device, or LRAD, capable of projecting a strip of sound 15–30 inches wide at an average of 120 dB (maxing at 151 dB) that will be intelligible for 500–1,000 metres (depending on which model you buy – see a demonstration at https://www.youtube.com/watch?v=QSMyY3_dmrM accessed 25 March 2022). LRADs are in use for domestic crowd control by police departments, as well as by the military in for example Iraq. It is also a medium of specifically musical violence, capable of directing music selected by individual soldiers sourced from their CD and MP3 players (see further Johnson and Cloonan 2008: 186–187). Sonic assault has also been used in the torture and interrogation of prisoners, as for example by the British armed forces from the period of Mau Mau rebels in Africa in the 1950s and 'The Troubles' in Northern Ireland in the 1970s (Johnson and Cloonan 2008: 149). This has become widespread in the so-called 'war on terror', perhaps most notoriously in Guantanomo Bay, where detainees, often locked in shipping containers, have been subjected to continuous high volume rock and rap, and such apparently innocuous songs as Barney the Purple Dinosaur's 'I Love You' (for this and a more general discussion, see Johnson and Cloonan 2008: 146–192).

Although these are extreme manifestations of the pathological impacts of modern sound, we don't need to go to spaces and places that are consolingly 'elsewhere' to experience forms of sonic assault. Our everyday soundscape is saturated with harmful components, and they are not always as obvious as high volume. Pitch is also a factor. We have made reference to LFN; in the increasingly noisy modern environment, it is LFN which, within the broader category of noise pollution, is the fastest growing cause of acoustic damage. The problems of LFN emerge from the convergence of numerous factors distinctive to modernity, including the physical shape of the contemporary city. Apart from cities built from scratch in the twentieth century, such as Brasilia in Brazil and Australia's national capital Canberra, modern cities are constructed upon a pre-modern grid. The old horizontal networks defined by the road system which developed in a pre-modern era and on which the original architecture had been constructed, now had superimposed upon them a completely new vertical order. High rise office and apartment blocks replaced old single to triple-storey terraces, bungalows and retail sites. The result is deep and resonant sonic canyons. Modern(ist) urban architecture is characterized by more sonically reflective and reverberant spaces and surfaces (like glass) than the sound-baffling structures they replaced. This makes them especially effective environments for the use of sonic weaponry. During the 2004 siege of Fallujah in Iraq, US forces bombarded the city with music, reportedly with Metallica's 'Hells' Bells' and 'Shoot to Thrill' among other sounds. PsyOps spokesman Ben Abel explained to reporter Lane DeGregory of the *St. Petersburg (Florida) Times*, 'These harassment missions work especially well in urban settings like Fallujah. The sounds just keep reverberating off the walls' (DeGregory 2004). Modern urban communities are also equipped with various electrically driven service installations, such as lighting and air-conditioning power plants, and elevator and escalator motors. In addition, high rise housing and office space stacks its occupants vertically rather than laterally. Sounds made both inside and outside will travel up and down. The relevance of this becomes apparent as we recall the Ubiquity Effect and its causes, as discussed in Chapter One.

At the same time, we have noted how profoundly the soundscape of modernity has changed. Taking the example of music, contemporary sound systems have enabled the projection of sound with far greater volume. The effects of this sonic environment are, however, far more pervasive than is generally recognized by public noise pollution legislation, which focuses on volume. Technologically mediated sounds, including music, marked the beginning of another change in the soundscape, relating to pitch (Johnson 2000: 111–135). We have already made reference to the role of low frequencies in setting up unbalanced power relations, particularly in various forms of ritual. The change in pop music frequencies has been accentuated by continuing developments in sound technology as well as by culturally based changes. These include the gradual disappearance of silence and the contraction of dynamic range in many genres – *pianissimo* has virtually disappeared. In recording, the process known as 'brickwalling' homogenizes the dynamics to bring every part of a track to the highest level possible, as part of 'the loudness wars' that began in the 1990s. Albums in which the musicians and marketers pressured for brickwalling include *Californication* (Red Hot Chili Peppers) and Metallica's *Death Magnetic* (Haskell 2022: 231). But there are historical precedents for the rise in the volume of recorded music. Some of the reasons for this are exemplified in the arrival of jazz in the early twentieth century, which was circulated primarily by early recording technologies. These had little sensitivity to dynamic variation; *forte* was the only option in pre-electric recording and was therefore a pervasive feature of early diasporic jazz performance modelled on recordings.

In addition, popular music has begun to deploy lower registers, and since the 1970s that downward movement has also been accelerated through improved bass speakers and manifested as highly amplified and accelerated bass percussion, power chords and drop tuning, the latter of which may lower the pitch of the bottom guitar string by 6 semitones to a B below its usual E of 41 Hz. That is, popular music has become a major contributor to a significant shift in the contemporary soundscape, to the lower registers of what is referred to as 'doof doof' music. This foregrounding of bass has become especially apparent on dance floors since the emergence of Jamaican sound systems cultures from the 1960s, spreading to a range of contemporary pop genres and subgenres, and has also become a feature of car stereo systems (Jasen 2017: 151–183, 192).

The subject of LFN has come up with increasing frequency as our attention has moved towards the modern soundscape, and it is timely, then, to consider more closely LFN-induced trauma. We have discussed pneumothorax and the bass trap in pop venues, but this is only one of a dismaying suite of pathologies specific to LFN. For example, it can activate the hearer's potential as a set of asymmetrical resonating chambers, generating such pathologies as motion sickness, or vascular diseases (Augoyard et al. 2005: 107). In 2005, it was reported that the Israeli air force 'was using sonic booms under the cover of darkness as "sound bombs" in the Gaza Strip'. Their LFN produced an effect that its victims likened 'to the wall of air pressure generated by a massive explosion. They reported broken windows, ear pain, nosebleeds, anxiety attacks, sleeplessness, hypertension, and being left "shaking inside"' (Goodman 2010: xiii).

As in other forms of sonic trauma, we don't need to or go to a war zone or a laboratory to be damaged by LFN; the following examples from everyday life in the contemporary world is the merest sample from a collection of articles in the academically peer reviewed collection, Hansen (2007). Workers and researchers in the field report a range of LFN-specific disorders, including feelings of 'oppression' (Inukai et al. 2007: 7), 'torment' (Møller and Lydolft 2007: 105), 'intrusiveness' and loss of control over their environment (Benton and Abramson-Yehuda 2007: 133). A woman whose flat was adjacent to a factory fan exhaust duct experienced psychological disorders of such magnitude as to require professional counselling (Kitamura et al. 2007: 191–192). 'LFN places an extra degree of demand upon individuals['] processing and coping strategies' (Benton 2007: 237). LFN also generates more quantifiable organic damage. Ten subjects experimentally exposed to infrasound for over one hour registered disturbances of systolic and diastolic pressure and heart rate, some changes being as high as thirty per cent (Qibai and Shi 2007: 309). Mood-altering organic changes are also suggested in the report that after two hours exposure to LFN at forty dB(A), 'the normal circadian decline in cortisol concentration was … significantly reduced' (Benton 2007: 235).

While a considerable spectrum of infrasound is below the human threshold of 'hearing', it nonetheless makes its presence felt in other ways, notably by vibration, and the impact of LFN is not confined to hearing. The vestibular system in the inner ear plays 'no direct role in audition', but is essential to our sense of balance and spatial orientation, and can be affected by bass sounds, producing various forms of spatial disorientation such as Meniere's disease (Jasen 2017: 110). Reports of the impact of immersion in infrasound (15–20 Hz) include

> dizziness and refusal to re-enter the afflicted rooms, along with bouts of shivering, perspiration and inexplicable fear … respiratory disruption,

nystagmus (ocular vibration), visual anomalies, piloerection (goosebumps), sudden chills and various other discomforts, ranging from the barely perceived to the intensely painful and the psychologically distressing. Panic attacks.

Jasen 2017: 45

Studies of long-term exposure to vibration associated with noise in workers found a link with 'pericardial thickening, pulmonary fibrosis and so on. They called the pathological changes "vibroacoustic disease"' (Takahashi et al. 2007: 250).

The broader and growing social impact of LFN is reinforced in a survey of schools conducted by Sweden's Occupational Board of Safety in 1997 which identified a

> ... growing body of data showing that low frequency noise (LFN) differs in its nature from other noises at comparable levels. ... Low frequency noise is not only ubiquitous in the general environment but also in the occupational environment (e.g., in industrial control rooms, office-like areas etc.). Ventilation systems, pumps, compressors, diesel engines, gas turbine power stations, means of transport, etc., may be quoted as some examples of common sources of LFN. Its prevalence in offices and control rooms is mainly due to indoor network installations, ventilation, heating and air-conditioning systems as well as from outdoor sources of noise and poor attenuation of low frequency components by the walls, floors and ceilings.
>
> Pawlaczyk-Łuszyńska et al. 2007: 319–320

This covers pretty much the full acoustic spectrum of contemporary urban life. Wherever the LFN problem is being recognized, it is found to be increasing in magnitude: as for example in Japan, Denmark, Sweden and the Netherlands. Regarding his own region, Rotterdam, an EPA inspector writing around 2003, made the following projection:

> In 15 years 1/3 (1/2 in all Holland) of the Rotterdam inhabitants will be over 55 years of age. At the moment most of the LFS[Low Frequency Sound]-complainants are in this age group. The shared use of buildings for 'industrial' and 'living' purposes is increasing ...At the moment only 3% of Dutch homes are provided with climate control installations. These are sources of LFS and the numbers will grow. Due to the lack of building space more underground infrastructure is being developed. Vibrations caused by traffic result in LFS via the foundations of residential buildings.
>
> Sloven 2007: 82

That is, a sonic profile which generates a range of traumas from anxiety to panic is an increasingly pervasive aspect of 'normal' life.

For the reasons I have sketched above, music is now one of the main sources of this trauma. In a 1985 study it was outranked in nuisance value by most other categories of LFN. In a 1989 study amplified music or 'discotheque' had climbed to second and among documented studies has remained in that position, behind the sound of a drop forge, both causing particular nuisance because they are impulse LFN (Poulsen 2007a: 181, 187; 2007b: 141; Qistdorff and Poulsen 2007: 89). We don't hear many drop forges, but we are constantly immersed in music, whether or not of our own choosing. All the evidence suggests that LFN is a growing problem overall, and that within that framework, amplified music is its fastest growing problem.

Ironically, it is likely to be overtaken, however, by a development designed to reduce a major environmental threat: that of climate change. The problems presented by LFN have often been buried under broader political issues, as in the case of wind farms, one of the fast developing alternatives to fossil fuels. The politics of what follows is so tangled that I want to begin by declaring my own support for wind turbine energy. At issue in what follows is a question that applies to all energy sources – fossil, nuclear, renewable: where are the generators to be located? In my own country, the closest we have come to a broad recognition of the growing problems of LFN has arisen in the course of controversies over wind turbines. They have produced strange bedfellows, drawing together climate change deniers with environmental groups in alliances in which the question of the need for alternative energy sources becomes conflated with the question of their effectiveness.

One of the primary factors in these concerns is LFN. Dr John Etherington is Reader in Ecology at the University of Wales, former Co-editor of the *Journal of Ecology*, and Thomas Huxley Medallist at the Royal College of Science. He discusses the two main sources of noise emanating from a wind turbine: the LFN of the turbine blades themselves, and the gearbox and generator. Apart from the noise of the wake vortices, as the blades pass the tower there is 'a pulsating quality' added to the sound pattern. In addition, where there are clusters of turbines, as they pass in and out of phase with each other, there are 'beat' sounds set up (Etherington 2009: 113), so that apart from LFN itself, there is a further nuisance factor, known as aerodynamic modulation; the profile is not unlike that of the impulse patterns associated with forms of pop music rich in LFN. Indeed, it is a sound which Etherington in passing, but instructively in this context, likens to the woofer in a music sound system (Etherington 2009: 114; see similarly 115). He reports that complaints about this noise extended up to one point nine kilometres away from the turbine, notwithstanding developer's claims that the limit is half a kilometre. He cites cases in which owners of properties in proximity to turbines have suffered health problems, even to the extent of having to abandon their homes (Etherington 2009: 117–119).

The reason that the problem of LFN has been under-recognized is that there is little crossover between the literature of popular music and of environmental ecology. Environmentalists don't read or write in the field of music and vice versa. Yet even within each of these fields, LFN has been able to hide or to camouflage itself as something else, just as a headache caused by a tumour can be diagnosed as a sinus problem. Because the wind farm debate ranges over so many issues, the specific role of LFN as a more general problem of contemporary life has been all but submerged under partisan political arguments over other issues. Likewise, in discussion of music, LFN as a distinctive and potentially traumatic element in its sonic profile has been eclipsed by debates about volume, anti-social lyrics or festival riots. Each of these areas of social policy has its own discourse, its own lobby groups and government instrumentalities. The ways of dividing up policy responsibilities discourage those who monitor urban acoustic issues such as entertainment licences, from interesting themselves in, for example, alternative energy sources.

As we shall see in the next chapter, in broader policy discussions about noise pollution, LFN is overwhelmed by questions of volume. If the increasingly pervasive phenomenon of LFN were to be extrapolated as a distinctive issue, then attention could be shifted to the policy problems presented by an acoustic phenomenon that affects the totality of the contemporary soundscape, a connection could be recognized between the death of a freshman university student at a party in London and the depression and organic damage suffered by someone living near a windfarm in rural Australia, or a pathological aberration in the life cycle of a marine species. If we were to redraw the map of the forces that traverse our society and our social welfare through acoustic taxonomies, new lines of force would appear, new policy continuities and priorities.

Notes

1 Mansell also provides a very useful 'Noise History' timeline (263–269) which discloses the weighting of constructed noise to the modern period, and a table of decibel readings for a range of everyday anthropogenic sounds (275–276).
2 An oddly similar phenomenon known as the Havana Syndrome has been reported since 2016, when members of the US diplomatic mission, including members of the CIA, in Cuba began experiencing similar problems associated with sound. This was followed by similar reports from other US diplomatic missions, and the fact that these were often from countries with problematic relations with the US, including China, led to a theory that the US personnel were targeted victims. While this theory has been widely debunked, more broadly it has been suggested that these 'attacks' were recent examples of 'mass psychogenic illnesses' (MPI) that have a long but inexplicable history. See further, for example, O'Sullivan 2022.
3 See among the examples of *Playboy* advertising at https://trendland.com/what-kind-of-men-read-playboy/ (accessed 2 April 2022); in general, this collection strikingly dramatizes the male:active:foreground/female:passive:background model.

Reading

Augoyard, Jean-Francois, Henry Torgue, Andra McCartney and David Paquette (eds). 2005. *Sonic Experience: A Guide to Everyday Sounds*. Montreal: McGill-Queen's University Press. Originally published in French, 1995.

Benton, Stephen. 2007. 'Low Frequency Noise Annoyance and the Negotiation Challenge for Environmental Officers and Sufferers'. In C.H. Hansen (ed.) [Hansen, Colin H. 2007. '(Undated; these are Reprints from the Journal of Low Frequency Noise, Covering the Period 2000–2005 Inclusive—See 'Introduction', VII—Though the Individual Papers Are Not Dated or Sourced. In Online Catalogues the Publication Date is given as 2007)'.], 227–244.

Benton, Stephen and Orna Abramson-Yehuda. 2007. 'Low Frequency Noise Annoyance: The Behavioural Challenge'. In C.H. Hansen (ed.), 131–136.

Connell, John and Chris Gibson. 2003. *Sound Tracks: Popular Music, Identity and Place*. London and New York, NY: Routledge.

Cusick, Suzanne 2008. '"You Are in a Place That Is Out of the World": Music in the Detention Camps of the 'Global War on Terror'. *Journal of the Society for American Music*, 2 (1): 1–26.

Daughtrey, J. Martin. 2015. *Listening to War: Sound, Music, Trauma, and Survival in Wartime Iraq*. Oxford and New York, NY: Oxford University Press.

DeGregory, Lane. 2004. 'Iraq and Roll'. *St Petersburg Times* online, 21 November 2004, https://academic.oup.com/book/9302/chapter-abstract/156050450?redirectedFrom=fulltext

DeNora, Tia. 2000. *Music in Everyday Life*. Cambridge: Cambridge University Press.

Etherington, John. 2009. *The Wind Farm Scam: An Ecological Evaluation*. London: Stacey International.

Goldsmith, Mike. 2012. *Discord: The Story of Noise*. Oxford: Oxford University Press.

Goodman, Steve. 2010. *Sonic Warfare: Sound, Affect, and the Ecology of Fear*. Cambridge, MA and London: The MIT Press.

Hansen, Colin H. 2007. '(Undated; these are Reprints from the *Journal of Low Frequency Noise*, Covering the Period 2000–2005 Inclusive— See 'Introduction', VII—Though the Individual Papers Are Not Dated or Sourced. In Online Catalogues the Publication Date is given as 2007)'. In *The Effects of Low-Frequency Noise and Vibration on People*. Brentwood, Essex: Multi-Science Publishing.

Haskell, David George. 2022. *Sounds Wild and Broken*. Collingwood: Black Inc.

Inukai, Yukio, Norio Nakamura and Hideto Taya. 2007. 'Unpleasantness and Acceptable Limits of Low Frequency Sound'. In C.H. Hansen (ed.), 7–13.

Jasen, Paul C. 2017 (first pub 2016). *Low End Theory: Bass, Bodies and the Materiality of Sonic Experience*. New York, NY and London: Bloomsbury.

Johnson, Bruce. 2000. *The Inaudible Music: Jazz, Gender and Australian Modernity*. Sydney: Currency Press.

Johnson, Bruce and Martin Cloonan. 2008. *Dark Side of the Tune: Popular Music and Violence*. Aldershot and Burlington, VT: Ashgate.

Kitamura, Toshiya, Masaki Hasebe and Shinji Yamada. 2007. 'Psychological Analysis of Complaints on Noise/Low Frequency Noise and the Relation between Psychological Response and Brain structure'. In C.H. Hansen (ed.), 191–198.

Lanza, Joseph. 2007. *Elevator Music: A Surreal History of Muzak, Easy-Listening, and Other Moodsong*. Revised and Expanded Edition. Ann Arbor, MI: University of Michigan Press.

Mansell, James G. 2017. *The Age of Noise in Britain: Hearing Modernity*. Urbana, Chicago, IL and Springfield: University of Illinois Press.

Møller, Henrik and Morten Lydolft. 2007. 'A Questionnaire Survey of Complaints of Infrasound and Low-Frequency Noise'. In C.H. Hansen (ed.), 105–118.

O'Sullivan, Suzanne. 2022. *The Sleeping Beauties And Other Stories of Mystery Illness*. Basingstroke: Pan Macmillan.

Pawlaczyk-Łuszyńska, Małgorzata, Dudariwicz Adam, Waszkowska Małgorzata, Szymczak Wiesław, Kameduła Maria and Śliwińska-Kowalska. Mariola. 2007. 'Does Low Frequency Noise at Moderate Levels Influence Human Performance?'. In C.H. Hansen (ed.), 319–341.

Pettan, Svanobor, ed. 1998. *Music, Politics and War: Views from Croatia*. Zagreb: Institute of Ethnology and Folklore Research.

Pieslak, Jonathan. 2009. *Sound Targets: American Soldiers and Music in the Iraq War*. Bloomington and Indianapolis, IN: Indiana University Press.

Poulsen, Torben. 2007a. 'Annoyance of Low Frequency Noise (LFN) in the Laboratory Assessed by LFN-Sufferers and Non-Sufferers'. In C.H. Hansen (ed.), 177–190.

Poulsen, Torben. 2007b. 'Comparison of Objective Methods for Assessment of Annoyance of Low Frequency Noise with the Results of a Laboratory Listening Test'. In C.H. Hansen (ed.), 137–156.

Qibai, Chen Yuan Huang and Hammin Shi. 2007. 'An Investigation of the Physiological and Psychological Effects of Infrasound on Persons'. In C.H. Hansen (ed.), 303–310.

Qistdorff, Frank Rysgaard and Torben Poulsen. 2007. 'Annoyance of Low Frequency Noise and Traffic Noise'. In C.H. Hansen (ed.), 93–103.

Russolo, Luigi. 2004 (first pub 1913). The Art of Noise. (Trans. Robert Filliou). Ubu Classics, online at http://www.artype.de/Sammlung/pdf/russolo_noise.pdf

Schwartz, Hillel. 2011. *Making Noise: From Babel to the Big Bang & Beyond*. New York, NY: Zone Books.

Sloven, Ing. Piet. 2007. 'A Structured Approach to LFS-Complaints in the Rotterdam Region of the Netherlands'. In C.H. Hansen (ed.), 71–85.

Sterne, Jonathan. 2003. *The Audible Past: Cultural Origins of Sound Reproduction*. Durham, NC and London: Duke University Press.

Takahashi, Yukio, Kazuo Kanada and Yoshiharu [2007] 'Some characteristics of human body surface vibration induced by low frequency noise'. In C.H. Hansen (ed.) 249–264.

Thompson, Emily. 2004. *The Soundscape of Modernity: Architectural Acoustics and the Culture of Listening in America, 1900–1933*. Cambridge, MA and London: MIT Press.

10
THE MODERN SOUNDSCAPE, SOCIAL WELFARE AND POLICY

Changes in sound technologies and music media clearly have exponentially extended the capacity of sound for unacceptable intrusiveness and intervention, leading to consequences that range from social friction to homicide (see below). Consider, then, how much sound is imposed upon us both privately and in public spaces. There are social and ethical implications here for every community that deploys sound technologies. The struggle for the right to make noise, or to suppress it by the imposition of silence, is one of the ways we can chart the emergence of modernity, in all forms of social analysis: cultural studies, cultural history, demographics, welfare, class, race and gender studies, studies of aesthetics and the arts. Modern sound technologies have destabilized the relationship between public and private space, upon which all conduct relies for the parameters of civilization as we understand the term. From the local to the global, they therefore raise urgent questions regarding cultural policy and regulation. More generally, where in this debate do we place the mantra of 'human rights', with its implications of universality, yet in a global music market characterized by profoundly unbalanced power relations?

We shall conclude by addressing these issues more directly and the measures that have been and might be taken to deal with them. Noise lies at the intersection of a growing range of social issues so it is useful to pause for a moment to consider this term. First, we can say that while 'sound' has a measurable existence 'out there' (though it has to be heard), the characterization of that sound as 'noise' is subjective. We look at our sound garden and decide what are weeds and what are not, relative to the particular circumstances in which it is used. The music of a late-night party that ecstatically energizes its participants is noise to the people trying to sleep in the apartment below. Examples of this underscore one of the motifs throughout our study: the complicity of

DOI: 10.4324/9781003042662-11

class in the understanding of noise nuisance. When a Mr Francis Newton took his upstairs apartment neighbour Mrs Richard T. Wilson (sister-in-law to a Vanderbilt) to court in 1921 for holding musical evenings that often continued well past midnight, her witnesses all testified to the 'artistic character' of the music, and that it therefore could not be construed as noise at any time of day or night (see further Thompson 2004: 128–129).

Trotta notes that comparing case studies in Edinburgh and in Brazil highlights the cultural relativity of noise nuisance, different ways of experiencing music and different expectations about the reasonable level of sound (Trotta 2020: 33). In Brazil, a law of 1977 forbids noises produced in 'residential buildings by animals, musical instruments, radio or television' (Article 3/IV) as well as public performance of 'bands, musical ensembles or sound reproduction devices' (Article 3/V). Interestingly, the same article also prohibits samba school rehearsals between midnight and seven o'clock in the morning, except thirty days before carnival season, when it is allowed (Article 3/VII. That is, there are cultural contexts which also frame the recognition of what sounds are objectionable (Trotta 2020: 173).

Most generally noise is sound that undesirably disrupts a specific activity, ranging from sleep, to concentration on solving a problem, to trying to maintain auditory focus such as listening to music or conducting a conversation. It is in this sense of 'unwanted sound' that I shall generally use the term, but one caveat is necessary, and it is relevant to the broader historical developments under investigation here. As we have noted, it has always been the case that some person or persons within the sonic space wanted the sound that others call noise. But from around the beginning of the twentieth century, there have been increasing numbers who have welcomed what has been termed noise. The most famous example is to be found among the Italian Futurists, exemplified in the work cited above of Luigi Russolo, who assembled 'noise orchestras'. But embrace of noise extends to less intellectually driven projects as well. As we have seen, from heavy industry to milking machines, sound can be a welcome sign of productivity. Late in the nineteenth century, industrial deafness could be regarded as a negligible price to pay for the noise of productivity (Bijsterveld 2008: 70).

Attitudes to the noises of modernity were thus often ambivalent. At the Philips laboratory in Amsterdam, the relative silence of early computers was disconcerting, and operators amplified their sound to create an 'auditory monitor' that gave assurance that the machines were operating correctly (Bijsterveld 2008: 78) We have already referred to the creation of noise as a manifestation of power. This includes operating the noisiest machine on the factory floor (Bijsterveld 2008: 78) and more recently removing mufflers on cars and motorbikes, and the phenomenon of 'boom box' competitions in car sound systems.

In the radical context of early Soviet Russia, there emerged in 1920 *Shumovyi orkestr* in response to the demand that music should express the labour conditions of modern society, adding to musical instruments the sounds of 'industrial engines, turbines, dynamos, sirens, hooters and bells to generate performances within factories' (Reimann forthcoming). Outside the US, the earliest jazz bands often equated the music with noises that included barnyard impersonations, pistol shots and banging on pans; German 'Lärm-Jazz-Orchesters' (literally, noise jazz orchestras), were exported and copied widely throughout northern Europe (Johnson 2020: 47, 108). The example of jazz was just the beginning of a tradition of deliberately incorporating 'noise' into modern music for reasons ranging from slapstick comedy (Spike Jones and His City Slickers) to more serious experimental attempts to challenge the noise/music distinction (such as Pierre Schaeffer's *musique concrète* 1948 compositions *Five Noise Studies*, the Fluxus movement of the 1960s); there are also the categories of contemporary 'Noise Rock', 'Noise Music' and in 'art music' composers including Steven Stucky and Julia Wolf (see Hegarty 2007; Iles 2014; Haskell 2022: 257). Unless otherwise indicated, however, I will use the word 'noise' in that sense of unwanted sounds that underpin the history of noise complaints and anti-noise measures.

Noise complaints are as old as the written human record. Akkadian, spoken in Assyria and Babylonia nearly 2,500 years before the Christian era, includes among its surviving literature the story *Atrahasis* which describes how the gods created the human race to labour for them. But as the race multiplies, it becomes unbearably noisy, attracting the earliest surviving record of a noise complaint:

> The land had grown numerous, the peoples had increased,
> The land was bellowing like a bull.
> The god became disturbed by their uproar,
> Enlil heard their clamor.
> He said to the great gods,
> "The clamor of humankind has become burdensome to me,
> "I am losing sleep to their uproar.
>
> Foster 2005: 241

Enlil visits various plagues upon the human race to silence them, including a deluge, but Atrahasis is given warning, and builds an ark by which he and numerous other humans and animals are saved. When the gods, however, then realise the full extent of their reliance on the human labour pool, they decide that because of the tumult humans create, their numbers must be regulated by various means including making them mortal (Foster 2005: 228; for the full story, see 227–280).[1] As we shall see, this would not be the last time that death was the penalty for creating noise nuisance.

Since then, objections to noise have been perennial throughout history, ranging from Buddhist scriptures from 500 BC listing ten objectionable urban noises to a fourteenth-century poet complaining of the noise of smithies who 'Drive me to death with the din of their dints' (Thompson 2004: 115–116). An official complaint from 1378 in London about the noise of an armourer was evidently the first noise complaint invoking the nuisance act introduced into English law by Henry II in the previous century (Goldsmith 2012: 42). By the end of the nineteenth century, various forms of smithy were disappearing or quarantined by zoning regulations (Bijsterveld 2008: 67). Ironically, however, the zoning of sources of industrial noise would in time also lead to more commuting, which in turn increased traffic density and noise (Bijsterveld 2008: 89). The combination of new public and domestic sound sources and urban congestion produced, as we have seen, a rising chorus of intellectuals and writers complaining bitterly of street noise, with Thomas Carlyle famously building a sound-proofed attic (Picker 2003: 43). By century's end, noise was being condemned as the enemy of progress and civilization (Thompson 2004: 120).

From the turn of the century, the clamour against clamour increased exponentially. The press was filled with complaints about noise (Mansell 2017: 1–2). Medical professional Dan McKenzie published *City of Din: A Tirade against Noise*, in 1916, declaring that 'Civilisation is noise', that by contrast with the countryside, the modern city constantly battered the nerves (Mansell 2017: 34, 35). In 1929, one Cecilia Winkler in New York City complained that 'The sound of the loud-speakers carries through windowpanes, floors, ceilings, walls', which she declared created the need for more psychiatric institutions (Schwartz 2011: 630). Complaints multiplied, particularly about traffic noise, to which was added in the interwar period, the sound of radios, record-players and in the street, loudspeakers coming from shops and even aircraft used for advertising (Thompson 2004: 149–151).

With increased urban congestion and technologized sound in the post-WW2 period, the problem continued to be exacerbated; from 1993–1994, English police received 131,153 complaints about noise, of which 372 resulted in convictions (Schwartz 2011: 858). Most recently, it was reported that

> New Yorkers file as many as 75,000 a month – but new 311 call data obtained by Patch has revealed that many recent complaints arise from those disturbed by their neighbors' late-night ventures. From 19 February 2021 to 9 February this year, the website reported, the official helpline received 277 complaints about noisy sex. Queens produced the most, with 103. Manhattan came second with 66 while Brooklyn produced 55, the Bronx 48 and Staten Island four.
>
> *The Guardian* online Tuesday 1 Mar 2022

The source of one of the most distinctively modern of all acoustic intrusions and complaints has been aviation. For the first half of the twentieth century, however, the sonic radius of piston-engine aircraft made them relatively unobtrusive. Around mid-century, two developments changed all that. One was the sudden and rapid rise in the popularity of commercial flight, and the other was the conversion of civil aviation to turbo-jet and jet-propelled aircraft, both requiring longer runways and surrounded by encroaching suburban development. In the late 1950s, London's Heathrow was the biggest airport in Europe in terms of the number of starts, departures, and passage, and it was also in the midst of densely populated areas that were therefore exposed to the 'screaming of the turbojet airplanes that succeeded the last generation of propeller-driven, piston-engined aircraft' (Bijsterveld 2008: 195).

At the same time, commercial aircraft traffic increased. In 1958, the first year that American commercial jets landed at Heathrow, more people were crossing the Atlantic by air than by boat (Keizer 2010: 123). On 25 January 1959, the first transcontinental commercial jet flight in the US left Los Angeles, flew to Idlewild in New York, and returned to LA that evening (Peterson 2021: 19). In 1961, Heathrow processed six million passengers; by 1965, the figure had risen to 10.5 million (Bijsterveld 2008: 196). Jet aircraft are not just a source of intense acoustic intrusion, but also are a significant cause of property damage, including cracks in walls and windows and dislodged roofing tiles (Peterson 2021: 114). The combined effects can become intolerable, and in Peterson's detailed case study of Los Angeles airport she reported that the area over which planes depart has become what has been termed a 'ghost town' (Peterson 2021: 171).

The modern soundscape has had various adverse social effects, as we have seen in the particular case of LFN (see further Johnson 2009a). In 2011, the World Health Organization (WHO) estimated

> that about one million healthy life years are lost every year because of traffic noise in Western Europe through cardio-vascular disease, cognitive impairment, and the stress-related illnesses resulting from sleep disturbance, tinnitus, and annoyance. To take a specific example, coronary heart disease killed 101,000 in the UK in 2006, and, according to WHO's analysis, 3,030 of those deaths were caused by chronic exposure to traffic noise.
>
> Goldsmith 2012: 244

Prolonged exposure to aircraft and road traffic noise has been found to impair the learning of reading skills (Goldsmith 2012: 233). Surveys by the EU found that up to 170 million of its citizens suffered serious noise nuisance, one in four suffered reduced quality of life, five to fifteen per cent suffered serious disturbance of sleep and more than 6.5 per cent of people between the ages of sixteen and sixty suffered moderate to extreme hearing impairment (Goldsmith 2012: 234–235).

With the proliferation of new forms of mediated and amplified sound, music has generated the most extreme manifestations of complaint, in the form of violence. In Chicago, neighbours whose complaints about a woman's loud radio received no action, bombed her apartment (Thompson 2004: 151; for an extended study of the various connections between popular music and violence, see Johnson and Cloonan 2008). Karaoke seems to be particularly provocative of injury and even death (Johnson and Cloonan 2008: 81); in 2009, the press reported an attack on a woman singing in a Karaoke bar in the US city of Stamford:

> Authorities say the six women, all under the legal drinking age of 21, knocked the 25-year-old singer to the floor, punched her and pulled her hair. The victim, who suffered bruises and a chipped tooth in the attack, has said she was singing A Dios Le Pido by Colombian superstar Juanes when the violence began.
> https://www.smh.com.au/world/karaoke-singer-attacked-over-performance-20091009-gp9j.html accessed 9 April 2022

Similar reports of Karaoke violence include, in 2017, a fatal stabbing frenzy by a Karaoke singer in Vietnam who was mocked for his performance. In the same year, 'two men were detained for murdering another patron after a heated argument at a karaoke bar in southern Ninh Thuan province', and another in Malaysia who was killed for hogging the microphone (https://www.theguardian.com/world/2017/may/25/vietnam-man-kills-karaoke-dispute accessed 9 April 2022). On the basis of press reports, Karaoke performances of the song 'My Way' are particularly risky. In November 2021, it was reported from Kabul that 'gunmen posing as Taliban fighters killed three people ... as they attacked a wedding in an attempt to stop the music being played' (James Rothwell, 'Wedding music provokes attack', *Sydney Morning Herald* 2 November 2021: 17). In any event, since humankind's earliest written records, the connection between death and noise has been reinforced.

These are extreme responses to noise nuisance. The most prominent of the adverse impacts of the modern soundscape on public health is, however, irreversible hearing damage. The symptoms of industrial deafness were recognized as early as 1713, and from the 1830s onwards the affliction was receiving increasing attention (Bijsterveld 2008: 71–72); by the early twenty-first century, 120 million people had hearing loss 'sufficient to disable them. And ... all adults are deaf to sounds above 15,000 cycles a second', or fifteen kilohertz (Goldsmith 2012: 7). Much of this deafening exposure to sound is voluntary, through MP3 players, causing up to five million children in the US to suffer from measurably impaired hearing; one American child in eight has noise-induced hearing loss (Goldsmith 2012: 29). As we have seen, measures to combat sonic nuisance have a long history, but it is the modern soundscape that has generated the most comprehensive array of noise monitoring and abatement measures.

The rising tide of noise particularly in relation to the street noise in increasingly congested urban centres has led to proliferating noise abatement measures. They included German philosopher Theodore Lessing's Antilärmverein (Anti-Noise Society) founded in 1908 in Hanover, while in Berlin in the same year, pharmacist Maximilian Negwer began manufacturing earplugs called Ohropax (roughly translated as 'earpeace') (Goodyear 2012: 20). Complaints about modern noise were made by Nietzsche and Schopenhauer (Goodyear 2012: 23); as Picker (2003) has documented, street music was a common target for 'mind workers'. In the mid-nineteenth century, Charles Babbage noted that over one period of eighty days, he had confronted street musicians 165 times and in one year had expended the then very considerable sum of 105 pounds in court proceedings against them. In his assessment, 'lower classes are the chief encouragers' (Schwartz 2011: 235). Given his status as a wealthy and eminent mathematician, engineer and philosopher, we are again presented with a theme that is now familiar: the role of class in soundscape politics. 'The quest for quiet is used to separate the middle and upper classes from the working class who did not have the luxury of – or supposedly even the desire for – silence in their lives' (Goodyear 2012: 23).

From the early twentieth century, noise abatement campaigns multiplied in the new urban soundscape (on the interwar period, see for example Bijsterveld 2008: 110–133). From November 1929 to May 1930, a formal survey of environmental noise was conducted in New York, leading to the formation of a Noise Abatement Commission; similar exercises were conducted in Chicago, Boston, London, Paris and Berlin (Goldsmith 2012: 167–169). In the UK, similar concerns led to the foundation of the Anti-Noise league (ANL) in 1933, in particular to protect those involved in intellectual work from the noises made by such modern inventions as gramophones, wireless and motor cycles (Mansell 2017: 21).

By the 1950s, recognition of damage caused by the modern soundscape led to the success of litigation to gain compensation for workplace hearing loss, following a successful court action in 1951 by a sixty-one-year-old employee of a drop forge company in Wisconsin (Schwartz 2011: 807); this was followed by the introduction of measures to protect workers from noise-induced damage (Bijsterveld 2008: 72). Such developments gave impetus to further campaigns targeting changes in the soundscape and urban demography, such as Citizens for a Quieter City in New York in the 1970s, the Right to Quiet Society in Vancouver and in the UK the Right to Peace and Quiet Campaign ran from 1991–1996 (Schwartz 2011: 832, 858). Other groups include the organization Noise Free America in California, The People's Environmental Protection Alliance in Australia and Noise Network in London (Bijsterveld 2008: 53).

Many of these campaigns have highly particularized targets that reflect changes in the modern soundscape in specific spaces. In 2006 in Sydney, the group Public Transport, was formed to fight audio advertising on trains and buses. The UK's Pipedown opposed the use of Muzak in supermarkets, hospitals and with notable success in the case of Gatwick airport; a 1997 survey found that seventeen per cent of its sample cited Muzak as the most detested feature of modern life (Johnson and Cloonan 2008: 179; for further listings of similar campaigns, see Bijsterveld 2008: 240–256; Johnson and Cloonan 2008: 178–181; Keizer 2010: 277–280; Goldsmith 2012: 158–180, 202–210, 222–225, 237–255; and Google Noise Pollution Clearing house).

Grassroots organizations have often been among the drivers of legislative changes that also seek to address the growing problem of noise pollution throughout the world. Such legislation includes the US Noise Control Act of 1972 which sought to restrict noise 'that jeopardizes … the health or welfare' of citizens (Keizer 2010: 124–125), and in France 'the first law covering most aspects of noise pollution was passed in 1992 … it covers town-planning, transport systems, and noise protection near airports' (Goldsmith 2012: 236). In the US, in late 1971, under the auspices of the Clean Air Act Amendments, hearings were conducted on sources of noise pollution that extended the emphasis on public nuisance and health to the broader remit of environmental protection, covering

> construction noise; manufacturing and transportation noise; urban planning, architectural design, and noise in the home; standards and measurements methods; legislation and enforcement problems; transportation noise (rail and other); urban noise problems and social behavior; physiological and psychological effects; agricultural and recreational use noise; technology and economics of noise control; national programs and their relationship with state and local programs … An investigation into the scope of the problem of noise, the hearings ultimately led to the formation of ONAC [Office of Noise Abatement and Control] … the hearings marked a moment in which diverse and divergent issues and interests related to noise come under the umbrella of the environment
> Peterson 2021: 92

The sources cited above are just samples of modern anti-noise campaigns that are far too numerous to list here. Some began as private individual noise complaints which gradually gathered enough critical mass to generate formal organizations; campaigns were assimilated into government policies and generated a body of formal legislation. If the former were the work of people with sufficient social capital, they often gained enough momentum to influence the latter. To exemplify, consider briefly two prominent case studies, one from the UK and the other from the US. Again, it is noteworthy that class was a crucial factor, not simply as the sensibility underlying the campaign, but also in terms of political influence.

The UK-based ANL, referred to above, was established in 1933 by Baron Horder of Ashford. While Horder sat in the House of Lords, he proclaimed the bottom-up dynamic of the organization in declaring that 'there has come upon us, as the result of increased motor traffic, increased transport, aeroplanes and louder forms of amusement, a spate of uncontrolled noise for the suppression of which *we must organize ourselves*' (Mansell 2017: 51; my italics). ANL's activities included publication of the journal *Quiet* (49), pamphlets and radio broadcasts that particularly addressed themselves to 'professional people and often emphasized that educated people's neurasthenic breakdown – because it deprived the nation of much-needed expertise – was an urgent concern' (Mansell 2017: 51). H. G. Wells was associated with the League, and was among the presenters at the Noise Abatement Exhibition held in London in June 1935 at the Science Museum.

The former Chief Inspector of Schools, Henry Richards, was also a member of the ANL, and identified noise as 'a modern danger which has increased, is increasing, and must be diminished' (Mansell 2017: 51). Some of the 'modern dangers' they targeted included 'loudspeaker abuse', finding that complaints about loud radios had risen from 298 in 1932 to 508 in 1933 (Mansell 2017: 55), and the use of loudspeakers in political campaigning was a 'flashpoint in the policing of noise in mid-1930s London' (Mansell 2017: 57). The ANL went through a number of iterations, dissolved in 1951 for lack of funds, but was reborn in 1959 as the British Noise Abatement Society (Bijsterveld 2008: 197). In this form, it became active in relation to aircraft noise (Bijsterveld 2008: 213) and remains active as the only registered UK charitable foundation with the sole mission of regulating noise.

> In 1960, recognizing that exposure to persistent, unwanted sound was detrimental to human health and wellbeing, productivity and quality of life, our founder John Connell OBE lobbied the Noise Abatement Act through the UK Parliament making noise a statutory nuisance for the first time in the UK.
>
> https://futuresoundfoundation.uk/home, accessed 10 July 2021.

A member of the House of Lords, an eminent intellectual, a senior public servant, an OBE: although initially presenting itself as a grass-roots self-help movement, this is hardly a proletarian project. Similarly with a US equivalent, spearheaded by Julia Barnett Rice from the early twentieth century. Rice was a physician, married to a wealthy businessman Isaac Rice, and lived in New York City, in a mansion within earshot of the tugboat steam whistles on the Hudson River, of which she counted nearly 3,000 blasts in one night. Apart from disturbing her own tranquillity, she was concerned about the impact of the sound on nearby hospitals. In 1906, she organized the Society for the Suppression of Unnecessary Noise. With the support of numerous doctors and a 3,000 signature petition, this well-connected woman became the driving force behind the 1907 'Bennett Act', named for a supportive congressman, which prohibited the unnecessary blowing of whistles in ports and harbours (Thompson 2004: 121–122; for a lengthy account of Rice's career, see Schwartz 2011: 505–550). The Society also campaigned against other sources of noise, including July Fourth fireworks. Its activities foreshadowed the formation of a succession of similar organizations in the US which targeted not only other urban noise, but which also sought to protect pristine rural silence. Under the aegis of the National Sounds Program formed in 2000, the noise abatement movement was extended to national parks and other outdoor recreational areas (see further Keizer 2010: 179–186). By the end of the twentieth century, noise abatement programmes were seeking to transcend the confusing diversity of national guidelines; in 2000, the European Commission proposed new approaches to the problem of noise that often superseded various national programmes (Bijsterveld 2008: 193–194).

For purposes of the present argument, we should note that Rice was a woman of considerable social capital, and also give particular regard to the word 'Unnecessary' in the name of her movement. It signals again the ambivalence and ambiguity built into noise abatement campaigns. 'Unnecessary' for whom? Although unimpeachable in their intent, these movements were largely driven by well-connected members of the bourgeoisie whose own affluence depended directly or indirectly on various forms of (noisy) industrial productivity. Rice did not want to prohibit all river tug noise, only that which she felt was 'social' rather than strictly commercial.

The Society for the Suppression of Unnecessary Noise 'recognized that much noise was simply unavoidable, and its members had no desire to interfere with the vital commerce and business of the city' (Thompson 2004: 122). For these reasons, noise abatement groups were more likely to target street noise than industrial noise. In the late 1920s, 'the Noise Commission of London claimed that street noise was a much more serious problem than industrial noise, because street noise, unlike industrial noise, had no rhythm' (Bijsterveld 2008: 74).

Early noise abatement campaigns were slow to take effect, and some historians attribute this to their elitist complexion, with disdain for the working class preventing what could have been an effective alliance with labour unions (Bijsterveld 2008: 102). This fundamentally class-based caveat would continue to frame and constrain legal action brought by victims of modern noise, including the sounds of industry, road, marine and air traffic. The *National Safety News* no 15 April 1927 declared that a successful defence against noise complaints only had to demonstrate that 'the noise was a part of the very necessary industrial processes and that the industry was a very necessary part of the community and therefore had to be tolerated as a necessary evil' (Thompson 2004: 120).

The subjectivity of the understanding of sonic 'nuisance', complementing the question of whether it is a cognitive or physiological problem, was not the only difficulty encountered by attempts to grapple with the growing problems of modern noise. One of the most persistent of these was the attempt to over-ride that subjectivity by the establishment of objective standards of acoustic measurement by which 'nuisance' could be quantified. Notwithstanding various attempts to measure sound in the nineteenth century (Thompson 2004: 85–86), when James Loudon addressed the American Association for the Advancement of Science as its President in 1901, he began by apologizing for choosing to speak about a subject that 'has been comparatively neglected by physicists for many years' (Thompson 2004: 59). As late as 1917, a report on the progress of noise abatement declared that 'Noise not only has no instrument of measurement but is even without a satisfactory definition' (Thompson 2004: 145).

It was the invention of the telegraph, telephone and radio valve that gave impetus to attempts at standardized acoustic quantification that could gauge the effectiveness of transmissions (Bijsterveld 2008: 105). Telegraph and telephone gave rise to the term MSC (Miles of Standard Cable), which measured deterioration of signal over one mile. A later unit of measurement proposed in 1924 by the Bell Telephone Laboratories was the TU (Transmission Unit), which was arrived at by more complex mathematics, and in 1928 Bell renamed it the decibel. Other units proposed for the measurement of noise in the 1930s included the sone and the phon, to measure perceived loudness, the mel and the bark 'to capture the subjective pitches of sound'; the watt was used in the study of underwater acoustics (Goldsmith 2012: 175). The first International Committee on Acoustics met in Paris in 1937 to formalize acceptance of two noise units, the phon (the level of loudness) and the decibel (intensity of sound) (Bijsterveld 2008: 106).

While the decibel has become the most familiar unit of acoustic measurement, it remains far from adequate to the full spectrum of the soundscape of modernity (on problems of sound measurement, see further for example Bijsterveld 2008: 104–110; Goldsmith 2012: 260–264). Some sense of its complexity is suggested by Bijsterveld: 'two sounds differed by 10 decibels, "when the louder is ten times the physical intensity of the fainter, by 20 decibels when the ratio is 1000, and so on" ... Once they had a zero level of noise as the beginning of the scale, they could start counting. This zero became the threshold limit of a tone of 1000 Hertz'. (Bijsterveld 2008: 105). It is not necessary to enter this highly complex technical area in detail in the present context; suffice to say that the measurement of sound is, and remains, problematic in attempting to determine when sound becomes the subjective evaluation as potential nuisance. Various refinements of the basic unit of the decibel have been introduced to register different sonic profiles. The most common of which is known as the A-weighting curve (dBA). This is 'a filtering algorithm ... that aims to conform data to the human ear across the frequency spectrum (a standard known as an equal-loudness contour). In other words it excludes virtually "all of the sounds we are not *expected* to hear"'(Jasen 2017: 62; italics in the original).

The dBA has been adopted for studies of environmental noise and for studies of noise-induced hearing impairment. As is recognized by the WHO, it is still, however, inadequate in dealing with one of the fastest growing problems in the contemporary soundscape, sounds below 200 Hz; the alternative dB curve is more effective, but still unreliable, below 60 Hz (Jasen 2017: 62). That is, the simple parameter of sound intensity or volume is insufficiently nuanced to address problems in the modern soundscape. In the context of densely populated urban space, and the lowering of pitch in ambient noise, especially in popular music, there has been a growing recognition of the distinctive problems of LFN. In 2007, Sydney's mayor, Clover Moore, insightfully called for the regulation not just of volume, but of the use of bass speakers in apartments (Johnson 2009a: 188–189), and licensing authorities are now taking into account LFN as a specific component of sound in applications for music festivals (see further Johnson 2009a).

A further (and sometimes overlapping) site of the difficulties of regulating noise problems is one we have briefly referred to above: aircraft noise. One of these difficulties springs from regional inconsistencies. Attempts to establish an international standard for the measurement and regulation of aircraft noise have foundered on the variations in local conditions and legislative frameworks (Bijsterveld 2008: 231, 244). Attempts to develop a uniform standard for what is a global phenomenon led to the establishment of The Noise and Number Index (NNI), which 'attempted to quantify the subjective noisiness of aircraft, and it used both measured sound levels and the number of aircraft per day (or night) as a key annoyance factor' (Goldsmith 2012: 209). The NNI was developed specifically for Heathrow, but then applied for other airports. It was replaced after two decades by L.Aeq, a 'measure of the total energy of a period over which noise is present ... and is still in common use' (Goldsmith 2012: 212).

Given all the difficulties in scientifically quantifying noise nuisance, it is testimony to the severity of the impact of changes in the modern soundscape on public health to find just how far noise abatement campaigns have been translated into formal government policies. In addition to measures already referred to, the US Noise Control Act of 1972 sought to restrict noise 'that jeopardizes ... health or welfare' of citizens (Keizer 2010: 124–125). In the US, the National Environment Policy Act (NEPA) was passed in 1969; it was augmented by the Noise Control Act (NCA) in 1972, as outcomes of the work of the US Environmental Protection Agency, who had warned Congress that thirty million Americans 'were exposed to noise high enough to cause hearing loss' (Goldsmith 2012: 212–213; on noise legislation, see further Bijsterveld 2008: 69–81).

In practical terms, there are various measures undertaken in noise abatement legislation. One of them is the imposition of curfews on social activities such as parties and music venues, and in the commercial sphere applying, for example, to industrial and aircraft noise. Complementing curfews is the policy of spatial zoning. In premodern cities, a lack of acoustically sensitive planning meant that various professions, trades, commercial and residential precincts were intermingled. One of the solutions to this problem was the growth of special function areas, such as the suburbs themselves – and ironically, as we have seen, the rise of noisy rail and road commuting (see further Johnson 2009b). There also developed occupation-specific precincts – business offices, professions, shopping, industrial – sometimes emerging spontaneously, sometime by formal regulation. And one of the criteria for regulation was noise. In the UK, in 1939, the government issued a bylaw

> for the use of local authorities that made it an offense to create noise in public places or within earshot of public buildings such as schools and hospitals. A whole section of the bylaw was given over to wireless and gramophone loudspeakers, proposing to make it illegal to use them in public places or in such a way as to cause disturbance to neighbours.
>
> Mansell 2017: 59

Goldsmith identifies the Chicago Zoning Ordinance of 1957 as 'the first noise ordinance in the world to specify maximum noise levels' (Goldsmith 2012: 191).

A further response to problems of noise nuisance has been developments in acoustic engineering in architecture, both domestic and commercial. At the beginning of the twentieth century, the opening of the Boston Symphony Hall on 15 October 1900 was celebrated as 'the first auditorium in the world to be constructed according to laws of modern science. Indeed, it not only embodied, but instigated, the origins of the modern science of acoustics' (Thompson 2004: 4). The chief consultant on the new concert hall was perhaps the most influential acoustic engineer of the new century, Wallace Sabine (in addition to Thompson 2004, Sabine's work is also discussed by Schwartz 2011: 457–471). But the distinctive soundscape of modernity introduced unprecedented complexities into the relationship between architecture and sound, and much of that was to do not simply with amplification, but also filtering, with growing concern that we have been tracing about the protection of elite culture from violation by plebeian noise. The owner of Boston Symphony Hall, Henry Lee Higginson, not only sought the perfect performance acoustics, but, in his words, also wanted to quarantine the sound, particularly of his favourite composer, Beethoven, from the 'sounds of the world' (Thompson 2004: 15). Higginson's objectives were thus both practical and ideological: producing a perfect acoustic for both hearing art music and sacralizing it by separating it from the vulgar noise of everyday life. Aesthetically, this represented the apex of attempts to address the problem of the sonic deluge of modernity, and central to attempts at the abatement and control of noise was the acoustic engineer.

The Acoustical Society of America was founded in 1928 and held its first official meeting on May 1929 (Thompson 2004: 60, 105–106). By the early 1930s, there was an increasing public awareness of sound, with a pamphlet on career options for youth predicting that acoustical engineers 'will become more and more indispensable to civilisation', and that they are increasingly important in building design (Thompson 2004: 60). Acoustic science and engineering became one of the central pillars in noise abatement projects. In the late 1960s, the Dutch Board of Public Health, an advisory body to the government, proposed four anti-noise measures: 'soundproofing, reducing the sound emission from consumer appliances, careful city planning, and public information campaigns' (Bijsterveld 2008: 183). Introducing her study of architecture and sound in the US from 1900 to 1933, Thompson summarizes the importance of acoustic engineering: 'Scientists and engineers discovered ways to manipulate traditional materials of architectural construction in order to control the behavior of sound in space. New kinds of material specifically designed to control sound were developed' (Thompson 2004: 2).

Conclusion

The Aural Renaissance of the late nineteenth century was a harbinger of a sonic order that has liberated many in giving them a public voice. Nonetheless, and notwithstanding the proliferation of noise abatement campaigns, policies and material interventions, noise has become such a significant form of pollution that in 1998 the WHO designated noise as one of only two exponentially increasing environmental threats (the other was allergies), for which no solution seemed possible. At the turn of the century, the Commission of the European Communities presented a monetized assessment of the damage caused by environmental noise, estimating it to be between thirteen and thirty-eight billion Euros, taking into account not just direct damage, but also such factors as 'a reduction of house prices, medical costs, reduced possibilities of land use and cost of lost labour days' (Johnson and Cloonan 2008: 167). This study clearly raises significant issues of social policy in the contemporary contexts of urban space and the character and portability of sound.

Since the WHO report, in spite of various noise abatement programmes instituted globally, the situation has continued to deteriorate. By way of some preliminary data immediately relevant to this discussion: A Johns Hopkins University study from July 2008 'reported that the incidence of hearing loss in the United States is approaching epidemic proportions. ... one in three Americans now suffer some degree of hearing impairment – much of it noise induced' (Prochnik 2011: 15). According to a 2004 report, seventy-five per cent of US farm workers have hearing impairment because of heavy machinery (Prochnik 2011: 42). A European Environment Agency report of 2008 estimated that in the EU alone, 'traffic noise regularly exposes upward of

67 million people to decibel levels exceeding safety recommendations in terms of both hearing and cardiovascular health' (Prochnik 2011: 155). The government run Australian laboratories trading as Australian Hearing have reported a significant narrowing in the range of hearing among young people.[2]

Rather than industrial or traffic noise, however, major causes are self-inflicted. Tom Roland, Director of NYU Medical Center's Department of Cochlear Implants declared that 'if you can hear someone else's music leaking through their headphone or earbuds, that person is causing themselves hearing damage'. A study conducted by the University of Colorado and the Children's Hospital Boston in the 1980s found that teens who listen to iPods at dangerous levels constitute between seven and twenty-four per cent of the population (Prochnik 2011: 167). A Hannah Montana in Concert Collection Doll, made by Disney, reaches 103 dB; a Tickle Me Elmo reaches 100 dB, comparable to a snowmobile (Prochnik 2011: 16). And these are children's toys!

The distinctive modern condition includes a radical change in the sonic order and its politics, requiring a reassessment of assumptions about human rights that have long been taken for granted. Citizens of the US have a right to bear arms, inscribed in the Second Amendment introduced in 1791 to the Constitution. But this right was guaranteed in a community that had only recently gained its independence through armed revolution, in a country that was still largely a frontier wilderness, and at a time when the private ownership of 'arms' was largely limited to single-shot muskets, swords and knives. Although now much vaunted by the gun lobby as a basic constitutional right, bearing arms simply does not mean the same thing in a modern city dense with personal frictions and grievances, in which the arms include easily obtainable assault rifles and portable missile launchers. So with sound. From the twentieth century, the level of noise that could be made by a human being suddenly increased to deafening levels, sometimes with lethal outcomes (see further Johnson and Cloonan 2008: 173).

Sound has become an instrument of enormous social power, even when dominant social discourses, from scholarship to politics, remain visually oriented. As recently as 2022, David Haskell reported the continuing visual bias of scientific training as a biologist: 'In my own training, not once was I asked to use my ears in a lab experiment' (Haskell 2022: 5). In the words of Feiereisen and Hill, 'Despite sound's importance in the medical field, the visual still serves as a synonym for the objective' (Feiereisen and Hill 2012: 5).

The less amenable to 'reading' (as opposed to 'hearing') a message is, the less authority it is felt to carry, especially by those whose cultural capital is sustained by print (see further Johnson 2006). Studies of culture and its history will benefit by paying sustained attention to the dynamics of sound in society. Sound is everywhere, both within and beyond the range of human hearing. We cannot close our ears in the way we can close or avert our eyes. Modern sound technologies have liberated millions who have been silenced by marginalization and illiteracy. But every liberation for some is a constraint on freedom for others. An understanding of modernity, its history and relations of power requires us to attend to sound in all its aspects, from the physiology of hearing and the mechanics of sonority, to the deployment of sound in all social and political formations.

Notes

1 Although the 'noise nuisance' is given as the reason for these divine interventions in some translations or adaptations of the better known *The Epic of Gilgamesh*, its source is in fact this poem, called *Atrahasis*, after its protagonist (named Utanapishti in *Gilgamesh*). My thanks to Professor Andrew George, editor of the 2019 Penguin, *The Epic of Gilgamesh* for this information (personal communication 16 October 2021).
2 My thanks to senior staff of Australian Hearing for discussion of contemporary Australian hearing impairment.

Reading

Bijsterveld, Karin. 2008. *Mechanical Sound: Technology, Culture, and Public Problems of Noise in the Twentieth Century.* Cambridge, MA and London: MIT Press.

Feiereisen, Florence and Akexandra Merley Hill (eds). 2012. *Germany in the Loud Twentieth Century: An Introduction.* Oxford: Oxford University Press.

Foster, Benjamin R. (ed.). 2005. *Before the Muses: An Anthology of Akkadian Literature* (3rd edition). Bethesda, MD: CDL Press.

Goldsmith, Mike. 2012. *Discord: The Story of Noise.* Oxford: Oxford University Press.

Goodyear, John. 2012. 'Escaping the Urban Din: A Comparative Study of Theodor Lessing's Antilärmverein (1908) and Maximilian Negwer's Ohropax (1908)'. In Florence Feiereisen and Alexandra Merley-Hill (eds), *Germany in the Loud Twentieth Century: An Introduction.* Oxford: Oxford University Press: 19–34.

Haskell, David George. 2022. *Sounds Wild and Broken.* Collingwood: Black Inc.

Hegarty, Paul. 2007. *NoiseMusic: A History.* New York, NY: Continuum.

Iles, Anthony. 2014. *Noise and Capitalism.* San Sebastian: Arteleku.

Jasen, Paul C. 2017 (first pub 2016). *Low End Theory: Bass, Bodies and the Materiality of Sonic Experience.* New York, NY and London: Bloomsbury.

Johnson, Bruce. 2006. 'Divided Loyalties: Literary Responses to the Rise of Oral Authority in the Modern Era'. *Textus*, XIX (Spring): 285–304.

Johnson, Bruce. 2009a. 'Low Frequency Noise and Urban Space', special issue, 'Music, characterization and urban space'. *Popular Music History*, 4 (2): 177–195.

Johnson, Bruce. 2009b. 'Sites of Sound'. *Oral Tradition*, 24 (2): 455–470.

Johnson, Bruce. 2020. *Jazz Diaspora: Music and Globalisation.* London and New York, NY: Routledge.

Johnson, Bruce and Martin Cloonan. 2008. *Dark Side of the Tune: Popular Music and Violence.* Aldershot: Ashgate.

Keizer, Garret. 2010. *The Unwanted Sound of Everything We Want: A Book About Noise.* New York, NY: Public Affairs.

Mansell, James G. 2017. *The Age of Noise in Britain: Hearing Modernity.* Urbana, Chicago, IL and Springfield: University of Illinois Press.

Peterson, Marina. 2021. *Atmospheric Noise: The Indefinite Urbanism of Los Angeles*. Durham, NC and London: Duke University Press.
Picker, John. 2003. *Victorian Soundscapes*. Oxford: Oxford University Press.
Prochnik, George. 2011. *In Pursuit of Silence: Listening for Meaning in a World of Noise*. New York, NY: Anchor Books.
Reimann, Heli. Forthcoming. 'The Dilemmas Around the Status of Jazz in Soviet Union: The Beginning of Anti-Jazz Rhetoric in 1920s'. In Bruce Johnson, Adam Havas, David Horn (eds), *The Routledge Companion to Diasporic Jazz Studies*. New York, NY: Routledge.
Schwartz, Hillel. 2011. *Making Noise: From Babel to the Big Bang & Beyond*. New York, NY: Zone Books.
Thompson, Emily. 2004. *The Soundscape of Modernity: Architectural Acoustics and the Culture of Listening in America, 1900–1933*. Cambridge, MA and London: MIT Press.
Trotta, Felipe. 2020. *Annoying Music in Everyday Life*. New York, NY and London: Bloomsbury Academic.

INDEX

abeng (musical instrument) 36
acousmatic sound 17, 55, 83, 85, 86, 90
acoustemology ix, 9, 15–32
Adventures of Jack O'Donohoe (song) 44, 45
Africa, African 34, 124, 149, 170
Ainsworth, William Harrison 100
aircraft 129, 131, 134, 140, 181, 186, 189; *see also* noise
Aitken, John 109
Alexander the Great 82
Alien (film) 92
Alone, Daniel 40
Always look on the bright side of life (song) 82
American-Indian 149
American Telephone and Telegraph Company, The 125
amplification 11, 26, 30, 123, 130, 190
amygdala 23
Anderson, Major Joseph 40
anechoic chamber 4, 27
anthropology vii, 2, 9, 12, 149, 150
antiquity 9, 26, 28, 35, 36, 51, 118, 123, 124, 146; *see also* Assyria; Babylon; Egypt; Greece; Rome
ANZAC Day (Australia) 114
archaeoacoustic 146
architecture 63, 185; ecclesiastical 10, 25, 27, 28, 56; secular 25, 135, 170, 190, 191; spatiality and acoustics 25, 27, 135, 170, 190, 191

Aristotle 145
Armstrong, Louis 8
Asia, Asian 149
Assyria 180
Atkinson, Isaac 108
Atrahasis (ancient epic) 180, 193
Attack of the 50 Foot Woman, The (film) 167
audion, the 130
auditory cortex 23
aurality 50, 55, 67, 80, 145; *see also* hearing
Aural Renaissance ix, x, 11, 12, 123–163
Australia, Australian 21, 27, 38, 114, 129, 148, 141, 152, 153, 154, 155, 157, 166, 170, 175, 184, 192, 193; Australian first nations people 24; bushrangers 44, 45, 47, 100, 111; convict settlement 39, 41, 42, 43, 46; punishment 42
Australian Hearing (research body) 27, 192, 193

Babbage, Charles 184
Babylon 180
Bacall, Lauren 21
Bach, Johann Sebastian 169
Bacon, Francis 56, 57, 61, 62
Banished Defender, The (song) 42
Banister, John 113
banjo 147
Bartok, Bela 149

Battle of the Sexes (film) 160
BBC, The 30
Beard, George M. 135
Beka-Record Company 149
Bell, Alexander Graham 125, 127, 188
Bell, Melville 125
Bell Telephone Laboratories 188
Bells 6, 25, 56, 116, 119, 124, 131, 135, 158, 159, 180
Berliner, Emil 127
Bible, The 25, 85, 103, 112, 126
Biggs, E. Power 28
Biggs, Ronnie 104
Birmingham (UK) 131, 135
Black Beauty (song) 148
Bodleian Library, The 113
Boer War, The 137
Bogart, Humphrey 21
Boilermaker's Disease 22, 131; *see also* deafness
Bold Jack O'Donohoe (song) 44, 45
Bonny Nell (song) 62
Bonny Sweet Robin (song) 81
Bonaparte, Napoleon 99, 127, 157, 160
Book of Common Prayer, The 69
Boom Box 9, 20, 179
Borwick, William 108
Boston 135, 184, 192; Boston Symphony Hall 26, 190
Bradford (UK) 135
Branch Davidian Sect 170
Brasilia, Brazil 170
Breton, Nicholas 120
Brian Boru (song) 37
Brighton (UK) 134
Britain, British 2, 10, 18, 25, 34, 36, 38, 45, 112, 137, 138, 145, 151, 170; British Museum 158; British Noise Abatement Society 186
Browning, Robert 126
Buddhism 180
Burghley, Lord 51
Burnet, Gilbert 68
Burns, Michael 40, 43

Californication (song) 171
Camden, William 131
Cameron, Donald, MP 46
Campbelltown, New South Wales 44
Canberra, Australia 170
Caribbean, The 150, 166
Car Radios 25
Carlyle, Thomas 181

Carnegie Hall 149
Carthage, Carthaginians 36
Catholicism 37, 42, 51
Cat-Women of the Moon (film) 167
celebrity 99, 100, 102, 104, 105, 107, 109–111
Chacksfield, Frank 168
Charge of the Light Brigade, The 92
Chartists 42
Chartists are Coming, The (song) 42
Chesterfield, Fourth Earl 98
Chicago, US 183, 184, 190
China, Chinese 149, 155, 175
Church, Church congregations ix, 10, 11, 25, 27, 28, 29, 33, 51, 53, 56, 57, 58, 69, 70, 71, 75, 95, 113, 116, 130–131, 135, 146, 168; *see also* Catholicism; Protestantism
City of Din: A Tirade against Noise 181
class relations ix, 10, 11, 37, 38, 41, 42, 43, 46, 51, 52–57, 69, 70–72, 77, 98–102, 104, 105, 109–111, 113, 114, 116–121, 129, 130, 152, 155, 156, 157, 168, 169, 178, 179, 184, 185, 187
Clay, Sonny and his Plantation Orchestra 148
Clayton, James 40
Cocteau, Jean 159–161
cognitive ecology 24
Colorado, University of (US) 192
concert halls 18, 25, 113, 149; acoustics 29, 149, 190; audience conduct 11, 113–114
Conniff, Ray 29
Cook, William 124
Cooke, Hezekiah 67
Copernicus, Nicolaus 51
Cotton Spinners' Farewell, The (song) 42
Cram, Ralph Adams 28
Cranz, Martin 35
Creole Rhapsody (song) 148
Croppy Boy (song) 43
Crosby, Bing 129, 169
Ctesibius 124
Cuba, Cuban 150, 175; Havana Syndrome 175
Cummings, Constance 161
Curlewis, Jean 152
Curnow, Thomas 47
Custom 10, 11, 48, 52, 53, 100, 102, 104–107, 111
Cyprus (ship) 43

Dallwitz, Dave 45
Dance, Dancing 9, 15, 20, 22, 41, 61, 112, 118, 119, 152, 153, 154, 172
Darrow, Clarence 127–128
Dauvois, Michel 16
Davenant, Sir William 73
da Vinci, Leonardo 124
deafness viii, 13, 22, 67, 115, 117, 131, 135, 137, 140, 146, 179, 183, 192
Death Magnetic (song) 171
de Forest, Lee 130
Delius, Frederick 169
de Mandeville, Bernard 109
de Mandeville, Édouard-léon Scott 126
Demosthenes 55
Denison, Sir William Thomas 41
Denmark 86, 92, 95, 173
Descartes, René 23, 51
Dickens, Charles 114, 131, 136, 161
DiPietro, Janet 5
Dr. Who 30
Disney, Walt 192
dissolution of the monasteries 51, 52; see also Reformation, The
Donne, John 71, 73
Donohoe, Jack 44–45
Doolan, Jack 44
Douie, Captain Charles 139
drums 8, 36, 39, 83, 85, 90, 117, 124, 125, 137, 148
Duke University Chapel 28

Easter Rising, The (Ireland) 33
Earthquake (film) 21
echea 124
echolocation 4, 26, 27, 166; see also reverberation
Edgeworth Bess 102
Egypt 126, 149
Eliot, T.S. 136
Elizabethan, Elizabeth I Queen of England 9, 10, 25, 54, 55, 56, 57, 58, 80, 81, 82, 89, 95, 99; Elizabethan acoustic world 60–63, 80, 114, 121; Elizabethan playhouse 67–77, 90, 93, 96–97 see also *Hamlet*; Elizabethan preaching 66–67
Ellington, Duke 148
El Sistema 35
Embodied Cognition 24
Enclosures, The 52, 105, 116
England, English viii, 6, 9, 10, 25, 34, 35, 36, 37, 42–45, 47, 50, 51, 52, 54, 56, 57, 59, 60, 61, 63, 66, 67, 68, 69, 71, 73, 74, 81, 93, 100, 102, 104, 105, 112, 114, 117, 120, 132, 135, 138, 181; see also Britain
Enlightenment, The 34, 39, 50
Environmentalism 12, 174, 175, 184, 185, 191
Environmental Protection Agency (EPA) 189
Epic of Gilgamesh, The 193
Epidaurus amphitheatre 16
Erasmus, Desiderius 98
Estonian language 6
Ethnomusicology 149, 150
European Commission, The 187
European Union (EU) 191
Examiner (newspaper) 127
execution 44, 45–46, 101, 102, 103, 107–109, 120; see also Tyburn Gallows
Exorcist, The (film) 5, 7
extended mind theory 24

Fallujah, Iraq 171
Father Knows Best (TV series) 167
Feilding, Rowland 1, 2, 137, 138
Felons of our Land, The (song) 33
Fielding, Henry 110, 115
film 1, 4, 7, 19, 21, 26, 38, 45, 71, 74, 75, 82, 85, 90, 92, 93, 127, 129, 130, 137, 149, 150, 151, 160, 167
Finland, Finnish 6, 13, 22, 25, 36, 146
Fitzgerald, Ella 8
flapper, the 152, 153, 155; see also gender
Flappers in the Sky (song) 153
Fluxus movement 180
France, French 7, 16, 21, 25, 36, 37, 55, 113, 117, 137, 138, 146, 185
Fraser's Magazine 110
frequency 12, 17, 19–21, 25, 75, 124, 135, 146, 153, 164, 165, 166, 171, 173, 188; see also pitch
Frost, John 42
Fry, Elizabeth 112

Galen, Aelius 145
Gaskell, Elizabeth 118, 136
Gatwick Airport, UK 185
Gay, John 103, 115
Gaza Strip 172
Gender 2, 9, 12, 20, 21, 30, 69, 125, 150, 153–158, 160, 167–168, 178
Gentleman's Magazine, The 107

Geschützund und Geschosslaute im Weltkrieg (Noises of Shells and Projectiles in the World War) 140
Gettysburg, Battle of 137
Germany, German 15, 18, 30, 34, 36, 37, 38, 113, 131, 137, 138, 139, 140, 149, 158, 180, 184
Glenrowan, Victoria 47
God Save Ireland (song) 33
God Save the Queen/King (song) 35
Goebbels, Joseph 30, 129
Gordon Riots 110, 117
grammar 56, 59, 69, 94
Graphic, The (Australian journal) 129
Graves, Robert 138
Great Depression 114, 128, 167
Greece, Greek 16, 36, 124, 131
Greensleeves (song) 81
Greville, Fulke 72
Guantanomo Bay 170
Guillemont, Battle of 37
Guitar 147, 152, 153, 171

Hail Glorious St Patrick (song) 33
Hall, Joseph 67
Hamlet/Hamlet ix, 7, 8, 10, 11, 51, 55, 72, 73, 74, 76, 77, 80–95, 96; Film 90; Music 81–82; Voice 74, 76, 82–83, 86, 92–95; *see also* Shakespeare, William
Handel, George Frideric 169
Hannibal 36
Hanover 113, 184
Hardy, Thomas 132–133, 141
Hastings, Robert 135
Hawks, Howard 21
hearing viii, ix, 2–6, 8, 10, 12, 15, 16–31, 33, 50, 53, 54, 55, 57, 59, 60, 61, 62, 63, 66–69, 72, 80, 82–83, 85, 87, 88–93, 99, 100, 107, 111, 114, 117–118, 119, 126, 127, 130, 134, 138–139, 156, 159, 164, 186, 172, 174, 178, 180, 182–184, 188–189, 190–193; listening skills and modernity 123, 140–148, 150; phenomenology 5, 16–31; physiology 16–31
Heathrow Airport, UK 182, 189
Heidegger, Martin 156
Hells' Bells (song) 171
Helmholtz, Hermann von 144, 146
Hendrix, Jimi 108
Henry Connor (song) 42
Henry II, King of England 181

Hero of Alexandria 131
Higginson, Heny Lee 190
highland clearances 105
Hindenburg, The (Airship) 128
His Master's Voice (HMV) records 130
Hitler, Adolph 18, 22, 27, 30, 129
Hobart (Tasmania) 41, 43, 169
Hobbes, Thomas 51
Hogarth, William 103, 108, 115, 116
Holdsworth, Thomas 40
Holmes, Sherlock 136
Home, Henry, Lord Kames 67
Hood, Robin 101
Hoover, Herbert 128
Hopkins, John 62
Horder, Baron of Ashford. 185
Howard, John (eighteenth century prison reformer) 112
'Hum, The' 164
Humperdinck, Engelbert (pop singer) 169
Hungary, Hungarian 6

Idlewild Airport, US 182
I Love You (song; Barney the Purple Dinosaur) 170
industrialization, industrial revolution 9, 12, 50, 52, 61, 99, 102, 105, 113, 115, 116, 118, 123, 130–135, 160–161, 164, 173, 179, 180, 181, 187, 189, 190, 192
interaural intensity difference 17, 18, 19
interaural temporal difference 18, 19
Inuit culture 6
iPod *see* personal stereos
Ireland, Irish 10, 33, 34, 37, 41, 42, 43–47, 51, 111, 113, 170
Irish volunteers, the 33, 34, 37
Ireland Boys Hurrah (song) 33
Irreversible, The (film) 21
Israel, Israeli 172
Italy, Italian 38, 113, 179

Jack O'Donohoe (song) 44–45
Jackson, Francis 107
Jackson, Peter 21
Jamaica 36, 172
James, Barbara 154
James Brothers, The (Frank and Jesse) 102
Japan 173
Järviluoma, Helmi 63, 146–147
Java 149
Jazz 37, 45, 129, 147, 148, 150, 151–153, 155, 168, 171, 180
Jericho 15, 18, 25

Johns Hopkins University (US) 5, 191
Johnson, Samuel 56, 100, 169
Joint Non-Lethal Weapons US Task Force, The 170
Jones, James Earl 21
Jones, Spike, and His City Slickers 180
Jonson, Ben 73
Jukebox 127, 130
Jünger, Ernst 139, 140
Junkers Ju 87 Stuka aircraft 18, 25
Juva, Johannes 36

Kabul, Afghanistan 183
Kalevala, The 25
Karaoke 183,
Keller, Helen 13
Kelly, Ned 37, 45–47, 102, 111
King Kong (film 2005) 21
Kings College, Cambridge 35
Kircher, Athanasius 124
Knudsen, Vern 145, 146
kymograph 126, 127

Laennec, Dr. René Théophile Hyancinthe 145
Lancaster aircraft 18
Lascaux Caves 7
Latimer, Hugh 67
Lautsprecherwagons 129
Law 10, 11, 48, 52, 53, 69, 81, 100, 105, 106, 107, 110, 111, 119, 128, 134, 151, 157, 179, 181, 185, 190; Nuisance Assize, 1378 119; The Combination Act of 1721 106; The Metropolitan Police Act of 1864 114; The Prison Act of 1865 112; The Riot Act of 1715 106; The US Bennett Act of 1907 187; The Waltham Black Act of 1723 106
Leavis, F.R. 30
Leeds 135
Leipzig 36, 113
Le Portel Caves 16
Lessing, Theofore 184
Life of Brian, The (film) 82
literacy, literate 10, 34, 46, 48, 53–55, 57, 58, 59, 62, 63, 67, 69, 70, 77, 98, 99, 109, 100, 107, 109, 116, 119, 120, 152, 155, 169
Little Richard 8, 154
Liverpool (UK) 63, 135
Livy 36
London 20, 52, 57, 60, 62, 63, 66, 69, 71, 75, 77, 100, 102, 103, 104, 106, 109, 110, 111, 113, 114, 117, 119, 120, 124, 126, 131, 134, 135, 158, 165, 175, 181, 182, 184, 186, 187
Long Range Acoustic Device (LRAD) 170
Los Angeles Airport, USA 182
Loudon, James 188
Low Frequency Noise (LFN) 19, 20–22, 75, 165, 170, 172, 173–175, 182, 189
Ludwig, Carl 126
Lusitania, The 125
Luther, Martin 51
Lydgate, John 114

Mach, Ernst 3
Maid's Lamentation, The (song) 43
Manchester 118, 135
Mandolin 152
Manilow, Barry 169
Manley, Colonel William 15
Mannerheim, Gustaf 22
Mantovani, Annunzio Paolo 29, 149
Marconi, Guglielmo 125
Marinetti, Filippo Tommaso Emilio 160
Marseillaise, The (song) 36
Marston Moor, Battle of 137
Maroons *see* Jamaica
Mau Mau force 170
McKenzie, Dan 181
Melachrino, George 29
Melford, George 151
Melville, Herman 136, 157
Memory 23, 52, 54, 57, 58, 63, 73, 95, 100, 140, 147
Meniere's disease 172
Mexico, Mexican 150
Microphone 20, 30, 75, 128, 141, 148, 154, 183
Middle Ages, The 28, 34, 53
Mildred Pierce (film) 167
mind/body split 17, 24, 59
Mistletoe and Wine (song) 169
Mitchell, John 42
modernity viii, 9, 11, 12, 28, 29, 34, 61, 115, 116, 117, 129, 132–133, 134, 135, 137, 144, 147, 150, 151, 152, 154, 160, 161, 164, 170, 171, 178, 179, 188, 190, 193
Montagu, James 68, 70
Mood Indigo (song) 148
Moore, Clover 189
Morrison, Herbert 128

Morrison, Scott 21
Morse, Samuel 124, 125, 127
Moses 102, 126
Mouth Organ 43
Mozart, Wolfgang Amadeus 169
music/musicality 3, 4, 9, 11, 12, 18, 19, 21, 23, 24, 25, 28, 29, 30, 34, 35, 41, 42, 63, 70, 71, 75, 76, 80, 81–82, 85, 99, 103, 113–116, 117–118, 119, 137, 138, 141, 145, 146, 147, 148, 150, 178, 179–180, 182–183, 184, 189, 190, 192; advertising 30; arousal 30, 33, 169; background 130, 135, 165, 167, 174; mechanical instruments 124, 127; popular 8, 18, 20, 38–39, 41, 42, 43, 44, 116, 120, 129, 152, 153–155, 159, 167, 168, 171, 174, 175, 189; social control 15, 25, 30, 39, 168–169; tuning 19, 81, 171; violence 35, 37, 41, 170–171, 183
musicology 149, 150
My Blue Heaven (song) 152
My Way (song) 183
Myanmar, formerly Burma 41
Myers, Charles 137

National Anthems 30, 35, 169
National Safety News, The (journal) 187
Nearer my God to Thee (song) 35
Negwer, Maximilian 184
Netherlands, The 173
Neurasthenia 24, 135
Newgate Prison 102, 103, 107, 109, 110, 112
Newton, Francis (Mrs) 179
Newton, Sir Isaac 144
New York 27, 134, 135, 181, 182, 184,
New York Department of Health, The 134
New York Times 149
Nietzsche, Friedrich 156, 184
nightclub noise 9
Noe, Gasper 21
noise 7, 8, 11, 22, 23, 26, 62, 83, 90, 98, 114, 116, 132, 145, 146, 148, 155, 159, 164, 173, 174, 176, 183, 192; abatement and suppression – organisations, policies, technologies 12, 17, 24, 120, 171, 184–187, 189–191; aircraft 165, 181–182, 189; class politics 11, 41, 99, 113, 114, 117, 118, 119, 120; complaints 119, 134, 180–181; definitions 41, 178–180; domestic 12,
166; electronic 12; industrial 61, 133, 134–135, 146; marine 166–170; measurement, decibel 188–189; military 18, 137–141, 160, 170, 171; neighbours 9, 183; office 157, 160–161, 165; orchestras 153; power 133, 179; rail, steam engine 133; regulation 11, 25, 48, 112, 117, 119 *see also* abatement and suppression; street traffic 9, 116, 117, 118, 131, 135, 147, 152, 165, 191–192; zoning 181, 190
Nolan, Captain Louis 92
Nolan, Sidney 45
Norden, John 57
Noriega, Manuel Antonio 169–170
Northern Miner, The (Newspaper) 46
Notre Dame Cathedral, Paris 29

Oceania, Oceanian 149
ocarina 152
orality, oral tradition ix, 6, 10, 11, 34, 43, 44–48, 52, 53–58, 59, 60, 63, 67, 69, 70, 73, 74, 89, 91, 94, 98, 99, 101, 105, 111, 116
organs (instrument) 18, 28, 33
Orpheus 25
Others, The (film) 7
otology 12, 144
Oxford 113

Panama 189
Paris 29, 114, 184, 188
Pepys, Samuel 73
personal stereos 22, 127, 167, 192
Perspective 1, 5
Philadelphia International Exposition, 1876 125
phonautograph 126, 127
piano 18, 19, 38, 39, 43, 44, 153, 158
Pickard, John 35
pitch 17, 18, 19–21, 25, 27, 30, 56, 81, 130, 164, 170, 121, 186, 189; *see also* frequency
playhouses ix, 9, 10, 29, 70, 71, 75, 93, 119; spatiality and acoustics 76; *see also* theatres
pneumothorax 20, 172
Poe, Edgar Allan 136
Pop Goes the Peeler (song) 33
Porilaisten marssi (song) 36
preaching 46, 66–68, 73, 76; congregational conduct 71
Presley, Elvis 101

print ix, 1, 8, 10, 11, 12, 19, 34, 44, 53–57, 59, 60, 62, 63, 66–70, 71–74, 76, 77, 80, 90, 91, 93, 94, 95, 98–100, 104, 110, 120, 123, 124, 127, 128, 145, 155, 156, 165
prisons 38, 100, 101, 102, 112, 113; Alcatraz 113; the silent system 112–113; *see also* Newgate Prison
Protestantism 28, 33, 37, 42, 66, 68
Pulpit ix, 9, 10, 18, 28, 66–68, 70; *see also* preaching; sermons
Puns 11, 55–56, 94
Puttenham, George 72
Pynchon, Thomas 92

Quiet (Journal) 186
Quintilian, Marcus Fabius 58

Rachmaninov, Sergei 169
radio 11, 12, 25, 27, 28, 30, 38, 123, 125, 126–130, 141, 145, 146, 147, 150, 153, 154, 155, 164, 165, 167, 179, 181, 183, 186, 188
Radio City Music Hall 26
Radio Corporation of America (RCA) 125
Ramus, Petrus (Pierre de La Ramée), Ramism 55
Rann, Jack 107
Rayner, Olive Pratt, *nom de plume* for Grant Allen 155, 158
recordings 11, 12, 15, 22, 26, 29, 38, 123, 126–130, 145, 147, 148, 149, 150, 153, 154, 155, 156, 167, 168, 171; dictaphone 127, 128, 155, 156, 157; high fidelity 148–149; recording studios 26, 29, 171; stereophonic 148, 149, 165
Reformation, The 10, 34, 51, 52, 68
Release Me (song) 169
Renaissance, The 11, 34, 53, 55, 61, 68, 113
resonance vii, viii, 16, 27, 28, 35, 124, 135, 144, 145, 146, 170, 172; *see also* reverberation
reverberation 4, 16, 25–29, 51, 75, 76, 105, 135, 145, 170, 171
Reznikoff, Iegor vii, viii, 16
rhetoric 54–55, 67, 73, 74
Rice, Julia Barnett 186–187
Richards, Cliff 169
Richards, Henry 186
Richardson, Samuel 70

Richardson, Tony 90
Riddle, Nelson 168
Riley, William 40, 43
Rimsky-Korsakoff, Nicolai 169
Robson, Mark 21
Rocky Road to Berlin. The (song) 33
Rogers, John 57
Roland, Tom 192
Rolling Stone (magazine) 168
Rome, Romans 38, 92, 131
Roosevelt, Franklin D. 128
Royal, Society, The 56, 67
Rum Song (song) 42
Russia 7, 36, 131, 179
Russolo, Luigi 140, 160, 164, 165, 179

Sabine, Wallace 26, 27, 190
Sarnoff, David 125
Schaeffer, Pierre 180
Schafer, R. Murray 63, 146, 147, 165
Schools, School Teaching 3, 11, 30, 47, 54, 55, 57, 58, 72, 74, 113, 153, 158, 173, 179, 186, 190
Schroeder, Christa 27
School Songs 30
Schopenhauer, Arthur 184
Schuyler, Montgomery 27, 28
scientific revolution, the 56, 67
Scot's Magazine 124
Scott, Ridley 92
Selborne, Lord 134
Sellers, Peter 160
sensorium 2, 8, 85
sermons 10, 28, 30, 53, 54, 57–58; *see also* preaching
Shakespeare, William ix, 1, 7, 10, 51, 55, 57, 59, 60, 61, 63, 68, 71–77, 80, 81, 82, 86, 91, 92, 94, 95, 96; *Henry the Fourth* 73; *The Winter's Tale* 61; see also *Hamlet*
Shaw, George Bernard 75
Sheik, The (film) 151
shell shock 137, 139
Sheppard, Jack 102–104, 107, 111, 120
She's The Most Distressful Country (song) 37
Shoot to Thrill (song) 171
Should a Girl Propose? (film) 151
Sinatra, Frank 168
Singapore 149
singing, song vii, viii, 3, 7, 8, 11, 20, 24, 25, 30, 31, 33, 35, 36, 38, 39, 40, 41, 42, 43, 44, 45, 47, 62, 81, 82, 83, 85,

111, 112, 114, 116, 117, 119, 124, 129, 132, 145, 146, 149, 153, 154, 168, 169, 170, 183
Slade, Ernest Augustus 40
Slessor, Kenneth 152, 157
Smith, Al 128
Smith, Henry 67
Soldier's Song, The (song) 33
Solzhenitsyn, Alexander 7
song *see* singing
songlines *see* Australia, Australian First Nations People
Songs For Swingin' Lovers (record album) 168
sonic telegraphy 124, 125, 126, 135, 145, 188; *see also* Radio Morse Code; telephone
sound waves 3, 125, 144, 145, 164
soundscape ix, x, 6, 8, 10, 11, 12, 20, 21, 26, 27, 56, 62, 63, 70, 71, 73, 74, 80, 114, 118, 120, 123, 130, 131, 132, 133, 134, 135, 136, 137, 140, 144, 146, 147, 149, 150, 151, 152, 154, 155, 160, 161, 164, 165, 166, 170, 171, 172, 175, 182, 183, 184, 188, 189, 190
South Africa 34
spatiality (and sound) ix, 4, 5, 9, 16, 17, 26, 27, 28, 29, 30, 73, 75, 146, 170, 171; *see also* reverberation
speech *see* voice
Spinoza, Baruch 23
spiritualism 126
sports songs 30, 35, 36, 167
Stamford, US 183
Stanhope, Philip *see* Chesterfield
Star Spangled Banner, The (song) 36
Star Wars (film) 21
stethoscope 12, 141, 145, 155
Stevenson, Robert Louis 136
Stokowski, Leopold 146
Story of the Kelly Gang (film) 37–38
St. Petersburg (Florida) Times 171
St. Thomas's Church, New York 27
Stucky, Stephen 180
Swallow, William 43
Sweden, Swedish 173
Sydney, Australia 27, 39, 40, 43, 44, 154, 184, 189
Sydney Morning Herald (Australian Newspaper) 183

Tait, Charles 38
Taliban 183

Television 38, 108, 127, 130, 179
Thailand 149
Thames River Police, The 106
Thatcher, Margaret 21
theatres 17, 21, 25, 51, 55, 57, 71, 72, 74, 75, 77, 88, 90, 96, 99, 113, 124, 151; audience conduct 71, 113–114, 148; *see also* playhouses
Thomas, Theodore 114
Thornhill, James 103
Thurber, James 160
Tillotson, Geoffrey 67
Titanic, The 35, 125
Tolpuddle Martyrs 42
Tolstoy, Leo 131, 133
Truth (Australian newspaper) 155
Tucker, W.S. 164
Turkey 149
Turpin, Dick 100–101, 102, 103, 104, 107
Twain, Mark 156
Tyburn Gallows 103, 107, 109, 110
typewriter 113, 155–161

Ubiquity Effect 15, 17, 19, 26, 171
Ulysses 25
urbanization 52, 99, 119, 134, 135, 165

Vallée, Rudy 154
van Beethoven, Ludwig 190
Venezuela 35
Vents solaires, les 147
Vesalius, Andreas 69
Vienna 114
Vietnam 183; Vietnam War 15–16
Vinegar Hill uprising, New South Wales 43
violin 116; bass 153
vision, visuality vii, viii, 1, 3, 4, 5, 6, 7, 10, 11, 17, 18, 25, 27, 28, 30, 51, 53, 54, 56, 58, 59, 60, 61, 62, 67, 68, 72, 73, 74, 77, 80, 83, 85, 89, 90, 91, 96, 98, 99, 100, 111, 114, 124, 125, 135, 136, 140, 145, 156, 173, 182
Vivaldi, Antonio 169
volume (sonic) 5, 12, 15, 17, 19, 20, 21–22, 30, 56, 61, 76, 118, 124, 137, 152, 164, 170, 171, 175, 189
von Mellenthin, General Friedrich 36
von Schlieffen, Alfred 140
von Suttner, Bertha 151

Waits, Tom 154
Walker, Steven J. 16

walkman *see* personal stereos
Wallace, Chris 21
Wallace, Jo-Ann 156
Wallington, Nehemiah 66
Waltzing Matilda (song) 111
war cries 35, 169; *see also* noise, military
War of the Worlds (radio broadcast) 128
Waterloo, Battle of 1, 137
Watson, Thomas 125
Watt, James 131, 133
Webbe, William 72
Welles, Orson 128
Wells, H.G. 186
Weskitt, John 107
Western Electric *see* American Telephone and Telegraph Company, the
Wheatstone, Charles 124

Wild, Jonathan 102
Wild Colonial Boy, The (song) 44, 47
Williamson, Nicol 90
Wilson, Mrs Richard T. 179
Wind Turbines 174
Winkler, Cecilia 181
Wisconsin, US 166, 184
Wizard of Oz, The (film) 7
Wolf, Julia 180
Wordsworth, William 117–118, 119, 131, 136
World Health Organisation (WHO) 182
Wrap the Green Flag (song) 33

Zama, Battle of 36
Zeffirelli, Franco 90

Printed in the United States
by Baker & Taylor Publisher Services